Contributions to Management Science

T0189741

For further volumes:
http://www.springer.com/series/1505

Jella Pfeiffer

Interactive Decision Aids
in E-Commerce

Physica-Verlag
A Springer Company

Jella Pfeiffer
Johannes Gutenberg-Universität Mainz
Lehrstuhl für Wirtschaftsinformatik und BWL
Jakob-Welder Weg 9
55128 Mainz
Germany
jella.pfeiffer@uni-mainz.de

ISSN 1431-1941
ISBN 978-3-7908-2948-8   ISBN 978-3-7908-2769-9 (eBook)
DOI 10.1007/978-3-7908-2769-9
Springer Heidelberg Dordrecht London New York

Physica-Verlag is a brand of Springer

Springer is part of Springer Science+Business Media (www.springer.com)

To my family

Acknowledgements

At the beginning of my doctorate, I had not anticipated that it would connect me to many people, bring me to many countries, and would follow a very evolutionary process inspiring me not to leave the scientific path. I am grateful for this interesting part of my life and I would like to express my thanks to some special people who have supported me throughout these past years.

First and foremost, I am very grateful to my supervisor Dr. Franz Rothlauf. Franz, you have always supported me no matter how complicated my ideas were and how far they carried me. Furthermore, you have taught me a lot about scientific writing and how to structure my thoughts, and I have the feeling that I will never stop learning from you. Whenever I needed your advice, you were there for me. You have quite simply played the role of "PhD Supervisor" – particularly in the German sense of the word – perfectly! But besides all that, I appreciate your friendship very much.

My second acknowledgment goes to Dr. Ulrich Hoffrage, who was very kind to serve as the second reviewer in the committee. His profound and extraordinary knowledge in the field of decision-making is remarkable. I am very happy to be able to share and discuss ideas with Ulrich and I am very much looking forward to do further research with him in the future.

Most importantly, I would like to say many thanks to my family for all their help and support. They have showed me the importance of being optimistic and earnest, and they have taught me to be curious about the world.

Next, I want to thank all my colleagues from my department for wonderful discussions and their immense support during these last few years. In particular, I would like to thank Heike Kirsch for all her help and support. I would also like to thank Dr. Daniel Schunk, who was the first to inspire me to undertake a research project during my studies in Mannheim, and who has given me valuable feedback on my present work. Daniel, I still remember endless hours of discussing and generating ideas well into the evening in the SFB 504 building. Similarly, I am also grateful to Dr. Martin Meißner, from whom I learned about preference measurement and with whom I had great discussions. Furthermore, I would like to thank Dr. René Riedl for his good ideas and cooperation in several projects, as well as Dr. Eduard Brandstätter for very inspiring discussions on decision-making behavior. Moreover, I would like to thank Felix Vogel who helped me a lot with implementing INTACMATO, and Melanie Bloos as well as my brother Thies Pfeiffer who both proofread parts of my dissertation.

I would like to express my thanks to those who participated in the studies and to several students who helped me to conduct the studies. The successful completion of my research is directly related to your support.

One very big thank you goes to Eric Bonabeau, Ph.D., from Icosystem Corporation. He is such an inspiring man, and has made many things possible for me, including allowing me to be part of a company, where both the science-world and the real-world go closely hand-in-hand. I also thank Dejan Duzevik from Icosystem, who is as excited as I am about decision-making behavior and with whom I had great discussions.

I would like to thank all my friends who were always there for me. My close friends, Silke, Susanne and my old friends from Mannheim, the friends I have found among my colleagues, and the friends I have found abroad during my time at Icosystem and Harvard in Cambridge (USA). Last but not least, I would like to thank Mine, who has not been discouraged despite coming into my life during the final and most strenuous stage of my doctorate.

Contents

List of Figures

List of Tables

Acronyms

ADD	Additive difference rule
ANOVA	Analysis of variance
COM	Compatibility test
CONJ	Conjunctive strategy
DIS	Disjunctive strategy
DOM	Dominance strategy
DSS	Decision support system(s)
EBA	Elimination by aspect strategy
ECP	Elementary communication process(es)
EIP	Elementary information process(es)
EQW	Equal weight heuristics
EV	Expected value
FRQ	Frequency of good and/or bad features heuristic
GA	Genetic algorithm
IDA	Interactive decision aid(s)
IIMT	Interactive information management tool(s)
INTACMATO	Prototype for interactive information management tools
LED	Minimum difference lexicographic rule
LEX	Lexicographic heuristic
LTM	Long-term memory
MAJ	Simple majority decision rule
MD	Median
M	Mean
RA	Recommendation agent(s)
SAT	Satisficing heuristic
SAT+	Satisficing-plus heuristic
SD	Standard deviation
SE	Standard error

SI	Search index
SM	Strategy measure
STM	Short-term memory
TTF	Task-technology fit
vs.	Versus
WADD	Weighted added rule

Symbols

α	Cronbach's alpha
a_{ij}	Attribute level of attribute i and alternative j
A_i	Vector of possible attribute levels of $attr_i$
$Attr^w$	Vector of attributes ordered decreasingly according to attribute weight
$alt_k = (a_{1k}, \ldots, a_{mk})$	Alternative vector
$attr_l = (a_{l1}, a_{l2}, \ldots, a_{ln})$	Attribute vector
$asp(\cdot)$	Aspiration level function (equals 0 in case aspiration level is met)
β_{ik}	Part-worth utility of occurrence k of attribute i
c	Fitness for correlation of attribute vectors
ct	Choice task
$d(alt_j)$	Deterministic component of $u(alt_j)$
df	Degrees of freedom
ds	Decision strategy
DS_u	The set of strategies without multiple mappings
ε_j	Error term of $u(alt_j)$
F	Fitness
$\hat{f}$	Effect size for ANOVA
F^{robust}	Robust fitness
$H(ct)$	Entropy of a choice task
l	The length of the genotype
n	Number of alternatives
m	Number of attributes
mp	Fitness for mapping
p	Mutation probability
$\pi(alt_j)$	The probability that alternative j is chosen
r	Pearson's correlation coefficient
r_{attr}	Number of attribute-wise transitions

s	Fitness for attribute range/attractiveness difference
$t(x)$	t-value of the T-test, x: degrees of freedom
$u(alt_j)$	Overall utility value of alternative j
$v(a_{ij})$	Attribute value of attribute i and alternative j
w_i	Attribute importance, attribute weight
X_{jik}	Binary variable is 1 if alt_j contains occurrence k of $attr_i$

Chapter 1
Introduction

Reason is, and only ought to be, the slave of the Passions.

David Hume

1.1 Motivation

The importance of online shopping has grown remarkably over the last decade. In 2009, every West European spent on average €483 online and this amount is expected to grow to €601 in 2014.[1] In Germany, the number of online shoppers has almost doubled since 2000, with 44% of all adults regularly buying products online today. In Western Europe, online sales reached €68 billion in 2009 and Forrester research forecast it will reach €114 billion by 2014 with a 11% compound annual growth rate.

The ease of product information acquisition for online shopping is one of the major drivers for the growth in the online retail business (Ariely 2000; Van den Poel and Leunis 1999). With easier access to information, the total amount of information considered in online shopping situations increases in comparison to traditional shopping situations (e.g., Lohse and Johnson 1996). Besides ease of information acquisition, three other factors may also account for the fact that customers consider an increased amount of information. In the first place, online shoppers rely solely on product information provided on websites and cannot experience the product physically or profit from a personal sales talk. For that reason, they may consider the provided information more intensely and in higher volume. In the second place, due to the anonymity in webstores, sellers do not know which customer needs which

---

[1]http://www.forrester.com/rb/Research/western_european_online_retail_forecast%2C_2009_to/q/id/56543/t/2.

J. Pfeiffer, *Interactive Decision Aids in E-Commerce*, Contributions to Management Science, DOI 10.1007/978-3-7908-2769-9_1, © Springer-Verlag Berlin Heidelberg 2012

kind of information. Consequently, sellers tend to give a large amount of product information per product (Ariely 2000; Donges et al. 2001). Finally, in addition to a lot of information per product, the amount of products offered is large. That is because a large variety in the assortment has been found to be the major criterion to increase consumer satisfaction (Hoch et al. 1999), and, in online stores, products can be profitably stocked, promoted and sold (Brynjolfsson et al. 2006; Hinz and Eckert 2010).

The drawback of the large amount of information is that information overload can become a serious threat. In many domains, such as organization science, marketing, accounting, and management information systems, information overload has been discussed for a long time (for an overview, see Eppler and Mengis 2004). These studies have found that the performance of individuals (i.e., the quality of decisions) increases only up to a certain point with the amount of information they receive. Beyond this point, the performance of individuals will rapidly decline (Chewning and Harrell 1990). Information overload can, for instance, have a negative effect on the webstore's sales, since it may prevent online consumers from making a purchasing decision (White and Hoffrage 2009). Further consequences can be stress or anxiety, low motivation, and a diminished decision quality (Eppler and Mengis 2004). This might be the reason why only 1–2% of online consumers who visit a website end up making a purchase, and over 80% of web shoppers leave electronic markets without even knowing what they want afterwards (Silverman et al. 2001; Sismeiro and Bucklin 2004).

In order to prevent information overload, webstores face the challenge to provide the right amount of information to every customer. If a store presents unnecessary information, the customer's ability to make accurate decisions is reduced, whereas, if information is incomplete, customers have no solid basis on which to come to a sound buying decision (Bettman et al. 1991; Jacoby et al. 1974; Malhorta 1982; Scammon 1977). In addition, the right amount of information is customer-specific and webstores usually do not know a priori the right amount and type of information needed by a single customer (Ariely 2000).

In their meta-study, Eppler and Mengis (2004) argue, "IT and its use and misuse are a major reason why information overload has become a critical issue" (p. 334). Although – due to advances in IT – there is an abundance of information available, it seems hard to get useful and relevant information when it is needed (Edmunds and Morris 2000). Therefore, several authors advocate the use of intelligent information management systems, such as decision support systems (DSS), that help decision makers to deal with a large amount of information (Cook 1993; Edmunds and Morris 2000; Eppler and Mengis 2004). However, current DSS in the field of consumer decision support still seem to lack an effective user support and do not satisfy users (Song et al. 2007). Hence, the deficient function of current DSS and search software has been made responsible for negative results for webstores (Silverman et al. 2001). Consequently, the competitiveness in the web retailing market is compelling Web retailers to further improve usability of their websites.

The most common DSS for facilitating the consumers' decision-making process are interactive decision aids (IDA) (Wang and Benbasat 2009). In general, DSS describe techniques that help decision makers to overcome cognitive deficits – caused by information overload – and avoid systematic errors (Beach 1997). The term *interactive* in IDA refers to the user's possibility to access and exchange information on demand, customize content, and receive and give real-time feedback (Ariely 2000; Joseph et al. 1997; Zack 1993). IDA should help consumers to find the right product with low effort by providing the appropriate information. Examples of IDA are recommendation agents and interactive information management tools (IIMT) (Gupta et al. 2009; Wang and Benbasat 2009; Xiao and Benbasat 2007).

Recommendation agents use question-and-answer dialogs to provide relevant information or to make suggestions to the customer (Bettman and Zins 1979; Gupta et al. 2009; Häubl and Trifts 2000; Qiu and Benbasat 2009; Todd and Benbasat 2000; Wang and Benbasat 2008; Wilkie 1975; Xiao and Benbasat 2007). In contrast, IIMT are "tools which enable buyers to sort through and/or compare available product alternatives" (Gupta et al. 2009, p. 163). IIMT leave the customers with full control over their own information search.

In order to optimally support consumers with IDA, we have to take into account how they process product information and how they make their purchase decision. Usually, we assume that customers follow some kind of decision strategy when choosing the preferred product. A decision strategy describes a decision maker's approach on how to select an alternative in a choice task. In the context of online webstores, we define a choice task as the problem to choose one product out of a finite set of products where each product is described by a number of attributes (product features). There are many different decision strategies that can be used in such choice tasks and both the characteristics of the decision makers as well as situational factors can influence which strategy is applied (Payne et al. 1993). While one consumer may make choices by choosing the product which is best on the attribute which he or she considers to be most important, another may carefully trade off the pros and cons of products (Adamowicz et al. 2008).

To the situational factors influencing decision-making behavior belongs the choice task complexity. Choice task complexity describes how difficult consumers arrive at decisions. It depends on several factors, such as the amount of product information, the degree to which the decision maker has to trade-off product features with each other, or how similar the products are to each other. Thus, with increasing choice task complexity, the risk for information overload increases as there is not only more product information but also the comparison of product information is more difficult.

In sum, owing to all these facts concerning decision-making behavior, it becomes plausible that only when decision processes are well understood, can we design IDA which are adapted well to users, offer them the best possible support, lead to an increased users' satisfaction and thus, reduce the problem of information overload.

1.2   Research Question and Contribution

Some researchers argue that approaches which address the information overload problem should be interdisciplinary because many of the open research questions in this field cross traditional disciplinary boundaries (Eppler and Mengis 2004). In the present work, we follow this notion and take both a psychologically oriented, behavioral perspective, as well as a design science, technological perspective to adress our two research questions:

1. How does the complexity of a choice task influence decision-making behavior?
2. How can we consider knowledge about decision-making behavior for the design of interactive information management tools?

As a consequence, the contribution of this dissertation is twofold. First, we contribute to current theory on decision-making behavior with behavioral experiments and, second, we develop a prototype of a decision support system which facilitates the usage of various kinds of decision-making behavior.

Regarding the first research question, our first hypothesis is that decision makers follow a two-stage decision process whose progression is influenced by choice task complexity. Following other work, we suggest that in the first stage of a decision, decision makers compare products across only few features and exclude inferior products (Bettman and Park 1980; Gilbride and Allenby 2004, 2006; Luce et al. 1997; Olshavsky 1979; Payne 1976; Payne et al. 1988; Russo and Leclerc 1994; Svenson 1979). If so, this behavior indicates the usage of rather simple strategies which ignore certain product features. We suggest further that in the second stage, decision makers evaluate all information of the remaining products in more detail. Furthermore, instead of comparing products across certain features as postulated for the first stage, in the second stage decision makers consider the complete information of one product before proceeding to the next one. Thus, the decision-making process is focused on whole products, rather than on the features of a single product. With regard to the influence of complexity on the two-stage decision process, we postulate that the more complex the choice task is, the more effort the decision maker invests. We further argue that this results in a later switch from the first to the second stage, in cases of high complexity.

Our second hypothesis does not focus on the decision process, but on the final purchase decision. Following others, we suggest that the more complex the choice task, the simpler strategies are applied (Bettman et al. 1991; Conlon et al. 2001; Ford et al. 1989; Payne et al. 1992, 1993). While this notion has been studied for a long time, we shed some light onto this field by analyzing the impact and the interaction of different measures of complexity (amount of product information, similarity and trade-offs) on the decision strategy applied. These different measures of complexity are correlated with each other. We elaborate on these different interactions of measures of complexity and their dependencies and we show how optimization methods can be used to systematically manipulate the values of the different measures of complexity in an experiment despite their interdependencies. Our approach is able to generate choice tasks with low vs. high levels of complexity for different measures of complexity for all respondents individually by taking into account their preferences and utility function. This controlled variation of complexity allows for causal inference. Moreover, our approach is able to generate choice tasks in a novel way that facilitates data analysis and reduces the number of observations to be made. As optimization method, we apply a genetic algorithm, which is a naturally-inspired optimization method from the field of artificial intelligence.

The results from the two empirical studies which address the first research question may be generalized to other contexts of multi-criteria decision making, besides the considered purchase decisions. This is because the choice tasks in the experiments have the same format as typical decision-making experiments in the field of multi-criteria decision making. The products represent different alternatives and the product features represent attributes by which the alternatives are characterized.

To address the second research question, we consider existent knowledge from decision-making literature as well as insights gained from tackling the first research question. The goal is to develop a set of IIMT that lead to increased user satisfaction and decreases the users' effort. Furthermore, we examine whether offering only a restricted set of decision aids influences the decision strategy chosen.

In order to reach this goal, we analyze which IIMT can support the application of which decision strategies. We develop a theoretical framework which describes the relationship between decision strategies and IIMT in detail. In the first step, we break down different decision strategies into subprocesses and describe current as well as new IIMT for supporting these subprocesses. This approach yields a close fit between decision process and decision support system which should increase user satisfaction and decrease effort. In the next step, we describe the process of decision making with and without support of IIMT. By extending Payne et al.'s (1993) effort-accuracy framework by the technological factor, IIMT, we then quantify the savings with decision support. Finally, we implement an IIMT-prototype and evaluate the theoretical framework, the usability of the IIMT as well as the achievement of the two goals (user satisfaction and decreased effort) empirically.

This dissertation does not only contribute to current theory, but also implements a prototype with high practical relevance. Hence, taking all the results from our own prototype, our empirical studies and theories from current literature into account, we are finally able to give recommendations for practitioners on which types of IIMT they should offer in order to increase user satisfaction.

To sum up, besides the theoretical contribution to the field of decision making and the influence of choice task complexity, the final product of this dissertation is an IIMT-prototype which supports decision makers in multi-criteria choice tasks. We call this prototype INTACMATO (INteractive inforMAtion MAnagement TOol).

1.3   Method

Standard information systems research usually follows two different research paradigms: behavioral science and design science (Nunamaker and Chen 1991; Simon 1996). While in behavioral science, researchers describe, explain and predict human and organizational behavior by developing and testing theories, the design science approach creates innovative artifacts in a creative and goal-oriented manner. Design science is a problem-solving approach, which belongs to the engineering disciplines (Simon 1996). It is fundamental to information systems since it creates, evaluates, and improves information technology (IT) artifacts. IT artifacts can mainly be described in four ways: constructs (vocabulary and symbols), models (abstractions and representations), methods (algorithms and practices), and instantiations (implemented and prototype systems) (Hevner et al. 2004). They have to be seen in an interdependent manner with humans and organizations, which – in confluence with technology – form the realm of IS. According to Hevner et al. (2004), the two paradigms must be seen to be interdependent, because they form a complementary research cycle: new artifacts are designed based on current theory (active part) which, themselves, regard the application and impact of innovative artifacts (reactive part).

The particularity of our work is that we apply both methodical approaches and therefore cover the whole research cycle of design and behavioral research methods (see Fig. 1.1). We address the first research question of how complexity influences decisions with behavioral science methods, such as laboratory and on-line experiments. Hence, the current knowledge is not only screened in a literature review, but new theoretical insights are also added to the knowledge base by experimental behavioral science approaches. Consequently, the first part of the present work represents part of the *rigor-cycle*. The knowledge is then incorporated in the second part, where we build a new artifact: INTACMATO. The design of the artifact is retrieved from theory on decision strategies and the influence of complexity thereon. Furthermore, we follow guidelines taken from literature on how to design IDA such that a structured engineering approach is guaranteed (*build-cycle*). The newly built artefact is then evaluated with a behavioral science approach in two qualitative and one quantitative experiment in the *relevance-cycle*. Moreover, in the quantitative study, the interaction between humans and the new artifact is observed in detail and new knowledge can be added to theory in the *rigor-cycle*.

Usually, in behavioral science, theories are developed and tested by applying quantitative and qualitative methods, such as experiments, field studies, case studies, and simulations. Hereby, the research rigor is ascertained by choosing the appropriate data collection and data analysis methods. We extend current research methodology in behavioral science by establishing computational intelligence methods, specifically genetic algorithms, as a new method for the selection of stimulus materials. In our second study, we use a genetic algorithm to systematically manipulate choice tasks. This algorithm enables the customized generation of choice tasks for all respondents. If choice tasks are designed such that a choice can

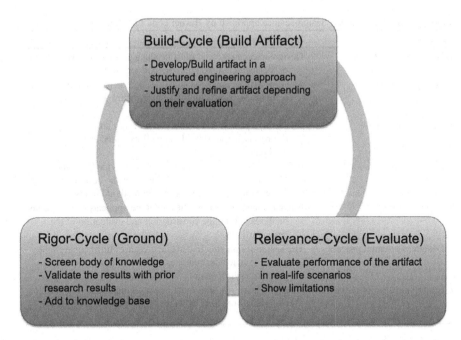

Fig. 1.1 The interplay of behavioral and design science represented by the rigor-, relevance-, and build-cycle

uniquely be explained by only one decision strategy, statements about the decision-making behavior can be retrieved from the observations easily and unambiguously. Furthermore, genetic algorithms facilitate the manipulation of variables describing the complexity of the choice task. This helps when analyzing the influence of the decision environment on the decision strategy. In other work, we have already shown that in addition to supporting the design of experiments, methods from computational intelligence provide more possibilities for analyzing data than ordinary testing of statistical hypotheses (Pfeiffer et al. 2009a). They are able to disclose new data patterns illuminating the observed behavior. However, in this dissertation, we only focus on the design of experiments. In this way, new strategies for describing the observed behavior can be explored.

Instead of developing and justifying a theory, in design science, the focus lies on the creative act of building an artifact and evaluating the latter with respect to its business need. In the different stages of this process, we use a variety of methods. While for evaluation, similar methods as for theory justification can be used, it seems harder to find appropriate research methods for creating an innovative artifact. In order to still assure the quality and rigor of a design science approach, Hevner et al. (2004) provide several guidelines which we also apply in our work, see Table 1.1. As Hevner et al. (2004) argue along with researchers in the behavioral science (Applegate 1999), "it is possible and necessary for all IS research paradigms

Table 1.1 Guideline for the design-science approach by Hevner et al. (2004, p. 83)

Guideline	Description
1. Design as an artifact	Design-science research must produce a viable artifact in form of a construct, a model, a method, or an instantiation.
2. Problem relevance	The objective of design-science research is to develop technology-based solutions to important and relevant business problems.
3. Design evaluation	The utility, quality, and efficacy of a design artifact must be rigorously demonstrated via well-executed evaluation methods.
4. Research contributions	Effective design-science research must provide clear and verifiable contributions in the areas of the design artifact, design foundations and/or design methodologies.
5. Research rigor	Design-science research relies upon the application of rigorous methods in both the construction and evaluation of the design artifact.
6. Design as a search process	The search for an effective artifact requires utilizing available means to reach desired ends while satisfying laws in the problem environment.
7. Communication of research	Design-science research must be presented effectively both to technology-oriented as well as management-oriented audiences.

to be both rigorous and relevant" (p. 88). In the following paragraphs, the methodical approach of this dissertation is further explained along these seven guidelines.

1. The first guideline is ensured by developing an IIMT-prototype. This artifact supports decision makers when comparing and evaluating alternatives.
2. The systematic *design* of IIMT is of high relevance for all kinds of non-risky multi-criteria decision making with complete information on alternatives. In the present work, we concentrate on purchase decisions on e-commerce websites but the same artifact could, for instance, be used for strategic management decisions.
3. Four different *evaluation* phases alternate with creation phases, so there are several feedback loops which focus on different criteria. In a first phase, in a review of current IIMT in the Internet and in the literature, it is assured that there is a lack of current consumer decision support in research and practice. Then, in a laboratory experiment, current approaches of IDA are compared to determine potential directions for new IDA. These first two evaluation phases ensure the relevance of the new artifact. In the third and fourth evaluation phase, the prototype is evaluated with a focus on research rigor. In the third phase, which is a qualitative evaluation phase including brainstorming and think-aloud approaches, the first version of the prototype is evaluated. Finally, in the fourth phase, we conduct a laboratory experiment with 120 students to validate utility, quality and efficacy of the new prototype and to validate our theoretical framework.
4. The *research contribution* of the present work is the design methodology and the application itself. In terms of the methodology, we test the feasibility of

systematically designing and implementing IIMT which are needed to closely assist various kinds of decision-making behavior. In terms of the design artifact, we develop a set of IIMT which assist the decision makers in choice decisions. The influence of the artifact on decision-making behavior can then be analyzed and the knowledge thus acquired can supplement the research field of decision making.

5. The fifth guideline aims at high *research rigor*. We ensure this guideline by several means. First, the ideas for the artifact are based on a detailed literature review and own empirical results. Therefore, we ensure a profound knowledge of the requirements of the artifact, namely how to support the "natural" decision-making process. We describe in detail the decision-making process by breaking it down into steps. From these steps, we retrieve the IIMT needed to support decision making. The advantage of this approach is the high degree of comprehensibility. Second, we extend a current theoretical framework for measuring decision effort in case of IIMT support. We analyze in detail the effort of different kinds of decision strategies with and without IIMT support and are thus able to quantify the saving of effort with the proposed artifact. Third, in the three empirical studies throughout the design process we repeatedly ensure research rigor by carefully designing the studies according to standards of psychological research.

6. As Hevner et al. (2004) point out, "design is essentially a search process to discover an effective solution to a problem" (p. 8). However, effectiveness, or optimality, is hard to reach, in particular if the problem and the environment cannot fully be specified, for instance mathematically. This is the case for our problem of optimal decision support for decision makers. Therefore, we follow Simon's suggestion to find one satisfactory approach which fits well to the given problem environment (Simon 1996). The satisfaction of the artifact is ensured in a lab experiment by the satisfaction consumers experience when using the new artifact.

7. Concerning the seventh guideline, presentations in the computer science community, the IS community, and the management community already have ensured the *communication* to different research groups (Pfeiffer et al. 2009b; Pfeiffer 2010). Based on this work, several journal publications are planned. Besides that, while you are reading the present work, you are already part of the ongoing communication process to the research community and/or management-oriented audience – depending on your professional background.

1.4   Structure

The structure of the present work follows our two main contributions and is henceforth divided into two large parts. In the first part, we provide the fundamentals on decision-making behavior (Chap. 2) and contribute to existing theory by studying the influence of complexity on decision-making behavior in two empirical studies

(Chaps. 3 and 4). In the second part, we apply this theory to the development of
a new DSS – an IIMT-prototype (Chaps. 5–8). Finally, we summarize the major
contributions of the present work and describe its implications, particularly for the
management-oriented audience.

Proceeding this chapter, which has motivated the two research questions and
discussed the methodology of the present work, we describe the fundamentals on
decision-making behavior in Chap. 2. Since research on decision-making behavior
is manifold, we refer to only those aspects which are relevant for the present
work. We start with defining choice tasks and decision strategies in detail because
they are the central elements of the present work. Specifically, we point out that
characteristics of choice tasks, such as its complexity, can influence which decision
strategy people apply. In order to be able to study this relationship between choice
task characteristics and decision strategies, we point out approaches for empirically
analyzing decision-making behavior in Sect. 2.3. We distinguish between outcome-
based approaches that analyze final choices, and process-tracing approaches that
analyze the decision process. Afterwards, in Sect. 2.4, we discuss the choice task
characteristic (i.e., complexity) which is central to the first part of the present
work. We distinguish between task-based and context-based complexity, which
we both address in the empirical studies throughout the rest of our work. The
main contribution of that section is a detailed literature overview about measures
of complexity and current research deficits. The identified deficits motivate the
following empirical studies.

In Chap. 3, we empirically study the influence of context-based complexity on
decision processes.[2] In this study, our concern is it to both measure context-based
complexity and the decision process as accurately as possible. To this end, we
measure each subject's preferences individually with two advanced techniques from
marketing research, rather than relying on less precise estimates of preferences.
Furthermore, we use eye tracking methodology to trace the decision processes
precisely. With eye tracking, we are able to distinguish between alternative-wise
and attribute-wise information acquisition. An alternative-wise search describes
a decision process where the decision maker first evaluates a given alternative
completely and then proceeds to the next one. An attribute-wise search, in contrary,
assumes the decision maker to compare alternatives across attributes, such as price.
Our results show that low context-based complexity leads to less information
acquisition and more alternative-wise search. Moreover, people search information
attribute-wise in the first stage of the decision process, then eliminate alternatives,
and search alternative-wise in the last stage. We also found evidence that in
situations of low context-based complexity, people switch earlier to alternative-wise
processing. In essence, our findings suggest that people not only select decision
strategies from an adaptive toolbox (Gigerenzer and Selten 2001) but that they also
switch between different strategies in situations of varying complexity.

---

[2]The experimental study was jointly carried out by Martin Meißner (University of Bielefeld),
Eduard Brandstätter (University Linz), and René Riedl (University of Linz).

In Chap. 4, our contribution is twofold. First, we again study the influence of complexity on decision-making behavior.[3] Unlike the preceding chapter, we study not only context-based complexity, but also task-based complexity as well as the interaction of different complexity measures. Furthermore, we do not observe the decision process, but analyze decision-making behavior based on the respondents' final choice. Besides contributing to theory onto complexity of choice tasks and decision-making behavior, our second contribution is to the field of optimal design of experimental stimuli. Specifically, we show how to use an optimization algorithm to design choice tasks. The proposed algorithm is able to simplify the analysis of choice tasks, create choice tasks with a certain level of complexity, and minimize the effects of estimation error on the generated choice tasks. In correspondence with Chap. 3, we again find a large influence of context-based complexity as well as interaction effects between some context-based measures of complexity, which we were able to study due to the optimal design of experiments. We also find that respondents exhibit sufficient propensities in their decision-making behavior that we can cluster them according to the applied decision strategy.

In Chaps. 2–4, we address our first research question, which deals with the influence of complexity of choice tasks on decision-making behavior. In the second part, we incorporate the gained knowledge into the design of IDA, and in particular IIMT.

In Chap. 5, we define IDA and distinguish between recommendation systems with IIMT. We find a lack of research on IIMT. A lack is also present in the Internet: a descriptive study on 100 websites reveals that only a limited number of IIMT are offered. Moreover, in an empirical study, we compare recommendation agents as one kind of recommendation system and IIMT. The results show that our sample of participants prefers IIMT to recommendation agents. Thus, both the lack of research, the lack of IIMT on current webstores, as well as people's preference for IIMT, motivates us to examining IIMT in detail in the next chapters.

Since there is only little research on IIMT, we assume that the main reason for the lack of IIMT in the Internet is that online sellers do not know which IIMT they should offer and what they should exactly look like. Hence, in Chap. 6, we address these two aspects. We review literature on IDA in the field of human interaction and discuss several drawbacks of current approaches as well as the resulting requirements for the design of new IIMT. Moreover, we describe the typically-observed decision-making process by breaking it down into steps. These steps indicate which IIMT would offer appropriate decision support. Based on these findings, we implement an IIMT-prototype, called INTACMATO, in an iterative approach where two qualitative usability studies and implementation phases alternate. This prototype is evaluated, first from a theoretical perspective and then in an empirical study, in the following two chapters.

---

[3]The experimental study was conducted in cooperation with Dejan Duzevik (Icosystem Corporation, consulting agency, USA), and Koichi Yamamoto (Dentsu Incorporated, advertising agency, Japan).

In Chap. 7, we analyze to what extent INTACMATO meets the requirement of low effort which has been specified in the previous chapter. We take an existing effort-accuracy model, extend and adapt it to INTACMATO and show analytically the savings of effort achieved. The results reveal that INTACMATO is able to reduce effort for all different kinds of decision strategies which we could find in the literature. The main contribution of this chapter is a new way of quantifying both mental and system effort for all different kinds of decision strategies.

The main purpose of the empirical study which we present in Chap. 8 is to evaluate INTACMATO empirically. The evaluation criteria are: perceived ease of use (effort), perceived usefulness, shopping enjoyment, confidence, and satisfaction. The results show that – compared to a control group of more than 30 students who just saw a product-comparison matrix without any IIMTs – the webstore with INTACMATO was evaluated more positively on all five evaluation criteria.

In the final Chap. 9, we summarize the most important results and draw conclusions. We have pointed out before that besides rigor, we intend to create also relevant research. That is why, as one part of the conclusions, we discuss in detail some practical implications of our work and give recommendations for practitioners on the design of webstores.

Part I
Analysis of Decision-Making Behavior

Chapter 2
Fundamentals on Decision-Making Behavior

This introductory chapter describes the fundamentals for later analysis, modeling and discussion of choice tasks and behavior. Figure 2.1 depicts the basic elements of the choice process which are relevant for the present work. On the left hand side, we see the general problem the decision makers are faced with: the choice task. Generally speaking, a choice task defines the problem of choosing the preferred out of a discrete and finite set of alternatives. The decision makers' preferences determine what the preferred alternative is. Thus, in Sect. 2.1, we define both choice tasks and preferences.

In recent decades, a large stream of research has shown empirically that choice behavior is contingent on the characteristics of both choice tasks and the decision makers (Einhorn and Hogarth 1981; Gigerenzer and Selten 2001; Payne et al. 1993). Following this body of literature, we assume that decision makers have a number of decision strategies in their mind and apply them contingent upon such factors such as the complexity of the choice task, which describes how difficult a choice task is for a decision maker (Payne et al. 1993). Hence, in Sect. 2.2, we provide a review of the different decision strategies which have been described in the literature so far.

In the subsequent Sect. 2.3, we then allude to different methods how researchers can observe and measure the decision process and determine the decision strategies which best explain the observed behavior and the final choice.

Finally, we provide a detailed literature review on different measures of complexity and the influence of complexity on decision-making behavior in Sect. 2.4.

2.1 Choice Tasks and Preferences

Choice tasks belong to the class of preferential decision problems. Preferential decision problems are characterized by the information elements which are given to the decision maker and by the goal statement of the decision (Payne et al. 1993). Concerning the information elements, preferential decision problems consist of three different components: (1) a number of alternatives, (2) events or contingencies

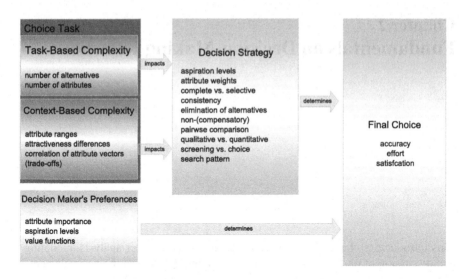

Fig. 2.1 The choice process with its central elements discussed in this chapter

that relate actions to outcomes and the probabilities for these events, and (3) values associated with outcomes (Payne et al. 1993, p. 20). Some information elements might be unknown. For instance, some alternatives might not be given but have to be generated by some optimization algorithm (Gettys et al. 1987; Keller and Ho 1988). The goal statement describes the outcome of the decision. Either the decision makers (1) select the most attractive alternative, or they (2) rank order the alternatives according to their attractiveness, or (3) they give a numerical value representing the attractiveness of every separate alternative.

In the present work, we focus on preferential decision problems in the context of purchase decisions. Following others, we refer to them as *choice tasks* (Bettman and Zins 1979). We define choice tasks as preferential decision problems with a limited number of alternatives where all information elements are known and there are no uncertainties. Thus, we do not deal with probabilities of events but assume that the outcome of alternatives is known. Furthermore, the goal of a choice task is to select the most attractive alternative, e.g., the product the consumer likes to purchase.

More formally, a choice task is a multi-alternative multi-attribute problem, which consists of n alternatives alt_j, $j = 1, \ldots, n$, $n \geq 2$ which are described by a_{ij} *attribute levels*, one for each of the m attributes, $attr_i$, $i = 1, \ldots, m$ (Harte and Koele 2001; Keeney and Raiffa 1993). Attribute levels are concrete occurrences of the attributes, where each attribute can have a different number of possible occurrences $|A_i|$. As an example, imagine a set of different cell phones (alternatives) which are described across different attributes, such as price, brand, and battery runtime. Each cell phone is specified by the three attribute levels it takes for each of the three attributes, such as €100, Samsung, and 48 h battery runtime for cell phone A or €150, Nokia, and 60 h battery runtime for cell phone B. For example, if

Table 2.1 Example of a product-comparison matrix with two alternatives and three attributes

Attribute	Cell phone A	Cell phone B
Price	100	150
Brand	Samsung	Nokia
Battery runtime	48 h	60 h

there are 10 different brands available, $|A_{brand}|$ would be equal to 10, as the attribute brand can take 10 possible levels. We assume that each alternative is described by the same attributes.

Typically, in the context of purchase decisions, choice tasks are displayed in form of *product-comparison matrices* (Häubl and Trifts 2000). A product-comparison matrix displays each alternative in a column. An example of such a product-comparison matrix is given in Table 2.1.

The space of attribute levels differs with respect to scales and ranges, which makes it hard to compare and trade-off alternatives against each other; e.g., while the price is measured as a ratio level in a currency, the color is described by words and induces only a nominal scale.[1] We assume that decision makers have preferences over attribute levels. These preferences can have a simple ordinal form "yellow is preferred over red". Sometimes, it is further assumed that decision makers assign so-called attribute values to attribute levels (Eisenfuhr and Weber 2002). These attribute values reflect the degree of attractiveness the decision maker assigns to the attribute level. Each decision maker hence has m value functions, v_i, that assign attribute values to all available attribute levels, $v_i(a_{ij})$. Typical examples of value functions are displayed in Fig. 2.2. In this figure, v_{price} is a decreasing function, as the highest attribute value is assigned to the lowest price. However, value functions do not have to be monotonic, as is often the case for the attribute *size*. The figure shows an example, where the decision maker prefers a medium sized product to small or large ones. Finally, the right figures shows an example of the attribute color, which has nominal attribute levels.

2.2 Decision Strategies

"The aim of research on multi-attribute evaluation processes is to describe the process taking place between the presentation of the information and the final evaluation" (Harte and Koele 2001, p. 30). Many researchers have formalized common operations which describe people's decision-making behavior and inferred decision strategies which describe the process of acquiring, evaluating, and comparing information elements of choice tasks (Beach 1990; Hogarth 1987; Payne et al.

---

[1]Nominal scales use mere labels; ordinal scales indicate a relative position (e.g., graduations); interval scales indicate the magnitude of differences without a fixed zero point (degree Celsius), and ratio scales indicate the magnitude of differences and fix a zero point (e.g., size, price).

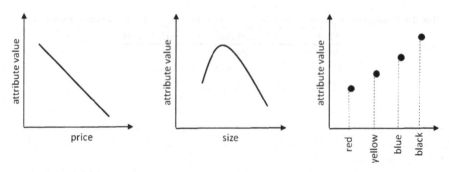

Fig. 2.2 Three examples of value functions

1993; Russo and Dosher 1983; Tversky 1969, 1972). Generally speaking, a decision strategy is defined as "a sequence of operations used to transform an initial stage of knowledge into a final goal state of knowledge in which the decision maker feels that the decision problem is solved" (Payne et al. 1992, p. 109). In our context, a decision strategy describes the process which decision makers follow when choosing an alternative in a choice task.

This section reviews decision strategies in detail, as they are the state-of-the-art for describing consumer purchase behavior. Yet, to gain a deep understanding of the common elements of and differences between decision strategies, we start by pointing out decision strategy characteristics which we retrieved from another literature review (e.g., Payne et al. 1993; Riedl et al. 2008).

2.2.1 Characteristics

2.2.1.1 Compensatory Versus Non-Compensatory

Decision strategies consist of compensatory and non-compensatory strategies. In compensatory strategies, a low value of an attribute of a product can be compensated by a high value on a different attribute. A typical statement of a consumer applying a compensatory strategy would be "I would prefer a cell with integrated navigation system, but not if I have to pay too much extra for that". Thus, compensatory strategies allow for trade-offs among attributes. In contrast, non-compensatory strategies do not allow attribute values on one attribute to compensate for low values on another attribute. An example for a non-compensatory strategy is "I choose the cheapest product."

2.2.1.2 Attribute Weights

Attribute weights, w_i, reflect how important each attribute is. Hence, they express how much each attribute influences a decision. For a decision maker with a high weight for price, for instance, the product price is a very important attribute. While some strategies involve an explicit weighting of attributes and thus assume a ratio scale on their values, others require an ordinal scale, assume equal importance of all attributes, or assume no order at all.

2.2.1.3 Attribute-Wise Versus Alternative-Wise Processing

A strategy can induce an attribute-wise or an alternative-wise comparison. Attribute-wise behavior describes a decision maker who picks one attribute, compares its attribute levels across all alternatives, and then moves to the next attribute. Comparing all products first regarding their color and then regarding their price is an example of attribute-wise processing. Alternative-wise strategies, by contrast, assume the decision maker to sequentially evaluate alternatives regarding all or at least several of their attribute levels.

2.2.1.4 Pairwise Comparison

Some strategies compare alternatives sequentially in pairs. Usually they eliminate the weaker alternative of that pair and keep the stronger alternative for forming a new pair.

2.2.1.5 Aspiration Levels

In some strategies, attribute levels are compared to aspiration levels. Aspiration levels (or cutoff-values) can be interpreted as thresholds or acceptable levels. Formally, for each attribute level, a_{ij}, we can assign whether the aspiration level is violated, $asp(a_{ij}) = 1$, or not $asp(a_{ij}) = 0$. Dependent on the strategy, an alternative is either immediately excluded from further consideration once an aspiration level is not met or this attribute level is marked to be negative. An example of an aspiration level would be a maximum price we are at most willing to pay for a product.

2.2.1.6 Consistency Across Attributes/Alternatives

A consistent decision strategy evaluates the same number of attribute levels per attribute/alternative. For an inconsistent strategy, the number of attribute levels which is considered per attribute/alternative varies.

2.2.1.7 Complete Versus Selective

A complete decision strategy considers all attribute levels. Therefore, each complete decision strategy is by definition consistent. A selective strategy leaves out certain attribute levels from consideration. This can be done in a consistent way (leaving out the same amount of attribute levels per alternative/attribute), or in an inconsistent way.

2.2.1.8 Elimination of Alternatives

Some decision strategies eliminate alternatives to narrow down the choice task until only the preferred alternative is left.

2.2.1.9 Qualitative Versus Quantitative Reasoning

Decision strategies can be distinguished by the way they evaluate attribute levels. Quantitative strategies require counting, adding, or multiplying, while qualitative ones evaluate by simply comparing attribute levels or values with one another.

2.2.1.10 Screening Versus Choice

This characteristic describes a tendency rather than a strict characteristic. Decision strategies differ in their goal to either narrow down a larger set of alternatives quickly in the screening process, or to choose one out of a small set of alternatives. The result of the screening phase is the consideration set which consists of only a few alternatives which the decision makers prefer most. Some of the strategies are more capable of building a consideration set than leading to a final choice. Although very similar at first glance, this characteristic is different to *elimination of alternatives*. While all screening decision strategies eliminate alternatives, choice decision strategies can either further eliminate alternatives or just choose an alternative out of the whole consideration set without explicit elimination of inferior ones.

2.2.2 Types

In the following paragraphs, we describe different strategies in detail. By means of an analysis of the literature, we have identified fifteen decision strategies. Therefore, our summary extends current overviews (Payne et al. 1993; Riedl et al. 2008). Moreover, in contrast to current overviews, we aim at a more formal description.

Table A.1 in the appendix lists all strategies, the main literature sources, as well as alternative name conventions of the strategies. In addition, Fig. A.1 gives an overview of the different strategies and their characteristics.

1. **EQW (Equal Weight Heuristic):** Decision makers select the alternative with highest utility, ($\max_{j=1,\ldots,n}[u(alt_j) = \sum_{i=1}^{m} v_i(a_{ij})]$). Each attribute is assumed

to be of equal importance to decision makers. Thus, the utility of an alternative is defined as the sum of all attribute values.

2. **WADD (Weighted Additive Rule):** The normative rule in the decision making literature. It assumes that a decision maker computes a utility for each alternative. WADD defines the utility function as the sum of the weighted attribute values ($\max_{j=1,...,n}[u(alt_j) = \sum_{i=1}^{m} w_i v_i(a_{ij})]$).

3. **ADD(Additive Difference Strategy):** When using this strategy, a decision maker iteratively performs pairwise comparisons of alternatives until only one candidate is left. The decision maker computes the utility difference between two alternatives as $diff(alt_k, alt_l) = \sum_{i=1}^{m} w_i[v_i(a_{ik}) - v_i(a_{il})]$. If $diff(alt_k, alt_l) > 0$, alt_l is eliminated and alt_k is compared to the next alternative. If $diff(alt_k, alt_l) < 0$, alt_k is eliminated.

4. **MCD (Majority of Confirming Dimensions Heuristic):** Analogous to ADD, a decision maker compares alternatives pairwise. In contrast to ADD, however, decision makers do not assign utility values, rather they decide whether they prefer a_{ik} over a_{il}. The difference of two alternatives is computed as: $diff(alt_k, alt_l) = \sum_{i=1}^{m} D(a_{ik}, a_{il})$, where $D(a_{ik}, a_{il}) = 1$ if $v_i(a_{ik}) > v_i(a_{il})$, $D(a_{ik}, a_{il}) = -1$ if $v_i(a_{ik}) < v_i(a_{il})$, and 0 otherwise.

5. **FRQ (Frequency of Good and/or Bad Features Heuristic):** The decision maker distinguishes between good, neutral, and bad attribute values. For this purpose, $frq(a_{ij}) = 1$ if a_{ij} has a desired attribute level, $frq(a_{ij}) = 0$ if the attribute level of a_{ij} has no influence on the decision maker's choice decision, and $frq(a_{ij}) = -1$ if the attribute level of a_{ij} is not attractive for the decision maker. The literature describes three variants of FRQ. A decision maker can choose the alternative (a) with the highest number of good attribute levels, (b) with the lowest number of bad attribute levels, or (c) a decision maker could consider both good and bad attribute levels ($\max_{j=1,...,n}[\sum_{i=1}^{m} frq(a_{ij})]$).

6. **COM (Compatibility Test):** An alternative alt_j is eliminated if its attribute values violate the corresponding aspiration levels more than k times, where k is specified by the decision maker: $\sum_{i=1}^{m} asp(a_{ij}) > k$.

7. **CONJ (Conjunctive Strategy):** A decision maker removes an alternative alt_j if at least one of its attribute values violates an aspiration level: $\sum_{i=1}^{m} asp(a_{ij}) \geq 1$.

8. **SAT (Satisficing Heuristic):** Decision makers sequentially consider alternatives in the order in which they occur in the choice task. They select the first alternative where all attribute levels are above the corresponding aspiration levels ($\forall i$ $asp(a_{ij}) = 0$). In contrast to CONJ, which assumes the decision makers to evaluate every alternative, SAT stops as soon as one alternative which meets all aspiration levels is identified.

9. **SAT+ (Satisficing-Plus Strategy):** A variant of SAT. Decision makers consider only m^* attributes. They select the alternative where all m^* attribute levels are above the corresponding aspiration levels.

10. **DIS (Disjunctive Strategy):** The decision makers remove an alternative alt_j if all of its attribute values violate an aspiration level:
$$\sum_{i=1}^{m} asp(a_{ij}) = m.$$

11. **DOM (Dominance Strategy):** A decision maker chooses the alternative that dominates all other alternatives. An alternative alt_k dominates alt_l if all attribute levels are at least as good and at least one attribute level is better : $\forall i \; v_i(a_{ik}) \geq v_i(a_{il}) \wedge \exists i \; v_i(a_{ik}) > v_i(a_{il})$. If no alternative dominates all other alternatives, the decision maker chooses no alternative.

12. **MAJ (Simple Majority Decision Rule):** Same as DOM – but the decision maker always chooses an alternative. The decision maker chooses the alternative whose attribute levels are best on the highest number of attributes.

13. **EBA (Elimination by Aspect Strategy):** Decision makers sort the attributes $attr_i$ according to their weight w_i. Starting with the attribute with the highest weight, they iteratively remove alternatives alt_j if the value of the ith attribute does not meet the aspiration level $(asp(a_{ij}) = 1)$. The strategy stops if there is only one alternative left or all attributes are considered. In the original version, EBA considers attributes not deterministically but probabilistically according to attribute weights (Tversky 1972).

14. **LEX (Lexicographic Heuristic):** Decision makers consider the attribute $attr_h$ with the highest attribute weight and select the alternative alt_j whose attribute value has the highest value: $max_{j=1,...,n} v_h(a_{hj})$. If this returns more than one alternative, they iteratively compare the remaining alternative across the next most important attribute until there is only one alternative left.

15. **LED (Minimum Difference Lexicographic Rule):** This rule selects an alternative analogous to LEX, but two attribute values a_{ij} and a_{ik} are considered to be equal if $v_i(a_{ij}) - v_i(a_{ik}) < \Delta_i$, where Δ_i is the threshold above which a decision maker notices a difference between two attribute values (Luce 1956; Tversky 1969).

2.3 Measuring Decision-Making Behavior

We aim at explaining and understanding observed decision-making behavior and hence follow a descriptive approach. There are basically two descriptive research paradigms for studying choice behavior. The outcome-based approach fits the mathematical models of the relation between attribute values and evaluations of alternatives (Harte and Koele 2001; Rieskamp and Hoffrage 1999). Structural modeling and comparative model fitting are the two representatives of this paradigm. The second research paradigm is process-oriented and focuses on the sequence of information acquisition and evaluation steps. Representatives of process tracing techniques are verbal protocols, Mouselab, and eye tracking which record the attribute levels observed, the length of observation time as well as the sequence in which they are looked at (Einhorn and Hogarth 1981).

2.3.1 Outcome-Based Approach

2.3.1.1 Structural Modeling

Structural modeling assumes that decision makers maximize their utility. The structural modeling approach then predominantly uses regression analysis to find the parameters which achieve the best fit given the assigned values or the final choice and a predefined utility model (Brehmer 1994). Usually, the assumed utility model is the weighted additive rule (WADD, Sect. 2.2.2), which is fitted to the data by linear regression. WADD is a very robust model and currently provides the best fit compared to competing utility models (Dawes and Corrigan 1974; Dawes 1979; Harte and Koele 2001).

Since the full range of decision strategies is not covered and only parameters of utility maximizing models are estimated, researchers try to approximate non-compensatory decision making from the parameters (Swait and Adamowicz 2001). If, for instance, one attribute has a much higher weight than others, one could infer that this attribute predominantly determines the decision, speaking in favor of a non-compensatory strategy.

The basic assumption of structural modeling approaches is that the overall utility value $u(alt_j)$ of an alternative j can be decomposed into two additively separable parts, (1) a deterministic component $d(alt_j)$, and (2) a stochastic component – the error term ϵ_j – representing, for instance, unobserved attributes affecting choice: $u(alt_j) = d(alt_j) + \epsilon_j$. The deterministic component $d(alt_j)$ is assumed to have an additively separable linear form. Given m attributes with each $|A_i|$ possible attribute levels it can be written as

$$d(alt_j) = \sum_{i=1}^{m} \sum_{k=1}^{|A_i|} \beta_{ik} X_{jik} \qquad (2.1)$$

where X_{jik} is a binary variable indicating whether the alternative j contains the occurrence k of attribute i. β_{ik} is the part-worth utility of occurrence k of $attr_i$. The part-worth utility reflects with which value each occurrence contributes to the utility of an alternative. In case of WADD, which assumes the weighted linear additive utility function, for instance, if the occurrence k is included in alt_j, $X_{jik} = 1$, $\beta_{ik} = w_i v_i (a_{ij})$. In case of EQW, it would be $\beta_{ik} = v_i (a_{ij})$. The part-worth utilities for each respondent can be estimated via a Multinominal Logit model or a Hierarchal Bayes approach (Lenk et al. 1996).

The range of part-worths for an attribute i can be used to evaluate the importance of this attribute (Verlegh et al. 2002). If, for instance, the part-worths for price have a high range, this indicates that prices might be very important to the individual. While, if part-worths of, for instance, color, differ only slightly for the different colors, this might indicate that the individual does not care much about color. Hence, we can compute attribute weights from part-worths and $\sum_{i=1}^{m} \sum_{k=1}^{|A_i|} \beta_{ik} X_{jik} = \sum_{i=1}^{m} \sum_{j=1}^{n} w_i v_i (a_{ij})$.

Although WADD explains large portions of the final decisions, many researchers have examined that WADD is remote from describing the actual decision process. First, WADD assumes no interaction among attribute values. This means that attribute values contribute to the utility of an alternative independently from other attribute values of the same or other alternatives. Yet people report that their value functions depend on what other alternatives are available (Ford et al. 1989; Payne 1976). Second, weighting and summing up the attribute values of all alternatives does not describe the actual process decision makers follow (Maule and Svenson 1993). This loose link between the assumed utility model and the observed behavior is the main problem of structural modeling approaches. Bröder and Schiffer (2003a) argue that structural modeling approaches can only reveal information about the process "in case there is a clear formal link between theoretical descriptions of these processes and the expectations about decision outcomes" (p. 195). They point out that using regression to estimate, for instance, the WADD strategy is lacking this formal link. Consequently, WADD is less a model to describe human decision making but rather a kind of a general-purpose analytical tool to make general conclusions. For further discussion on structural modeling and a description of the analysis of variance as another method for fitting mathematical models, see Harte and Koele (2001).

2.3.1.2   Comparative Model Fitting

Bröder and Schiffer (2003a) recently introduced the term *comparative model fitting* for an approach which gains increasing interest. In comparative model fitting, several models compete for the best explanatory power for a given data set (Dhami and Ayton 2001; Garcia-Retamero et al. 2007; Gilbride and Allenby 2004; Hoffrage et al. 2000). Parameters of the competing models are defined a priori including appropriate error models, and maximum likelihood methods are used to compare final choices with the predictions of the models (Glöckner 2009). Thus, in contrast to structural modeling approaches, different decision strategies and not just a utility-maximizing strategy are assumed. Furthermore, the final choice is sufficient for comparing the explanatory power of competing models.

Bröder and Schiffer (2003a), for instance, use a Bayesian method to assess whether a simplified variant of LEX, EQW, or WADD provide the best likelihood function for explaining observed decision-making behavior. If for an observed decision, the likelihood of one strategy exceeds the likelihood of the other two, it is classified accordingly. Furthermore, the authors assume that respondents make errors when applying one or the other strategy and they incorporate a uniform distribution for modeling this error.

Recently, also other researchers have developed approaches for identifying non-compensatory strategies, such as the conjunctive and disjunctive strategies and elimination by aspects (Gilbride and Allenby 2006; Hauser et al. 2010; Kohli and Jedidi 2007).

According to Cutting (2000) the problems of comparative model fitting are the specification of measures a priori and an equally balanced number of free parameters per model to ensure that each model provides the same degree of flexibility. Furthermore, comparative model fitting still has the same problem a structural modeling approach has: if strategies make the same predictions, then we cannot distinguish between different strategies (Glöckner 2009; Rieskamp and Hoffrage 1999). Unfortunately, is it not unusual that strategies explain the same choices (Batley and Daley 2006; Bröder 2000; Bröder and Schiffer 2003b; Lee and Cummins 2004; Louviere and Meyer 2007; Rieskamp and Hoffrage 1999, 2008). Thus, the authors propose to use additional measures, in particular decision times and confidence judgment in order to differentiate between strategies.

2.3.2 Process Tracing

In contrast to outcome-based approaches, where parameters of decision strategies are estimated such that they best explain the final choice, in process tracing, patterns of information acquisition are observed. Thus, process tracing methods should be able to detect which information is acquired when and for how long. From these patterns, many of the characteristics which have been described in Sect. 2.2.1 can be identified. Process tracing techniques can, for instance, distinguish whether the decision maker acquires information selectively and consistently. These characteristics, in turn, suggest that certain strategies were applied by the decision maker (Payne 1976). Since some characteristics cannot yet be identified with process tracing techniques, often only subgroups of strategies but not the exact strategy can be determined. When we observe a complete, consistent and alternative-wise information acquisition process, for instance, WADD, EQW, FRQ might have been used (see Table A.1 for a listing of decision strategies and their characteristics). In the following section, we describe the three most prominent techniques for process tracing: verbal protocols, Mouselab and eye tracking.

2.3.2.1 Verbal Protocols

Verbal protocols can be recorded simultaneously or retrospectively, depending on whether the decision makers describe their behavior during the search process or thereafter. Retrospective processing is criticized for a potential lack of validity, as the decision maker might describe the decision-making behavior based on their own psychological theory rather than an accurate description of the own cognitive steps during the search (Fidler 1983; Svenson 1989). The more common approach is therefore to ask decision makers to think aloud simultaneously to the decision process (Ball et al. 1998; Bettman and Park 1980; Biggs et al. 1985; Nisbett and Wilson 1977; Selart et al. 1998; Todd and Benbasat 2000).

An analysis of the validity of the simultaneous approach of thinking aloud showed that although it tends to slow down the process, it does not seem to change the sequence of thoughts during the process (Ericsson and Simon 1980, 1993). Furthermore, as long as the respondent only reports contents of the short-term memory which are simple to verbalize, the protocol reflects the decision making sufficiently. However, Russo et al. (1989) criticize both simultaneous and retrospective verbal protocols. They argue that simultaneous protocols might interfere with the decision task and found that in retrospective protocols respondents did forget or not report truly what had actually happened.

Besides a potential lack of validity, several other disadvantages have caused a more and more rare usage of verbal protocols. First, transcribing and coding of statements is time-consuming (Reisen et al. 2008). Now, much more sophisticated and automatized techniques are available due to the advancement in information technology in recent years (see Mouselab and eye tracking). Furthermore, coding is prone to biases since sometimes it is unclear which model to fit to the verbal statement. Third, verbal protocols are usually incomplete and do not fully cover the thinking process (Someren et al. 1994). Someren et al. (1994) remark, "occasionally protocols contain 'holes' of which it is almost certain that an intermediate thought occurred here" (p. 33).

2.3.2.2   Mouselab and Information Display Boards

Mouselab is currently the predominant method used in research and is an improved, automatized version of an older method, the so-called Information Display Boards (Bettman et al. 1990; Payne 1976; Payne et al. 1993; Reisen et al. 2008). When using Information Display Boards, decision makers have to manually pull cards out of envelopes to retrieve the attribute level information and put them back in the appropriate envelope afterwards. Thus, at most one attribute level is uncovered at any one time. Besides a higher effort for the decision makers to acquire information on the attribute levels, data observation in Information Display Boards is tedious, as data is recorded just by observing decision makers' behavior and there is no automated way of data collection.

Mouselab is a software that keeps track of information acquisition, response time, and choices by recording mouse movements in a product-comparison matrix on a computer screen (Bettman et al. 1990). At the beginning of the choice task, all attribute levels are hidden behind boxes. Only by clicking or moving the cursor on each box can the respondent retrieve the attribute level. In the original version, the box is hidden again once the cursor moves away (Payne et al. 1988).

Mouselab covers the decision process more completely than verbal protocols but because of the complete coverage, we no longer can distinguish the pure information acquisition stage from the cognitive evaluation stage (Svenson 1979). In a newer version of Mouselab, the so-called MouseTrace, the authors try to overcome these deficits (Jasper and Shapiro 2002). MouseTrace incorporates the notion of decision stages by allowing the software to record different process measures for different time periods. However, as the number of stages as well as the number of mouse clicks, movements, or choices per stage must be defined in advance, a certain structure of the process is assumed which might not reflect the actual way of decision making at all.

Besides the problem of ignoring the difference between pure information acquisition and the evaluation and comparison of alternatives which neither Mouselab nor eye tracking can resolve currently, a main disadvantage of Mouselab is the potential lack of external validity as it might bias the decision process. First, moving the mouse for turning cards causes additional effort and might therefore keep the decision makers from considering certain attribute levels. Second, a matrix of hidden information does not reflect the situation consumers are faced with in online webstores and is therefore not appropriate for analyzing online purchase behavior. For an overview on 45 studies which either used Information Display Boards or verbal protocols, see Ford et al. (1989).

2.3.2.3 Eye Tracking

Due to the increased speed of computer processors and computer vision techniques as well as reduced costs for the required hardware equipment, eye tracking has become an alternative way to keep record of the decision process (Duchowski 2007; Lohse and Johnson 1996; Reisen et al. 2008). In the field of human computer interaction, Nielsen (1993) was one of the first to provide the idea that eye trackers could be used to infer the users' intentions by reading their eye movements. Eye tracking is the process of measuring eye gazes or eye movements with eye tracker systems which differ with respect to the different video techniques they apply (Duchowski 2007). In desktop-based human computer interaction, for instance, the currently applied systems are head-mounted, stationary eye trackers (Pfeiffer 2010). They consist of two units. The user wears a camera unit, while at the PC a computer-vision system is installed.

In contrast to Mouselab or its variants, with eye trackers it is unnecessary to hide information since the eye tracker system is able to precisely record fixations on attribute levels or other pieces of information (Lohse and Johnson 1996; Reisen et al. 2008). It keeps track of not only the exact position and sequence of the fixations, but also of the length of fixations. There is a pre-specified time threshold for eye fixations which must be met in order to interpret the fixation as actual information acquisition.

The lack of external validity of Mouselab is addressed by eye tracking as it allows to capture information acquisition on the level of the decision maker's visual system and creates a situation which is closer to a natural purchasing process than other techniques do (Russo 1978; Russo and Dosher 1983; Russo and Leclerc 1994). Others even argue that eye tracking does not affect information acquisition costs at all if compared to natural purchasing decisions (Lohse and Johnson 1996). Svenson (1979) found that if the amount of information is too high (i.e., the number of alternatives and attributes is large), process tracing is imprecise. However, in our days, eye tracking has become a precise method for studying user behavior and interface design. Already in 1996, Lohse and Johnson pointed out:

> It is also important to mention that the discussion of eye tracking equipment in the literature [...] is based on equipment that is over 20 years old. Just as computers have rapidly increased in power and performance, eye tracking equipment has also improved significantly. Old eye equipment had limited precision and accuracy for detecting small regions on a display. Current eye tracking systems are able to detect regions as small as 1.5 square centimeters. [...] Thus, it seems time to reevaluate the importance of eye tracking equipment as a tool for process tracing studies (p. 42).

Now, in 2010 eye tracking is able to detect regions as small as $0.38\,\mathrm{cm}^2$.[2] Typically, current systems operate in a spatial volume of $30\,\mathrm{cm}^3$ around the screen and sample with rates around 600 Hz.

Lohse and Johnson (1996) were the first to address the question whether Mouselab and eye tracking techniques influence the decision process. In their study, when using eye tracking, respondents needed less time for the decision, looked more often at attribute levels already looked at before (reacquisition), but the proportion of cells accessed at least once (breadth of search) was lower than when using Mouselab. Furthermore, when using eye tracking, respondents had a more inconsistent search and they looked more attribute-wise. Reisen et al. (2008) did a comparable study and confirmed that when using eye tracking, respondents needed less time, did more reacquisitions, accessed more cells in total and had a more inconsistent search. However, they contradict some other findings by Lohse and Johnson (1996). First, the percentage of attribute levels which were considered at all was not significantly different from Mouselab. Second, they did not find any difference in the the sequence in which information was acquired. Under both conditions, respondents compared alternatives across their attributes. Because of the contradicting results, the two research groups draw different conclusions. While Lohse and Johnson (1996) concluded that the process tracing method does influence the decision process, Reisen et al. (2008) concluded the opposite.

Negative effects stemming from Mouselab were found by Dieckmann et al. (2009): They argue that decisions can be less effective when measured with Mouselab since moving the mouse causes additional cognitive effort. Hence, less effort is spent on the information acquisition itself. A consequence might be that different decision strategies are used when Mouselab instead of eye tracking is chosen for process measurement.

In a recent study, we compared Mouselab and eye tracking to shed more light on the discussion. We did not only analyze whether the process tracing method influences the decision-making process but also whether it influences the final choice (Meißner et al. 2010). In line with Lohse and Johnson (1996) and Reisen et al. (2008), respondents needed more time in the Mouselab condition, but in contradiction to both studies, they acquired the same amount of information as in the

---

[2]The SMI EyeLink II eyetracker system used in the present work, for instance, has a gaze position accuracy of $0.5°$ and respondents posit themselves in 40–60 cm distance from the screen $(\tan(0.5°) \times 40\,\mathrm{cm} = 0.35\,\mathrm{cm})$. A 0.35 cm radius forms a circle of $0.38\,\mathrm{cm}^2$.

eye tracking condition. We confirmed all other results by Lohse and Johnson (1996) in that when using eye tracking the respondents had a more inconsistent and a more attribute-wise search. The difference for the search pattern was highly significant, and in total in Mouselab respondents searched more alternative-wise than with eye tracking. Yet, in the eye tracking conditions, respondents switched from a more attribute-wise search to a more and more alternative-wise search, the more tasks they had already completed. In summary, we agree with Lohse and Johnson (1996) that the process tracing method influences the process, in particular since both the consistency of search and the search pattern differed in the Mouselab vs. the eye tracking condition. However, when comparing final choices, we found no significant difference with respect to the estimated preference model. We estimated the linear additive model (WADD) with a structural modeling approach based on the choices respondents had made and found no differences in the estimated utility functions. Thus, although the process tracing method influences the decision process, the final choices were similar.

In summary, we argue along the lines of Lohse and Johnson (1996), who claim that the relevance of the difference in the decision-making process depends on the nature of the research question. Because of the differences, a pure descriptive research has its limits since observed information acquisition patterns are dependent on the used measurement instrument and, thus, generalizations should be made with caution. However, as soon as the effect of independent variables on the decision process is tested, the process measuring technique only affects the result if there is an interaction between manipulation and measuring technique. If there is no such interaction, the process measuring technique may only increase or decrease the main effect and therefore should not influence the nature of the research conclusion. Nevertheless, such interaction effects can hardly be anticipated in advance. We therefore suggest that as long as resources for eye tracking are available, eye tracking should always be the preferred method as it is able to record the decision process more precisely (Norman and Schulte-Mecklenbeck 2010; Seth et al. 2008).

2.3.2.4   Outcome-Based Versus Process Tracing

In this section, we have discussed the differences between two methods for determining peoples' decision-making behavior: outcome-based and process tracing methods. While the outcome-based approach estimates parameters of decision strategies based on observed final choices, the process tracing approaches, Mouselab and eyetracking, observe the sequence and the amount in which people retrieve information. Thus, they measure information acquisition. Verbal protocols, in contrast, also may provide information about what information the participants actually process.

The question remains whether, in general, outcome-based or process tracing methods should be applied when analyzing decision-making behavior. Since outcome-based and process tracing approaches focus on different aspects of decision making, we argue that they can complement one another well. There are only few studies which have used such a multi-method approach (Biggs et al. 1985; Lohse and Johnson 1996; Rieskamp and Hoffrage 1999, 2008). Among them Covey and Lovie (1998) conclude, "(...) a skilfully combined approach can help to draw up a more complete picture which could not be so easily achieved by either method on their own" (p. 33).

Yet, because of cost and time restrictions experimental researchers might not have the resources (time, money, technical possibilities, etc.) to use both approaches. In general, we share the belief that novel steps in the study on individual decision-making behavior should first start with the observation of final choices (a widespread procedure in decision theory and economics, see e.g., Bröder and Schiffer 2003a; Caplin and Dean 2010). One reason is that one has to take into account that process tracing techniques are only able to record acquired information, which does not necessarily mean that all this information is also processed and evaluated (Payne et al. 1978). Second, the insights almost always relate to general categories such as overall alternative-wise or attribute-wise information acquisition, rather than to the level of the particular strategy used. Thus, it is hard to determine the exact decision strategy which has been applied just based on process data (Bröder and Schiffer 2003a). Nevertheless, as several researchers have shown, when applying the outcome-based approach, competing models might lead to the same choices, although they rely on different decision-making processes (Batley and Daley 2006; Bröder 2000; Bröder and Schiffer 2003b; Lee and Cummins 2004; Louviere and Meyer 2007). In these cases, process tracing methods are obligatory to learn about how decision makers actually behave.[3] Adomavicius and Tuzhilin (2005) point out that in these cases, one should refrain from only using outcome-based approaches which serve as "as if" models because they are only judged by the degree to which they predict behavior, and not by the degree to which they actually explain real decision-making behavior.

For studying consumer purchase decisions, predicting market shares is the most important goal. Therefore, outcome-based based methods seem to be most appropriate. On the other hand, for studying human decision-making behavior and understanding cognitive processes from a psychological perspective, process tracing methods seem to be most appropriate, as they reveal more details of the decision process.

2.4 Complexity of Choice Tasks

2.4.1 Task-Based Versus Context-Based Complexity

Faced with a choice task, previous research has found that besides personal characteristics (e.g., cognitive ability and prior knowledge) and the social context (e.g., accountability and group membership), certain problem characteristics

---

[3] We will present a novel approach, which addresses this problem, in Chap. 4.

influence decision-making behavior (Ford et al. 1989; Payne et al. 1993). Problem characteristics influence how difficult the choice task itself is for the decision maker and how much effort the decision maker needs for the decision. Similar to Payne et al. (1993), among the problem characteristics, we distinguish between *task-based complexity* and *context-based complexity* effects. We define task effects to be general aspects of the decision task which are independent of attribute levels and from the decision maker's preferences while context effects depend on particular attribute levels and often depend on decision makers' preferences.

In this section, we provide a literature review of empirical studies on the influence of task-based complexity and context-based complexity on decision-making behavior. Since there are many different task and context effects and their influence has been tested on many different aspects of decision-making behavior, we have structured this section into four parts. In the first part, we explain different task and context effects. In Sect. 2.4.2, we describe the variables which are used to measure the effect on decision-making behavior. Thus, from a methodological perspective, in the first section, we discuss the independent variables and in the second part, the dependent variables of the experimental studies which follow in the third and the fourth part. The third part summarizes studies on task-based complexity and the fourth part studies on context-based complexity. In addition to that, we provide a detailed summary of the reviewed literature in the appendix in Table . This table resumes the experimental design, process tracing methods, independent and dependent variables, and results.

2.4.1.1   Task-Based Complexity

As defined above, task-based complexity describes general aspects of choice tasks such as the number of alternatives and attributes (amount of information), time pressure, information display (e.g., sequential vs. simultaneous presentation of alternatives), and the response mode (e.g., selecting one alternative vs. stating a rank order of alternatives). There is a huge body of literature on the influences of these different task effects on decision-making behavior (Bettman et al. 1991; Conlon et al. 2001; Ford et al. 1989; Payne et al. 1992). Hence, it is beyond the scope of the present work to give a complete review of all different kinds of task-based complexity. Therefore, we need to focus on those aspects which are relevant for the overall goal of the present work: the design of a DSS for webstores which supports consumers' decision-making behavior. Because of the anonymity in the Internet, operators of online webstores have limited knowledge about some aspects of the choice task environment of the online shoppers. For instance, they do not know whether the online shopper is under time pressure. Other aspects are pre-specified by the setting of an online webstore (e.g., is the response mode usually the selection of one product rather than a rank order of products). Hence, from our viewpoint, the most interesting factor is the amount of information displayed, that is, the number of alternatives and attributes. For details on other effects which are not addressed in the present work, the reader is referred to Ford et al. (1989) and Payne et al. (1993).

As the number of alternatives and attributes increases, people use simplifying decision strategies which neglect information rather than more effortful compensatory strategies (Bettman et al. 1991; Conlon et al. 2001; Ford et al. 1989; Payne et al. 1992). An increasing number of alternatives and attributes, for example, makes a decision more difficult since the decision maker has to consider more information for making a choice (Biggs et al. 1985; Payne et al. 1993; Timmermans 1993) and experiences information overload.

2.4.1.2 Context-Based Complexity

Concerning task effects, we focus on the number of attributes and alternatives. But what information is actually shown about the products? Context effects deal with that question. They concern the particular attribute levels, such as the price of each product (e.g., low, medium, high price) and their relationship to one another. Moreover, they might also require knowledge on the decision maker's preferences if they take into account not only attribute levels but also attribute values or weights (see Sect. 2.1).

Payne et al. (1993) provide an overview of different context factors: *Framing effects, the quality of the alternative set,* and *similarity.* Among them, *framing effects* and the *quality of the alternative set* are less relevant in the context of online purchase decisions. The quality of the alternative set plays a role in risky decisions, for instance decisions between gambles, and are thus irrelevant for the context of purchase decisions in non-risky environments. Framing effects usually refer to wording effects, such as whether choice tasks are formulated as gains or losses. In one famous study, Tversky and Kahneman (1981) asked subjects to choose between two alternative programs to combat an outbreak of an Asian disease which is expected to kill 600 people. In the one condition, alternatives are formulated in positive wording, for instance, "the program will result in 200 people being saved", in the other condition the wording was negative "the programm will result in 400 dead people". Even though both alternatives resulted in the same number of deaths, subjects decided for different alternatives, depending on the wording. Although, framing effects are very relevant and an interesting research area, from our viewpoint, they are less relevant for online purchase decisions. We will examine choice tasks where alternatives (products) are described by the technical details where the wording plays a minor role and there is little flexibility to frame the details in either negative or positive wording.

Hence, we will now focus on the remaining factor, the *similarity of alternatives.* Consider two situations: one in which the attribute values of prices, designs, and brands are similar, and another in which several attributes vary sharply. The general observation is that the more similar alternatives are, the harder the choice task is (higher complexity). One reason might be that the more similar the values, the harder it is for the decision maker to eliminate one of the alternatives based on only few attribute-wise comparisons (White and Hoffrage 2009).

According to Payne et al. (1993), similarity of alternatives can be measured in different ways, namely *dominance structures*, *trade-offs* reflecting the degree of conflicting alternatives, *attribute ranges*, and *attractiveness differences*. It is rather unlikely that there is a dominant alternative in the context of purchase decisions, as a lower price usually compensates low values on other attributes and vice versa (Fasolo et al. 2003). It is therefore of little interest to investigate the influence of a dominant alternative for the present work. Thus, we will consider only *trade-offs*, *attribute ranges* and *attractiveness differences*. For details on dominance structures, the framing effect and the quality of the alternative set, the reader is referred to Klein and Yadav (1989), Payne et al. (1993), Garbarino and Edell (1997), and Swait and Adamowicz (2001).

A *trade-off* occurs when there are two different attributes, $attr_l$, $attr_k$, and two different alternatives alt_p, alt_q, where alt_p is better for $attr_l$ and worse for $attr_k$ than alt_q: $v_l(a_{lp}) > v_l(a_{lq})$ and $v_k(a_{kp}) < v_k(a_{kq})$. Each trade-off requires the decision maker to balance one against another attribute level and hence increases complexity (Payne et al. 1993). Trade-offs are measured by computing the average pairwise correlation of attribute vectors (Fasolo et al. 2009; Luce et al. 1997), where the attribute vector of $attr_l$ consists of attribute levels and is defined as: $attr_l = (a_{l1}, a_{l2}, ..., a_{ln})$. When attribute vectors are correlated positively, one alternative beats the other alternatives on most attributes. Table 2.2 shows two examples with three alternatives each, $n = 3$, and three attributes, $m = 3$. Instead of attribute levels, we display their attribute values, $v_i(a_{ij}) \in [0, 1]$ for a fictive decision maker, so the larger $v_i(a_{ij})$ the better is a_{ij} for the decision maker. The price is best (0.8) for alternative 1 and gets worse for alternative 2 (0.3) and for alternative 3 (0.2) (see Table 2.2a). The two attribute vectors price and size are correlated positively ($CORR((0.8, 0.3, 0.2), (0.6, 0.5, 0.4)) = 0.93$). The same holds for the other pairs of attribute vectors, price and weight, as well as size and weight. The average correlation of all three pairs of attribute vectors is 0.9. Thus, the choice task has a high positive correlation and few trade-offs (in this case, there are even no trade-offs). In Table 2.2b price and size have a negative correlation ($CORR((0.8, 0.3, 0.2), (0.4, 0.7, 0.9)) = -0.97$). Prize and weight also have a negative correlation of -0.36, while weight and size have a slightly positive correlation of 0.11. On average this choice task is correlated negatively (-0.4). This negative correlation indicates strong trade-offs.

Table 2.2 Example of positive and negative correlation of attribute vectors

Attribute	alt_1	alt_2	alt_3
(a) Positive correlation of attribute vectors			
Price	0.8	0.3	0.2
Size	0.6	0.5	0.4
Weight	0.7	0.6	0.3
(b) Negative correlation of attribute vectors			
Price	0.8	0.3	0.2
Size	0.4	0.7	0.9
Weight	0.3	0.5	0.3

In consumer decision making, DM often have to trade off attribute levels against each other because they generally want low prices but high quality (Fasolo et al. 2005). Often, decision makers avoid dealing with trade-offs and use simplifying, non-compensatory strategies (see LEX, EBA, etc. in Sect. 2.2), "to escape from the unpleasant state of conflict induced by the decision problem itself" (Shephard 1964, p. 277).

The second context-specific effect refers to *attribute ranges*, which can be measured by the number of different attribute levels displayed per attribute. For instance, the number of different brands or the number of different colors that are available for the products. If alternatives all have similar attribute levels, then this might reduce the effort as there are few distinct attributes that will have to be considered (Shugan 1980). Instead of counting the number of different attribute levels, a more advanced approach is to measure the standard deviations of the attribute values (Böckenholt et al. 1991; Iglesias-Parro et al. 2002). Most researchers have argued that decision makers find more similar alternatives more difficult to solve and this is the reason why they spend more time on the decision (Biggs et al. 1985; Böckenholt et al. 1991).

Finally, the *attractiveness differences* describes the differences in utilities of the offered alternatives and thus relies on some utility maximizing strategy, such as WADD. If one alternative has a much higher utility than others, in other words the attractiveness difference is large, then it should be easy for decision makers to find this utility maximizing alternative, and thus complexity is low (Böckenholt et al. 1991; Swait and Adamowicz 2001).

In contrast to other works, we like to separate attractiveness differences clearly from attribute ranges (see Payne et al. 1993; Böckenholt et al. 1991 for a less clear separation). While attribute ranges measure to what extent the single attributes differ from one another, for instance measured by computing the variance of attribute values on each attribute, the attractiveness differences refer to the difference of utilities of alternatives. The following examples display two choice tasks with high attribute ranges (see Table 2.3). In Table 2.3a, the alternatives hardly differ with respect to their total utility (0.425 vs. 0.475 vs. 0.425), while in Table 2.3b the alternatives differ a lot in respect to their total utility (0.8 vs. 0.375 vs. 0.225). However, both have the same average variance of attribute levels (attribute range) of 0.11.

Swait and Adamowicz (2001) introduced a measure of complexity which captures both the (1) complexity resulting from the quantity of information presented in a choice task and (2) the attractiveness difference: the entropy $H(ct)$. The entropy of a choice task, ct, is defined as

$$H(ct) = -\sum_{j=1}^{n} \pi(alt_j) \log \pi(alt_j),   \tag{2.2}$$

where $\pi(alt_j)$ is the probability that alternative j is chosen. The choice probability $\pi(alt_j) = \frac{u(alt_j)}{\sum_{j \in CT} u(alt_j)}$, of an alternative j results from the utility value $u(alt_j)$ of that alternative in relation to the utility values of all alternatives in the set of

Table 2.3 Two examples with both high attribute ranges but different attractiveness differences

Attribute	alt_1	alt_2	alt_3	Variance
(a) High range and low utility difference				
Price	0.8	0.5	0.2	0.09
Size	0.1	0.5	0.9	0.16
Weight	0.2	0.8	0.2	0.12
Brand	0.6	0.1	0.4	0.06
Total utility	0.425	0.475	0.425	0.11
(b) High range and high utility difference				
Price	0.8	0.3	0.2	0.10
Size	0.6	0.3	0.2	0.04
Weight	1	0.5	0.1	0.20
Brand	0.8	0.4	0.4	0.05
Total utility	0.8	0.375	0.225	0.11

choice tasks, CT. The utility values are estimated by means of a MNL model and Hierarchical Bayes for each individual.

If there is an alternative in a choice task with choice probability one and the others therefore have probabilities of zero, the entropy, $H(ct)$, reaches its minimum value of zero. On the contrary, if the choice probability of all alternatives in a choice task is equal, the entropy will reach its maximum value of log n, where n is the number of alternatives. Thus, the entropy depends not only on the similarity of the utilities of alternatives but also on the number of alternatives in the choice task. The more alternatives are in the choice task, the higher the entropy can be. For a given number of alternatives, n, the entropy is always greater or equal than for any other set with less alternatives n': $2 \le n' \le n$.

The authors argue that the number of attributes and their correlation only effects entropy indirectly, since they influence the choice probabilities, $\pi(alt_j)$. From our viewpoint, this effect should be included more directly into the model as the indirect influence stays vague.

In the following paragraphs, we will review studies on the influence of the number of alternatives and attributes on decision making as well as the influence of the context-based measurements described above. Before we summarize the empirical evidence for the influence of complexity on decision-making behavior, we want to describe how decision-making behavior is typically measured.

2.4.2   Variables for Describing Decision-Making Behavior

In Sect. 2.3, we discussed how decision-making behavior can be analyzed with outcome-based and process tracing approaches. In general, research on outcome-based approaches focuses more on the development of better models and methods and less on the influence of complexity (for an exception see Conlon et al. 2001; DeShazo and Fermo 2002; Swait and Adamowicz 2001). Thus, the following literature review summarizes mainly process tracing studies. As we will see in the following paragraphs, some of the variables typically measured correspond to characteristics of decision-making behavior as described in 2.2.1. Thus, Table A.1 can be used to determine which decision strategies fit best to the observed behavior.

1. *Depth of search* measures the absolute number of attribute levels which were assessed, including repeated processing of the same attribute levels (Huber 1980).
2. *Breadth of search* measures the number of considered attribute levels in relation to the amount of available information (Biggs et al. 1985). Thus, it counts whether an attribute level was assessed at least once, excluding repeated processing of the same attribute levels. A respondent who considers each attribute level at least once has a breadth of search of 1, and thus would use a decision strategy which is complete (see characteristic *complete* in Sect. 2.2.1).
3. A related measure describes the *consistency* of search (see characteristic *consistent* in Sect. 2.2.1), which is determined by the number of different attribute levels considered per alternative and per attribute or the time they were considered (Biggs et al. 1985; Timmermans 1993). In case the number of considered attribute levels per attributes is the same for each attribute, the search is consistent with respect to attributes. In case the number of considered attribute levels per alternatives is the same for each alternative, the search is consistent with respect to alternatives. This measure helps us to determine whether a compensatory or non-compensatory strategy was used. A consistent search with a breadth of search of one, for instance, militates in favor of a compensatory strategy (see Table A.1, the only consistent and complete but non-compensatory strategy is DOM).
4. The *search pattern* describes the sequence in which information is acquired. When decision makers tend to consider first several attributes of the same alternative before proceeding to the next alternative, the search pattern is alternative-wise. When, in contrast, they compare alternatives across attributes, we speak of attribute-wise search patterns. The most common form of operationalizing search patterns is the search index (SI) (Payne 1976). The SI sets the number of attribute-wise transitions (r_{attr}) and alternative-wise transitions (r_{alt}) in relation. It varies from -1 to $+1$, with -1 indicating completely attribute-wise search and $+1$ indicating completely alternative-wise search:

$$SI = \frac{r_{alt} - r_{attr}}{r_{alt} + r_{attr}}. \tag{2.3}$$

Alternative-wise and attribute-wise transitions can be measured with Mouselab and eye tracking methods. In case verbal protocols are used, researchers count statements reflecting comparisons among alternatives vs. comparisons among attributes (Timmermans 1993). Other researchers using verbal protocols, approximate the search pattern by analyzing how often decision makers mention the elimination of alternatives (Klein and Yadav 1989). Furthermore, when respondents spend more time on alternative-wise (attribute-wise) processing, this speaks in favor of alternative-wise (attribute-wise) search patterns (Bettman et al. 1993).

5. Another prevalent measure is *effort*. This can be measured by the total time taken for the choice. Sometimes, in addition to using time for measuring effort, researchers also measure the respondents' self-reported effort (Iglesias-Parro et al. 2002; Luce et al. 1997).

6. Besides effort, decision *accuracy* is an interesting factor, but few studies are able to measure it. That is because accuracy is usually defined as the relation between the utility value of the chosen alternative and the utility value of the alternative selected when using the normative WADD strategy. Thus, highest accuracy is achieved when the WADD strategy is applied. Since only very few studies determine the utility function, they are not able to measure accuracy. Some studies use self-reported accuracy measures instead (i.e., Klein and Yadav 1989) or they present subjects inference tasks where the optimal choice is independent from people's preferences (Rieskamp and Hoffrage 2008).

In the following two sections, we describe what effects task-based and context-based complexity have on these variables which describe decision-making behavior.

2.4.3 Influence of Task-Based Complexity

The influence of the number of alternatives and attributes has been the subject of a number of studies. In a meta-study by Ford et al. (1989), for example, 20 out of 33 studies examine that influence. These results as well as a newer study by Timmermans (1993) report that an increasing amount of information leads to decreasing depth of search and decreasing search time. This indicates the limits of decision makers' cognitive capabilities which are not sufficient for processing all available information. Hence, decision makers apply selective and non-compensatory strategies.

Timmermans (1993) finds that an increasing amount of information leads to an increased depth of search. However, for an increasing number of attributes this only happens until decision makers exceed their cognitive capabilities. When this point is reached, increasing the number of attributes does no longer lead to an increased depth of search. Furthermore, with an increasing amount of information, the breadth of search decreases. The reason might be that in such cases, decision makers apply selective and non-compensatory strategies which, in general, do not consider attributes with low importance and hence the more attributes there are, the more information is just neglected.

Studies on search patterns lead to similar results as the studies on the depth and breadth of search. When the amount of information is low (complexity is low), complete and compensatory strategies are used. An increasing amount of information increases the usage of non-compensatory strategies (Billings and Marcus 1983; Johnson and Meyer 1984; Olshavsky 1979; Staelin and Payne 1976). Biggs et al. (1985) and Shields (1980) measure the number of observed attributes per alternative and conclude that a relationship between the search pattern and the amount of information exists. With increasing amount of information, the variance of considered attributes per alternative increases, thus more inconsistent strategies are applied. The authors further argue that this result indicates an attribute-wise search and – according to Billings and Marcus (1983) and Crow et al. (1980) – might stand for strategies which are based on elimination such as EBA and CONJ. They further observe that at the end of the search process, people tend to use more alternative-wise search.

Timmermans (1993) reports similar results of a study in which she uses verbal protocols. In choice tasks with low complexity, respondents show more alternative-wise search. With an increasing amount of information, however, they compare alternatives more attribute-wise and eliminated more alternatives. She concludes that this indicates a two-step decision process.

Finally, studies reveal that respondents spend more time, the more complex the task is (Olshavsky 1979; Onken et al. 1985; Payne and Braunstein 1978).

In general, the influence of the number of alternatives on the depth and breadth of search, the search pattern, and the time is quite clear, while the influence of the number of attributes is still not completely understood. Furthermore, conclusions on the applied strategy are sometimes retrieved solely from search patterns, for instance researchers often conclude a compensatory strategy from alternative-wise processing (Conlon et al. 2001; Crow et al. 1980; Lee and Lee 2004; Olshavsky 1979; Payne et al. 1993). However, as can be seen in Table A.1, not all decision strategies with alternative-wise processing are compensatory (i.e., CONJ, DIS, SAT), nor are all strategies with attribute-wise processing non-compensatory (i.e., ADD, MAJ, and MCD). Hence, conclusions on the actual decision strategy applied based on only one or two process tracing measures should be drawn with caution.

2.4.4 *Influence of Context-Based Complexity*

Whilst the influence of the number of attributes and alternatives has come under a lot of academic scrutiny, the influence of context-based complexity is barely understood. We address this lack of research and start by providing a detailed overview of the context-based measures that influence the different dependent variables. As pointed out earlier, we focus only on three measures relevant to our later studies, namely *attribute ranges*, *trade-offs*, and *attractiveness differences*.

2.4.4.1 Attribute Ranges and Depth/Breadth/Consistency of Search

Several studies show that the smaller the attribute ranges, and thus the more similar the alternatives are, the higher is the depth and breadth of search. In Payne et al. (1988), subjects have to choose one out of two gambles. They operationalize the attribute range by the variance of probabilities of the two alternative gambles (low vs. high). If the variation of probabilities is high, the alternatives have low similarity. They show that subjects process less information (less depth of search) in case of high variance. Two follow-up studies support this result and also show that the complementary effect is true: high similarity, thus low variance, leads to an increased depth of search. Results are even stronger if many trade-offs are prevalent (Bettman et al. 1993; Payne et al. 1993).

In the first of their two studies, Böckenholt et al. (1991) also manipulate the attribute range. They show respondents two alternatives with attribute levels ranging from −6 to +6. In the small range condition, the two alternatives differ between 0 to 3 levels per attribute, while in the high range condition, they differ either 4 or 5 or 6 attribute levels. Their results show that respondents increase their breadth of search in case of low attribute ranges. Although the authors call this manipulation *attractiveness difference*, this is rather a manipulation of attribute ranges since they do not calculate the overall attractiveness of alternatives.

Biggs et al. (1985) draw similar conclusions by also manipulating the range of attributes. Instead of computing the variance, they design choice tasks where attribute levels differ at least one and at most three levels on a scale with a total of eleven levels. They combine this with the manipulation of the task complexity (operationalized through the number of attributes and alternatives). The authors observe that in case of constant task complexity, a high similarity causes an increase of both breadth and depth of search.

The same studies show that the lower the variance of attribute levels, the more consistent is the search. Subjects spend an evenly distributed amount of time on both attributes and alternatives (Bettman et al. 1993; Payne et al. 1988). Furthermore, subjects consider a constant amount of attribute levels per attribute in case of low variance and an inconsistent amount in case of high variance (Biggs et al. 1985).

In summary, in cases of high similarity, decision makers tend to search for more information, both in terms of breadth and depth of search, and they acquire information more consistently. Most strategies which are consistent and complete strategies are compensatory, such as ADD, EQW, FRQ, MAJ, MCD, WADD (see Table A.1). The only exception is DOM, which is consistent and complete but non-compensatory.

2.4.4.2 Attribute Ranges and Search Pattern

Studies on search pattern and attribute ranges are less common and results are less clear. Payne et al. (1988) and Bettman et al. (1993) find a positive SI, i.e. alternative-wise processing, in cases of low variance of attribute levels and a negative one in cases of high variance.

In contrast, Iglesias-Parro et al. (2002) do not find any influence of attribute ranges on the search patterns with Mouselab. They only find a negative SI in both conditions of low and high attribute range, indicating an overall attribute-wise search. In their study, they pre-define a utility function as well as specific weights. The subjects were then asked to behave as though this utility function were their own. In choice tasks with two alternatives, they then vary the variance and the mean of differences for the two attribute levels of each attribute, as well as the correlation of attribute vectors. In three studies, they examine the influence of these three context-based measures of complexity in different combinations.

Biggs et al. (1985) also partly considered search patterns with Information Display Boards and verbal protocols yet they did not explicitly report their results in the paper since they use the pattern only indirectly assigning one out of four strategies to the observed choice behavior. They report some evidence that subjects might use compensatory strategies in cases of increasing similarity, but use non-compensatory strategies in cases of increasing amount of information. However, their results must be interpreted with caution as they observed only seven subjects.

In general, people have a tendency to use more alternative-wise search patterns and to apply more compensatory strategies in cases of low variance. However, due to the small number of respondents in Biggs et al. (1985) the latter result needs further evidence.

2.4.4.3 Attribute Ranges and Effort and Accuracy

Payne et al. (1988) observe that decision makers need less time and thus spend less effort in case of high variances than in case of low variances. Moreover, Bettman et al. (1993) report high interaction effects between the attribute ranges and another context effect, the trade-offs measured in terms of the correlation of attribute vectors (see Sect. 2.4.1.2). In case of low variance and negative correlation (many trade-offs), subjects need the most amount of time for the decision. Furthermore, the relative accuracy as well as the number of utility-maximizing decisions decreases in case of low variance and negative correlation. Thus, in decisions where attribute ranges are small and there are a lot of trade-offs among the alternatives, decisions seem to be very difficult, because decision makers spend more effort but achieve low accuracy.

In their first study, Iglesias-Parro et al. (2002) do not control for trade-offs. They observe an increased amount of time and thus more effort with increasing attribute range when measured with the mean difference of attribute values for each attribute. However, it is hard to interpret these results without controlling for the amount of trade-offs inherent in the decision, as high variances can occur in scenarios with a dominant alternative (easy task) as well as in scenarios with a lot of trade-offs (difficult task). Consequently, in their following two studies, they also manipulate the amount of trade-offs but do not find significant interaction effects. They find again that with increasing attribute range, the time increases – an observation which is not in agreement with others (Bettman et al. 1993; Payne et al. 1988).

In summary, the results concerning the influence of attribute ranges on effort and accuracy are contradictory. We think that this is because attribute ranges alone cannot describe the difficulty of a choice task sufficiently. As explained before, low variance can occur in cases with low complexity where there is one dominant alternative which is only slightly better than others. But low variance can also occur in situations with high complexity where we have many trade-offs and no dominant alternative.

2.4.4.4 Trade-Offs and Depth/Breadth/Consistency of Search

In the previous paragraph, it was suggested that trade-offs were an important factor influencing the decision-making process. Trade-offs are usually measured by computing the average pairwise correlation between attribute vectors. In case of negative pairwise correlation between attribute vectors, there are trade-offs in the choice task. Imagine a choice task of two alternatives, where alt_1 dominates alt_2. In this case, the attribute vectors correlate positively as attribute values always decrease, going from alternative 1 to alternative 2. If, on the other hand, there are trade-offs and no dominant alternative, some attribute values increase and some decrease, because across some attributes alt_1 beats alt_2 and across others it is the other way around. Thus, the average correlation between all pairwise attribute vectors would be low.

In case decision makers adopt compensatory strategies, and hence actually consider all trade-offs, negative correlations make a choice more complex (Fasolo et al. 2009; Payne et al. 1993). Positive correlations, though, simplify choices, since simpler, non-compensatory strategies can be used in order to early eliminate "weaker" alternatives early on without losing too much accuracy (Bettman et al. 1993; Luce et al. 1997).

Correlation structures, and hence trade-offs, influence the depth of search and the consistency. Bettman et al. (1993) observe an increased depth of search as well as a more consistent search with negative correlations. Luce et al. (1997) also observe an increased depth of search. In one of their studies, 41 students had to choose among five jobs which were described along four attributes on a 7-point scale ranging from *best* to *worst*. In the group with few trade-offs, the average correlation between all pairs of attribute vectors was 0.14, in the group with high trade-off, it was −0.31 (the authors call the conditions "high" vs. "low conflict"). In a pre-study, the authors also acquire subjects' individual attribute weights. Thus, in contrast to the attribute values which were prescribed by the Likert scale on the subjects, the attribute weights were directly rated by each subject. The authors take the attribute weights to also manipulate in-between subjects whether the trade-offs involve more important attributes (high trade-off difficulty) or less important attributes (low trade-off difficulty). They find a main effect for the first variable, the attribute correlation. In case of negative correlation structures, subjects' depth of search increases. For the second independent variable, the trade-off difficulty, no main effect was found.

However, there was a significant interaction effect. In case of negative correlations on important attributes, the depth of search was highest.

To sum up, the more trade-offs among the alternatives, the more information is considered and the more consistent is the search. Thus, more trade-offs might result in the application of more compensatory strategies. Recall that literature on attribute ranges and depth/breadth/consistency of search and search patterns has come to the conclusion that the more similar alternatives are, the more compensatory strategies are used. Depending on how we define similarity in the context of trade-offs, these two results do contradict each other. Payne et al. (1993) have said that "In general, if the alternatives are similar, the attributes will be positively correlated; if they are very dissimilar, the attributes are negatively correlated" (p. 59). If we follow this interpretation, the results contradict. The more similar alternatives are with respect to their attribute range, the more compensatory is the search. The more similar alternatives are with respect to trade-offs, the less compensatory search is. From our viewpoint, the statement by Payne et al. (1993) neglects an important fact which we have already brought up in the discussion on attribute ranges and effort/accuracy. Alternatives with positive correlations can either have low attribute range or high attribute range. In the first situation, where we have positive correlation and low attribute ranges, alternatives only differ slightly. Hence, we have high similarity among alternatives. In contrast, in case of positive correlations and high attribute ranges one alternative, or at least a few, stand out clearly from the others and might even dominate them. In this case, we would speak of low similarity among alternatives. Thus, a choice task cannot be interpreted to be similar or non-similar alongside trade-offs alone. We always have to take into account other measures, such as attribute ranges and differences in attractiveness, in order to speak of similar or dissimilar alternatives. From the studies, we can therefore only conclude that the more trade-offs, the more likely is it that more compensatory strategies are used, but we should be careful to interpret these results in terms of similarity.

2.4.4.5 Trade-Offs and Search Pattern

Both Iglesias-Parro et al. (2002) and Luce et al. (1997) find no effect of trade-offs on the search pattern. Luce et al. (1997) find significant influence in the conditions with negative correlations where the trade-offs are along the most important attributes. In these cases, subjects process information attribute-wise. In a further analysis, the authors show tentative evidence that subjects start off with attribute-wise processing and then switch to alternative-wise processing. Furthermore, they support the view that subjects search longer attribute-wise in case of negative correlations on the most important attributes.

In contrast to Luce et al. (1997) and Iglesias-Parro et al. (2002), Bettman et al. (1993) and Fasolo et al. (2003) measure a positive search index in the context of negative correlations and thus an alternative-wise search. Fasolo et al. (2003) for instance, let subjects choose four times between five different digital cameras described by eight attributes and record their process with a web-based process tracing technique, while Bettman et al. (1993) let subjects choose between gambles. Because of the contradictory results, more research needs to be done in order to draw clear conclusions.

2.4.4.6 Trade-Offs and Effort and Accuracy

All studies observe that in case of negative correlations, the time increases significantly. Thus, in case of trade-offs, the choice task seems to be more complex and increases effort (Bettman et al. 1993; Fasolo et al. 2009; Iglesias-Parro et al. 2001; Luce et al. 1997). Some also show that accuracy decreases with increasing trade-offs (Bettman et al. 1993).

2.4.4.7 Attractiveness Differences and Depth/Breadth/Consistency of Search

Böckenholt et al. (1991) manipulate attractiveness difference and overall attractiveness of alternatives. The overall attractiveness reflects whether both alternatives are very attractive (high utility) or rather unattractive (low utility) for the subjects. The attractiveness differences were manipulated by creating choice tasks which presented an overall difference in the first two attributes of either one level at most, or one level at least (large difference). Each subject has to make 30 choices among two alternatives. They find that subjects consider a higher percentage of attribute levels (breadth of search) if the attractiveness differences are low and if the overall attractiveness are low. However, no interaction effect between attractiveness differences and attractiveness of alternatives is found.

Swait and Adamowicz (2001) use a structural modeling approach to measure the influence of complexity on decision-making behavior. They hypothesize that the degree to which participants tend to be utility maximizers depends on the entropy in a choice task (see (2.2)). They compare the estimated attribute weights in choice tasks with low vs. high entropy. They find that subjects tend to focus on only a few attributes when entropy increases, because the estimated attribute weights from the model have a high variance. Thus, in case of high entropy, one can interpret the results in terms of an inconsistent search and a focus on only a few attributes.

2.4.5 Discussion

In this section, we have summarized how task-based and context-based complexity influences decision-making behavior. Specifically, we have focused on the amount of information, attribute ranges, trade-offs, and attractiveness differences. Furthermore, we have discussed that attribute ranges and attractiveness difference define how similar alternatives are, while trade-offs alone are not able to measure similarity.

The results which relate to the number of attributes and alternatives show that people use simpler strategies in case of an increasing amount of information. That is, they apply more non-compensatory strategies. This result is more distinct for the influence of alternatives than for the influence of attributes.

While there are plenty of studies on the amount of information, relatively few studies examine the influence of similarity and trade-offs, although the existing studies give evidence for their strong influence on decision-making behavior. Since we have not found any detailed overview of these studies in the literature, we gave a detailed overview of all studies and summarized them in Table in the appendix.

A large number of trade-offs as well as a small range of attribute values lead both to an increase in information acquisition (breadth and depth of search) and more consistent search. In combination, these two observations indicate the usage of more compensatory strategies in case of similar alternatives with many trade-offs.

Usually, compensatory strategies cost more effort than non-compensatory strategies. Thus, in case of low attribute ranges and many trade-offs, we would expect an increase in effort. However, there are contradictory results for the influence of the attribute range on effort, while the result for trade-offs is more clear. In case of many trade-offs, more time is spent on the choice task.

When we measure the influence of attribute ranges and trade-offs with search patterns, the results are unclear. The few studies on attribute ranges and search patterns find no influence at all (Iglesias-Parro et al. 2002) or lack a profound subject pool (Biggs et al. 1985). Furthermore, studies contradict in respect to the influence of trade-offs. One study finds some evidence of a more attribute-wise search in case of trade-offs on the most important attributes (Luce et al. 1997), others a more alternative-wise search (Bettman et al. 1993; Fasolo et al. 2003).

Consequently, literature suggests that trade-offs and attribute ranges might influence the usage of compensatory vs. non-compensatory strategies but not the search pattern. Because compensatory and non-compensatory strategies can both induce an attribute and alternative-wise search, these results do not necessarily contradict each other.

Only few studies exist on the influence of attractiveness difference. Böckenholt et al. (1991) find that more information is considered if the difference is low. Swait and Adamowicz (2001) find the contrary effect. If entropy is high, and thus the attractiveness difference is low, subjects focus on only a few attributes. However, as their entropy measure takes into account both the number of alternatives and attractiveness difference, the two effects might overlap.

Swait and Adamowicz (2001) and Biggs et al. (1985) are two of the few studies which consider both task- and context based complexity. From our viewpoint, more research should not only focus on different measures of context-based complexity and their interactions, but more research should also follow the notion of analyzing both task- and context-based effects.

Most critical to all of the mentioned studies is that respondent's utility functions are not measured on the individual level. Already Böckenholt et al. (1991) outlined that one has to be aware that participants may value attributes and alternatives differently. Consequently, the similarity of alternatives and the amount of trade-offs depends on individual preferences and therefore is difficult to manipulate as an independent variable.

Hence, a large quantity of research has either neglected the existence of individual preference structures or used very restrictive assumptions for the part-worth utilities of attribute values (i.e., the attribute value which is ascribed to a certain attribute level is set to the same value for all respondents). Attribute levels are, for instance, displayed as integer values from 1 [very poor] to 10 [very good], so instead of naming an exact price, such as "coffee machine A is worth €189.99 and machine B €129.99", they record "coffee machine A is very poor in terms of price [value 1] and B is good [value 8] (Biggs et al. 1985). It thus appears that unless the value functions are measured accurately, the context-based measurement cannot be precisely determined.

2.5 Conclusions

In this chapter, we provided an overview of the fundamentals which are relevant to the present work. We defined the most important terms, such as choice task, decision strategy, preference as well as task- and context-based complexity. We have seen that a variety of different decision strategies have been described in the literature so far, covering all kinds of different decision-making behaviors. Moreover, we stressed the fact that decision-making behavior is contingent upon factors such as the characteristics of the choice task or of the decision maker. Hence, in order to build DSS that assist people in their decision processes, we need to understand these contingencies.

To study such contingencies it is necessary to empirically observe and analyze decision-making behaviors by using methods such as structural modeling, comparative model fitting and process tracing. Furthermore, we reviewed the literature pertaining to the influence of complexity on decision-making behavior. A main result of this literature review is the lack of research on different context-based complexities. Specifically, the effect of context-based complexity on search patterns is unclear. Moreover, the relationship between the two similarity measures, attribute ranges and attractiveness differences, and trade-offs needs to be scrutinized further. Another gap in current research is that many studies use rough estimates for measuring parameters and recording the observed data. First, they use process tracing methods such as Mouselab that might influence the decision process. Second, they do not measure decision makers' preferences in detail, but use some simple proxy and aggregated utility functions (for an exception see Klein and Yadav 1989).

We postulate that a more thorough measurement of both preferences and the decision process, by, for instance, using advanced preference measurement methods from marketing and by recording the decision process with eye tracking will improve validity.

Chapter 3
The Influence of Context-Based Complexity on Decision Processes

In this chapter, we present an empirical study which investigates the influence of context-based complexity on decision processes.[1] To determine context-based complexity accurately, we measure each subject's preferences individually with two advanced techniques from marketing research: choice-based conjoint analysis (CBC, Haaijer and Wedel 2007) and pairwise-comparison-based preference measurement (PCPM, Scholz et al. 2010), rather than relying on less precise estimates of preferences. Furthermore, we use eye tracking to trace the process of information acquisition precisely. Our results show that low context-based complexity leads to less information acquisition and more alternative-wise search. Moreover, people search information attribute-wise in the first stage of the decision process, then eliminate alternatives, and search alternative-wise in the last stage. We also found evidence that in situations of low context-based complexity, people switch earlier to alternative-wise processing. In essence, our findings suggest that people select decision strategies from an adaptive toolbox in situations of varying complexity, starting with lexicographic and elimination by aspect type rules and ending with strategies that imply an alternative-wise search.

3.1 Theory and Hypotheses

In this experiment, we use the eye-tracing technique to observe whether peoples' search patterns are attribute-wise or alternative-wise. Hence, let us first recapitulate exactly the definition of attribute-wise versus alternative-wise processing. Consider, for example, the choice between alternative models of coffee machines each one characterized by attributes such as price, brand, or design. When investigating choices like this, an important question is whether people process the

---

[1]The experimental study was joint work with Martin Meißner (University of Bielefeld), Eduard Brandstätter (University of Linz), and René Riedl (University of Linz).

If you were in the market to buy a new single-cup coffee brewer and
these were your only options, which would you choose?

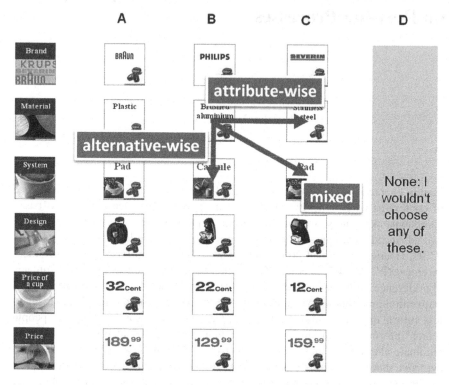

Fig. 3.1 Example of a choice task. Only cells 12 to 29 are used to calculate search patterns

different pieces of information either within alternatives or within attributes. In
alternative-wise processing, the attribute levels of one product are considered before
information about the next alternative is processed. This is the case when people
consider, for example, price, design, and brand name of one coffee machine alone,
before they go on to the next alternative. In attribute-wise processing, the values of
several alternatives on a single attribute are processed before information about a
further attribute is considered. For example, people might first compare the prices
of different coffee machines and then compare the machines' designs.

Eye tracking directly uncovers the cognitive processes that take place between
the onset of a choice task and the decision maker's choice. An example of a choice
task which our subjects had to decide on is displayed in Fig. 3.1. Here a transition is
defined as alternative-wise if a person looks at two boxes within an alternative, and
attribute-wise if a person looks at two boxes within an attribute. Mixed transitions
are both alternative-wise and attribute-wise.

In Chap. 2, we have learned that people can apply decision strategies that imply a more attribute-wise or an alternative-wise information search. Furthermore, some strategies exclude alternatives step-by-step from further consideration during the decision process (see characteristic *elimination* in Table A.1). Russo and Leclerc (1994) have divided the decision process into stages. In the first stage, the so-called screening stage, decision makers try to reduce choice task complexity by eliminating alternatives. In the second stage, they put more effort into comparison of the remaining alternatives (Olshavsky 1979; Payne 1976; Payne et al. 1988; Svenson 1979). Hence, in the first stage, they use simple heuristics and focus on only a few attributes, while in the second stage they consider the choice task holistically using more effortful strategies (Bettman and Park 1980; Gilbride and Allenby 2004, 2006; Luce et al. 1997; Payne 1976).

The most prominent decision strategies which eliminate alternatives are the EBA, LEX, and CONJ (see Chap. 2.2 and Table A.1). Let us recall briefly, how these strategies are defined. In a first step, EBA eliminates alternatives that do not meet the aspiration level for the most important attribute. The elimination process then proceeds with the second most important attribute. The elimination process stops when there is only one alternative left to choose. LEX chooses the alternative(s) with the best value on the most important attribute. Other variants of LEX, such as LED, choose alternative(s) only if their value is substantially better than the other values. In the case of a tied decision, LEX and LED proceed with the second most important attribute, etc. CONJ eliminates each alternative which does not meet the aspiration level at least once. Thus, CONJ compares the alternatives alternative-wise and accepts only those alternatives that meet the aspiration levels at all attributes.

Results of decision studies investigating decision strategy application in the various stages of a decision process are mixed. Some researchers have hypothesized that people use EBA or CONJ in the first stage, but empirical evidence for favoring one or the other strategy is diverse (Gilbride and Allenby 2006; Payne 1976). In agreement with research by Russo and Dosher (1983) and Tversky (1969), we argue that eliminating alternatives after a first screening stage is easier to manage if alternatives are compared attribute-wise rather than alternative-wise. That is because it is cognitively easier to find out whether one specific alternative performs low on an attribute (e.g. elimination of an alternative because of a very high price compared with other alternatives) than eliminating an alternative based on low performance on several attributes. This notion is also supported by a study by Bettman and Park (1980) on verbal protocols. This study provides evidence that decision makers usually start with an attribute-wise rather than an alternative-wise search. Therefore, we assume that information acquisition changes from an attribute-wise to alternative-wise search at a later decision stage.

Hypothesis 1:   People process information attribute-wise in the first stage of the decision process, but alternative-wise in the last stage.

The fact that people switch from attribute-wise processing to alternative-wise processing indicates a shift in strategies. Following other studies (Gilbride and Allenby 2006; Luce et al. 1997), we conclude that people first eliminate alternatives and then compare the remaining alternatives holistically. This gives rise to our second hypothesis:

Hypothesis 2:   People eliminate alternatives during a decision task. Consequently, they consider fewer alternatives in the last stage of the choice than in the first stage.

While much research addressed the influence of task-based complexity on decision-making behavior, little is known about the influence of context-based complexity and, particularly of the similarity of alternatives (see Sect. 2.4). As we have pointed out before, one reason for this lack of research might be that for assessment of context-based complexity, people's attribute utilities have to be known. Existing approaches mostly neglect this fact (see Sect. 2.4. We overcome this lack of research by using two sophisticated preference measurement approaches, CBC analysis and PCPM. Rather than using simplified proxies such as "very poor", we use real attribute levels (e.g., real prices). CBC and PCPM make it possible to calculate the attribute value of each attribute level for each person.

Unlike previous studies, we conceptualize complexity based on people's individual preferences. These preferences determine the perceived context-based complexity for each person. To this end, we use the context-based complexity variables discussed in Sect. 2.4:

1. The variation of attribute values for measuring attribute ranges
2. The average correlation of all pairs of attribute vectors for measuring trade-offs
3. The standard deviation of the overall utility values across alternatives for measuring attractiveness differences

We pointed out in Sect. 2.4 that the entropy measure (see (2.2)) takes into account both the number of alternatives and attractiveness differences. Since we use a fixed number of alternatives in this study, the entropy measure and the attractiveness difference (3) differ only slightly and lead to equivalent interpretations. Hence, to complete the analysis, we also report statistical results for the entropy measure, but refrain from mentioning it explicitly in the following discussions.

Our third hypothesis, thus, concerns the impact of context-based complexity on information acquisition. We predict that low complexity, operationalized as high dissimilarity between alternatives and positively correlated attribute vectors, leads to alternative-wise information acquisition. This is because people can easily recognize inferior alternatives and eliminate them. In a second phase, decision makers can use more effortful, alternative-wise comparisons between the remaining alternatives. Such a stepwise procedure saves cognitive effort because not all information must be considered. According to hypotheses 1 and 2, we assume that people examine information alternative-wise after having eliminated alternatives. This leads to hypothesis 3.

Hypothesis 3:   The lower the context-based complexity, the more people will search alternative-wise.

Concerning the influence of trade-offs on search pattern, with hypothesis 3 we argue in agreement with Luce et al. (1997), but contradict the research carried out by Bettman et al. (1993) and Fasolo et al. (2003) (see Sect. 2.4.4). We also contradict Biggs et al. (1985), Payne et al. (1988) and Bettman et al. (1993) who find a more alternative-wise search pattern with decreasing attribute range. Furthermore, we address the lack of research about the effect of attractiveness differences, where only few process-tracing studies exist (for an exception see Böckenholt et al. (1991), who, however, do not measure search patterns).

In our extensive analysis of the literature we found only one study, Russo and Dosher (1983), that also investigated the influence of context-based complexity on eye-movements and accessed people's utility functions individually. This study found no evidence that context-based complexity affects decision processes. However, two factors might explain why no effect was found. First of all, eye tracking techniques were relatively immature in the early 1980s, and second of all, measurement of people's utility functions was executed based on simple, rather than today's sophisticated techniques. These two factors are possible explanations of why Russo and Dosher (1983) did not find evidence for the influence of context-based complexity on information acquisition behavior in their eye tracking study.

In our experiment, the complexity of a choice task is operationalized with the four variables described above. At first, this operationalization seems counterintuitive, because people who do not consider all information (thereby using simple strategies such as LEX and EBA), are hardly able to calculate the alternatives' overall utilities, estimate variances of attribute values or calculate pairwise correlations of attribute vectors at the beginning of the decision process. So how can people know whether a decision task is complex or not when they do not use a strategy that (1) uses all information and (2) calculates overall utilities, variances, or correlations?

We argue that people are able to estimate these measures of complexity, although they only consider the most important attributes. For instance, if alternatives are better than other alternatives already across the most important attributes, it is very likely that this difference cannot be traded off against other less important attributes. Therefore, the higher the standard deviation of alternatives' overall utility values, the higher is the chance that the alternatives' utility across only the most important attributes is a valid proxy for the alternatives' overall utility value. For instance, a decision maker might eliminate an alternative with a very high price immediately, as there is only a low probability that the high price will be offset by good attribute levels on other less important attributes.

A similar argumentation holds for attribute ranges and pairwise correlations. If attribute levels differ sharply on the most important attributes, people might infer that alternatives overall differ sharply. In the context of correlations of attribute vectors, several studies have even observed whether subjects are able to assess correlations. Bettman et al. (1986) find that their subjects are good in assessing correlations, while Alloy and Tabachnik (1984) draw the opposite conclusion from their study. However, one has to take into account that these studies use Mouselab and Information Display Boards where one attribute level is only shown once at a time. This will make it more difficult to assess correlation and variances of attribute values (Bettman et al. 1993). Even if subjects might not be able to assess correlations exactly, they are able to perceive whether they are positive or negative (Klein and Yadav 1989). To sum up, in support of hypothesis 3, we argue that subjects are able to estimate context-complexity of the choice tasks even before having considered all information and even without explicitly calculating all attribute values, correlations, and variances.

If people estimate context-based complexity by only considering few attributes, this estimation process should take longer, the more complex the choice task is. This is because it is necessary to evaluate more attributes before an alternative can be eliminated, if, for instance, the alternative are very similar to each other.

Consequently, following other research (see Sect. 2.4), we postulate that choice tasks with high context-based complexity imply that people search for more information.

Hypothesis 4:   The higher the context-based complexity, the more information people will search for.

In addition, we suggest that people would switch later in the process from attribute-wise to alternative-wise processing since it takes them longer to eliminate alternatives in the first stage of the decision process. This behavior can be motivated by the criterion-dependent choice (CDC) model which has so far only been supported for choice tasks with only two alternatives (Böckenholt et al. 1991; Russo and Dosher 1983; Schmalhofer et al. 1986). The CDC model posits that two alternatives are evaluated attribute-wise and that people accumulate the differences of attribute values over the processed attributes until the sum of differences exceeds a critical value k. Given a pair of alternatives, a large k implies that many attributes are considered before the final choice is made, while a low k means that the respondent stops the choice process early on. Furthermore, in scenarios with similar alternatives, it is harder to obtain the critical value k, as more attributes have to be processed in the case of similar attribute levels and many trade-offs (Böckenholt et al. 1991). Hence, the CDC model explains the decision-making behavior we anticipate for the beginning of the choice process: In situations with a low attractiveness difference, a low range, and a lot of trade-offs, people have more difficulty in obtaining the critical k value, and therefore they search longer attribute-wise before they can eliminate alternatives from the decision process and switch to alternative-wise processing.

Hypothesis 5:   The higher the context-based complexity, the later people will switch from attribute-wise to alternative-wise processing.

The next section introduces quantitative measures for operationalizing the theoretical constructs. Then, we describe the design of the eye tracking experiment and the results. We close by discussing core findings, potential limitations, and possible directions for future research.

3.2   Operationalization

Hypothesis 1 states that people process information attribute-wise in the first stage of a decision process, but alternative-wise in the last stage. To establish different stages of the decision process, the stream of eye fixations within a decision task can be separated into an equal number of fixations. In contrast to Luce et al. (1997), who set a fixed number of thirteen fixations per stage for each respondent, in our experiment, we take into account respondents' differences in the total number of fixations per choice task and divide each participant's total number of fixations by three, resulting in three stages of same length for each participant. The same analysis with two and four stages yielded very similar results, which is why we only report results for a separation into three stages.

To measure whether information processing in a choice task is alternative- or attribute-wise, Payne (1976) developed the SI (see (2.3)).The value of SI varies from -1 to $+1$, with -1 indicating completely attribute-wise search and $+1$ indicating completely alternative-wise search.

The SI has been criticized by Böckenholt and Hynan (1994), who showed that it is biased towards alternative-wise processing if the number of attributes exceeds the number of alternatives (and vice versa). To overcome this bias, they proposed a strategy measure (SM), which is defined as:

$$ SM = \frac{\sqrt{N}((n\,\frac{m}{N})(r_{alt} - r_{att}) - (m - n))}{\sqrt{n^2(m - 1) + m^2(n - 1)}}, \tag{3.1} $$

where n denotes the number of alternatives, m the number of attributes (dimensions), and N the number of transitions. The SM value is not constrained to lie between -1 and $+1$, rendering its interpretation difficult. As we only distinguish attribute-wise from alternative-wise processing and do not take into account the strength of attribute-wise processing, this limitation is of minor concern. The crucial fact is that an $SM < 0$ indicates an attribute-wise search, while an $SM > 0$ indicates an alternative-wise search, and the higher the SM, the more alternative-wise is the search. As the Böckenholt measure can be calculated for each stage of the decision process separately, this measure can be used to indicate a possible shift from a more attribute-wise search in the beginning to a more alternative-wise search at the end of the decision process.

Hypothesis 2 states that people eliminate alternatives during a choice task. Consequently, they consider fewer alternatives in the last stages of the choice tasks that in the early stages. To test this hypothesis, we separately calculate the number of alternatives with at least one fixation for the different stages of the decision process. Hypothesis 2 consequently shows that less alternatives are considered at later stages of the task when compared to earlier stages.

Hypothesis 3 states that if context-based complexity decreases, people process information more alternative-wise. As argued above, we operationalize the complexity of choice tasks with four different measures. For computing the measures, we need to know the attribute values and attribute weights for each respondent. For this purpose, marketing research offers well-developed preference measurement techniques, which use either compositional (e.g. PCPM, Scholz et al. 2010) or decompositional (e.g. CBC, Sawtooth 2008) measurement approaches. To increase experimental validity, we use both techniques for measuring the respondents' preferences.

Decompositional conjoint analytic approaches, especially CBC, are one of the major contributions of marketing science (Netzer et al. 2008). When applying these approaches, the evaluations or choices between holistically described products of respondents are decomposed into utilities. In our experiment, we used the decisions of respondents for the choice tasks in order to estimate utilities with CBC. Every respondent has to choose his or her preferred alternative in a number of choice tasks. The part-worths for each respondent (see Sect. 2.3.1.1) were then estimated via a Multinominal Logit model and a Hierarchical Bayes approach (Lenk et al. 1996). Hence, CBC is a structural modeling approach which estimates the parameters of the WADD strategy (see Sect. 2.3.1).

Compositional approaches are based on the direct self-report of respondents' preferences concerning all attribute levels of an alternative. Rating scales are used very often to evaluate the desirability of attribute levels. However, compositional approaches are often criticized for not capturing the trade offs between attributes. There has been an ongoing controversy about the ability of compositional approaches, especially so-called self-explicated approaches, to elicit meaningful utilities (Nitzsch and Weber 1993). An improved compositional approach called PCPM was proposed by Scholz et al. (2010). It is based on the paired comparisons of attributes and attribute levels and allows for the handling of inconsistencies in preference judgments. To estimate the overall utilities of alternatives for respondents, we applied PCPM at the end of the experiment. Respondents had to answer pairwise comparison questions. The utilities were then calculated as described in Scholz et al. (2010).

In order to calculate context-based complexity, the utilities from CBC as well as from the PCPM approach were used. Each alternative can be represented by a set of attribute levels. Then $u(alt_j)$ is the overall utility value of alternative alt_j in the choice task.

We measured the *attribute range* with the mean sample standard deviation of all attribute values over all attribute vectors (similar to Bettman et al. 1993 and Payne et al. 1993):

$$SD_{range}(ct) = \frac{1}{m} \sum_{i=1}^{m} \sqrt{\frac{1}{n-1} \sum_{j=1}^{n} (v(a_{ij}) - \bar{v}_i)^2}, \tag{3.2}$$

where $\bar{v}_i$ is the average of all attribute values of attribute i.

We measure the *attractiveness difference* with the sample standard deviation $SD_{attract}(ct)$ of the overall utility values in a choice task, ct. This measure expresses how different the alternatives in a choice task are with respect to their overall utility values:

$$SD_{attract}(ct) = \sqrt{\frac{1}{n-1} \sum_{j=1}^{n} (u(alt_j) - \bar{u})^2}, \qquad (3.3)$$

where $\bar{u}$ is the average utility of all alternatives.

We measure the *correlation of attribute vectors* as described by Luce et al. (1997) for determining the amount of trade-offs, where AV is the set of the m attribute vectors, $attr_1 = (a_{11}, a_{12}, \dots, a_{1n}), \dots, attr_m = (a_{m1}, a_{m2}, \dots, a_{mn})$ and CORR stands for correlation (Pearson):

$$CORR(ct) = \frac{m(m-1)}{2} \sum_{\forall i,l; i \neq l; attr_i, attr_l \in AV} CORR(attr_i, attr_l). \qquad (3.4)$$

Furthermore, entropy is calculated as defined in (2.2).

Hypothesis 4 states that if context-based complexity increases, people will be forced to search for more information. We use two measures for quantifying the amount of acquired information: the total amount of eye fixations (depth of search) and the number of different attribute levels that were fixated at least once (breadth of search). Hypothesis 4 is confirmed when both measures correlate negatively with choice complexity.

Hypothesis 5 states that if complexity increases, people switch from attribute-wise to alternative-wise processing at a later stage. We can test this hypothesis by comparing the SM index at different stages for tasks with low versus high context-based complexity.

3.3 Experiment

3.3.1 Participants

Sixty-two respondents (37 females, 25 males) participated in an experiment where they were asked to choose a single-cup coffee brewer. Eighty-five percent of the subjects consumed 1–3 cups of coffee per day, and 15% consumed even more, indicating that participants had a high product experience with the product category.

3.3.2 Design and Procedure

One crucial aspect was to design choice tasks in a way that each participant's utility function could be estimated. To this end, the complete enumeration technique, implemented in the Sawtooth software, was used to create the choice tasks (Sawtooth 2008). Each of these choice tasks consisted of three alternatives and six

Fig. 3.2 Experimental
procedure

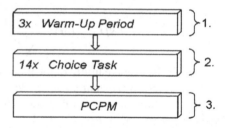

attributes (plus a no-choice alternative). Three additional choice tasks – presented at the beginning of the experiment – served as warm-up trials. All in all, each participant responded to 17 choice tasks (see Fig. 3.2). The first part consisted of three warm-up tasks. The second part, the core of the experiment, presented respondents with 14 choice tasks, which were then used for statistical analysis and, using CBC, were also used to estimate the utility functions. In the third part preference measurement with PCPM was carried out.

In a pre-study with 20 respondents, we used the direct dual questioning method (Myers and Alpert 1968) as it is common in marketing research practice to determine the most relevant six attributes of single-cup coffee makers. In the direct dual questioning method, respondents are first asked how important they find several attributes. They then have to describe to what extent they believe products differ in terms of that attribute. The most relevant attributes are the ones which respondents evaluate as highly important to them and whose levels appear to vary greatly between products. The most important attributes we determined were: price, brand, material, design, system, and price of a cup of coffee (see Table 3.1).

As recommended by Scholz et al. (2010), in the PCPM-part respondents had to conduct 12 pairwise comparisons to compare the six attributes and 25 pairwise comparisons for the attribute levels.

3.3.3   Eye Tracking

To record participants' eye movements we used the SMI EyeLink II System, which features two monitors – one for the participant and one for the experimenter. Each subject wore a light helmet with two fixed mini-cameras which recorded the eye movements. Four infrared sensors (installed on the participant's monitor) were used to adjust to changes in the seating positions of the. As indicated in Fig. 3.1, the screen was divided in a grid structure, consisting of 35 cells with different pieces of information, such as the instruction (cell 1), the names of alternatives (cells 2–5), the attributes (cells 6–11), the attribute level cells (12–29), the no choice option (cell 30) and the buttons to choose alternatives and go to the next screen (cells 31–35). The subjects' eye fixations were uniquely assigned to one of 35 cells. The cells 12 to 29 of each choice task displayed the attribute levels and were used for the analysis of participants' eye tracking patterns (excluding the warm-up tasks). Fixations in

Table 3.1 Design of preference measurement used in CBC and PCPM with attributes with either 4,3, or 2 levels

Attribute	Level 1	Level 2	Level 3	Level 4
Price	€99	€129	€159	€189
Brand	Braun	Krups	Philips	Severin
Material	Stainless steel	Plastic	Brushed aluminium	
Design	Braun	Krups	Philips	Severin
System	Pad	Capsule		
Price of a cup of coffee	€0.12	€0.22	€0.32	

one of the other cells were not evaluated in the present work, since they had no influence on the SM. Thus, if we observed a transition on the cells 12–6–8–14, the two fixations on the cells 6 and 8 would not be included in the analysis and we would count only the 12–14 transition as an alternative-wise transition.

3.3.4 Empirical Results

Of the 18 cells representing attribute levels in Fig. 3.1, participants fixated on average on 13.94 cells ($SD = 3.00$) at least once. The average number of fixations in a choice task decreased from 61 in the first to 37 in the last choice task. Results further indicate that participants became acquainted with the choice tasks since a decrease in the relative number of fixations outside the matrix (i.e., cells below 12 and above 29 in Fig. 3.1) was observed, the more tasks they had completed ($r = -0.276$, $p < 0.001$). Apparently, participants learned about the decision environment (cells 12 to 29) and avoided unnecessary fixations outside of the choice matrix.

Hypothesis 1 states that people process information attribute-wise in the first stage of the decision process but alternative-wise in the last stage. To test this hypothesis, for each participant and for each choice task we divided the number of fixations into three stages of equal length and calculated the SM index for each stage. If hypothesis 1 was correct, the mean SM index would be expected to be negative in the first stage of the decision process but positive in the last stage. We recall that negative values of the SM index indicate attribute processing, while positive values indicate alternative processing. Our results, indicated in Table 3.2, confirm this prediction. The results suggest that people use a type of attribute-wise search strategy in the first stage of the choice process ($M = -0.54, SE = 2$), while in the last stage they exhibit more alternative-wise search patterns ($M = 0.54, SE = 1.73$).[2]

These latter considerations lead us to the second hypothesis, which states that people eliminate alternatives during a choice task. Consequently, they are expected to consider fewer alternatives in the last stage of the choice task than in the first

---

[2]M: mean, SE: standard error.

Table 3.2 SM for the three stages

Mean (SD) Stage 1	Mean (SD) Stage 2	Mean (SD) Stage 3	F	p
−0.54 (2.0)	0.00 (1.92)	0.54 (1.73)	70.256	<0.01

Table 3.3 The number of alternatives with at least one fixation for the three stages

Mean (SD) Stage 1	Mean (SD) Stage 2	Mean (SD) Stage 3	F	p
2.83 (0.43)	2.65 (0.58)	2.45 (0.67)	97.065	<0.01

stage. To test hypothesis 2, we calculated the number of alternatives that were fixated at least once for each participant and for each stage. If hypothesis 2 turns out to be correct, this number declines with the succeeding stages. Table 3.3 supports this prediction. The mean number of alternatives that were fixated at least once declines ($p < 0.001$).

Hypothesis 3 states that if context-based complexity decreases, people will process information by alternatives. Context-based complexity is low, if (1) the attribute range is high (high SD_{range}), (2) the attractiveness difference is high (high $SD_{attract}$ and low entropy) and (3) if there are few trade-offs (high and positive $CORR$). Because a positive value of the SM index indicates processing by alternatives, hypothesis 3 postulates a positive correlation between all three context-based complexity measurements and the SM index.[3] Hypothesis 3 is supported for SD_{range} and $SD_{attract}$ for both preference measurement methods, CBC and PCPM. The correlations start from 0.087 ($n = 868$, $p < 0.05$, two-tailed) for SD_{range} and CBC and reach 0.142 ($p < 0.01$) for SD_{range} when measured with PCPM (see Table 3.4). With respect to the entropy measure and $CORR$, it makes a difference whether the attribute values are determined with PCPM or CBC. While for the CBC method we get no significant results, we get a highly significant result for the PCPM in the proposed direction ($r = -0.127$ and $r = 0.097$, $p < 0.01$). In summary, we recorded robust results, which suggests that people process information more by attribute when choices are difficult but more by alternative when they are easy.

Hypothesis 4 states that if context-based complexity increases, people will search for more information. Context-based complexity is high if the attribute range is low (low SD_{range}), the attractiveness difference is low (low $SD_{attract}$ and high entropy) and if there are numerous trade-offs (low and negative $CORR$). To quantify the amount of information search, we determined (a) the depth of search and (b) the breadth of search. Hypothesis 4 thus predicts negative correlations between context-based complexity and depth (breadth) of search (for entropy, we expect positive correlations). In support of these predictions, we found significant correlations starting from −0.086 for $CORR$ measured with CBC for the depth of search up to −0.181 for $SD_{attract}$ and breadth of search (see Table 3.4). Results are slightly stronger for breadth of search, and robust for both CBC and PCPM. Only for SD_{range}

---

[3]Because high entropy means high complexity, we expect a negative correlation for entropy.

Table 3.4 Correlations between measures of complexity and breadth and depth of search

Complexity	SM		Breadth of search		Depth of search	
	CBC	PCPM	CBC	PCPM	CBC	PCPM
SD_{range}	0.087[a]	0.142[b]	0.018	−0.164[b]	0.004	−0.141[b]
$SD_{attract}$	0.111[b]	0.093[b]	−0.181[b]	−0.143[b]	−0.146[b]	−0.134[b]
Entropy	0.006	−0.127[b]	0.147[b]	0.157[b]	0.149[b]	0.115[b]
CORR	0.036	0.097[b]	−0.114[b]	−0.161[b]	−0.086[a]	−0.125[b]

[a]Correlation is significant on 0.05 level
[b]Correlation is significant on 0.01 level

are results not significant in the case of CBC measurements. Hence, for SD_{range} the effect that with a low attribute range, people tend to search for more information, is only supported in the case of PCPM measurement. In summary, as expected, people search for more information if complexity is high.

Hypothesis 5 states that if context-based complexity increases, people switch later from attribute-wise to alternative-wise processing. To test this hypothesis, we took all 868 choices (62 participants × 14 tasks) and performed a median split of the context-based measure of complexity by separating choice tasks with low and high complexity individually for each participant. Then, we calculated the means of the SM measure for both groups across the three stages of the decision process. In support of hypothesis 5, Fig. 3.3 shows that participants switch later from processing by attribute to processing by alternative when the complexity of the choice task is high rather than low. This result is consistent for all measures. However, it is stronger when preferences are measured with PCPM instead of CBC (compare Figs. 3.3 and 3.4). In particular, we observed that respondents searched attribute-wise in the second stage when the complexity of the choice tasks was high but they searched alternative-wise if the complexity was low. Indeed, all SM for all combinations of complexity measures, for both CBC and PCPM are positive ($SM > 0$) in cases of low complexity and negative in case of high complexity ($SM < 0$). This finding strongly supports our hypothesis.

An analysis with paired t-tests on the different stages indicate further in which of the stages the search pattern significantly differs for the cases of low versus high complexity. Thus, the paired t-tests show where the results are particularly strong in the stages. We report the effect size as measure for the strength of the relation. The effect size is determined by calculating the Pearson r-value as $r = \sqrt{\frac{t^2}{t^2+df}}$ (Rosenthal 1991; Rosnow and Rosenthal 2005)[4]. The Pearson r ranges between 0 and 1 (strong relation). An r of 0.1 is interpreted as small, 0.3 as medium, and 0.5 as large effect (Cohen 1988, 1992).

When preferences were measured with PCPM, we obtained significant results for SD_{range} in the first and second stage ($t(61) = -2.836$, $r = 0.34$ (medium effect) and $t(61) = -2.968$, $r = 0.36$ (medium effect), both $p < 0.05$), $SD_{attract}$ in the

---

[4]df: degrees of freedom, t: t-value of the T-test.

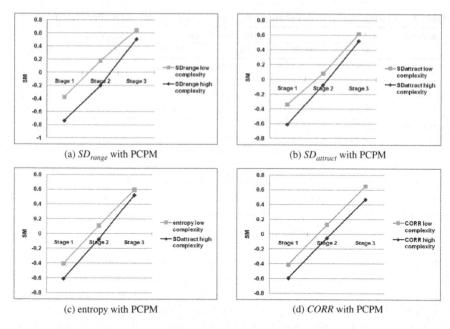

(a) SD_{range} with PCPM

(b) $SD_{attract}$ with PCPM

(c) entropy with PCPM

(d) $CORR$ with PCPM

Fig. 3.3 Results of the respondent-specific two-tailed analysis of variance with PCPM. The higher the strategy measure (SM) the more alternative-wise is the search

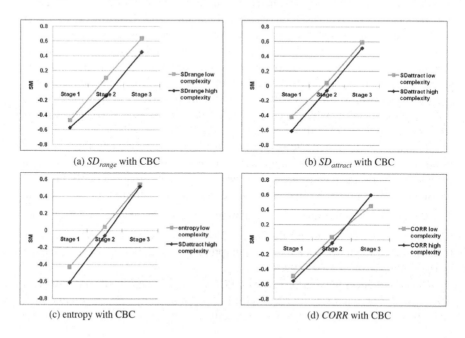

(a) SD_{range} with CBC

(b) $SD_{attract}$ with CBC

(c) entropy with CBC

(d) $CORR$ with CBC

Fig. 3.4 Results of the respondent-specific two-tailed analysis of variance with CBC. The higher the strategy measure (SM) the more alternative-wise is the search

first stage ($t(61) = -2.083$, $r = 0.26$ (small effect), $p < 0.05$) and *entropy* in the first and second stage ($t(61) = 2.781$, $r = 0.34$ (medium effect) and $t(61) = 1.86$, $r = 0.23$ (small effect), both $p < 0.05$). For *CORR* there is no significant difference. When preferences were measured with CBC, we get significant results for SD_{range} in the second stage ($t(61) = -2.007$, $r=0.25$ (small effect), $p < 0.05$) and *entropy* in the first stage ($t(61) = 2.345$, $r = 0.29$ (small effect), $p < 0.05$).

In summary, in cases where preferences are quantified via PCPM, we find that, when complexity is low, people acquire information more alternative-wise in earlier stages of the choice process. Thus, they switch earlier to the second stage of the decision process. In the last stage, all respondents search alternative-wise ($SM > 0$), independently of complexity. Moreover, the amount of trade-offs has the smallest effect. However, the other three measures, which represent similarity, indicate that the more similar the attributes are, the longer people search attribute-wise. This supports hypothesis 5.

3.4 Conclusions

3.4.1 Discussion and Contributions

The current study used advanced techniques to examine the influence of context-based complexity on human decision processes. We used two sophisticated preference measurement techniques from marketing research, CBC and PCPM, for a robust and accurate determination of people's utility functions. This was necessary because context-based complexity is dependent on the utility function of each single individual. Furthermore, eye tracking was used to follow the information acquisition process. Indeed, eye tracking records the decision process in greater detail than alternative methods (e.g., Mouselab), since it keeps track of quick comparisons between multiple pieces of information (Glöckner and Betsch 2008).

Context-based complexity was quantified via four different measures, namely (1) the variation of attribute values which is used to measure attribute ranges, (2) the average correlation of attribute vectors which is used to measure trade-offs, (3) the standard deviation of the overall utility values across alternatives and (4) entropy which is used to measure attractiveness differences. To quantify the information acquisition process we used the well-established SM index, which describes the information acquisition process as being either attribute-wise or alternative-wise in asymmetric matrices (i.e., with an unequal number of alternative and attributes). Furthermore, we described the information acquisition process by the depth and breadth of search.

We conjectured that attribute-wise versus alternative-wise information acquisition behavior changes within choice tasks. This behavior indicates a switch between decision strategies. At the beginning, decision makers tend to acquire information attribute-wise, whereas with increasing time this process changes to an alternative-wise search pattern. Dividing the entire decision process of each choice task into three stages, the SM index rose from -0.54 to 0 to 0.54, strongly supporting this hypothesis.

Besides the change in the information acquisition process within choice tasks, we proposed an influence of context-based complexity on this search pattern. We showed two interesting relationships: first, with increasing complexity, the search pattern is more attribute-wise. Second, with increasing complexity, people increase the depth and breadth of search. Together with the first result of a switch from an attribute-wise to an alternative-wise pattern of information acquisition, we are able to explain these results in terms of a staged decision process. We suggest that people start using decision strategies with an attribute-wise information search to compare alternatives, such as LEX or EBA. They use these strategies to determine which alternative(s) they can exclude from further consideration. They then focus on a few alternatives and compare them by using alternative-wise patterns. We conjecture that the less complex the task is, the earlier the switch happens. Since the elimination phase at the beginning of the decision process is harder in cases of high complexity, people will increase the depth and breadth of their search to eliminate only inferior alternatives; in this case, the switch from attribute-wise strategies to alternative-wise strategies will happen later, as in cases with low complexity.

Our results not only contribute to research on decision-making behavior but also on structural models used in marketing research. Einhorn and Hogarth (1981) contend that both process tracing and structural models consider two sides of the same coin. Conjoint analytic approaches provide estimates of systematic and error variance in judgments. While the relative importance of an attribute is difficult to determine in a process tracing model, conjoint analytic approaches can provide this information. On the other hand, results of eye tracking can be used to identify decision heuristics, which might seriously harm the validity of structural models because they rely on utility maximizing strategies. The empirical results show that information acquisition behavior is dependent on the context-based complexity of the decision situation. This implies that the predictive power of structural models will decline due to adaptive information acquisition behavior when context-based complexity is high.

As our work supports previous findings that the information acquisition process consists of several stages, researchers should consider explaining choices with a sequence of different decision strategies which might have been applied. Gilbride and Allenby (2006) recently proposed such a method. We recently also have examined the occurrences of mixed decision strategies (Pfeiffer et al. 2009a). In this latter experiment, we monitored the purchase decisions of 624 consumers shopping online. We studied how many of the observed choices can be explained by the existing strategies in their pure form, how many decisions can be explained if we account for switching behavior, and investigated switching behavior in detail. Since accounting for switching leads to a large search space of possible mixed decision strategies, we applied a genetic algorithm to find the set of mixed decision strategies which best explains the observed behavior. The results showed that mixed strategies are used more often than pure ones and that a set of four mixed strategies is able to explain 93.9% of choices in a scenario with 4 alternatives and 75.4% of choices in a scenario with 7 alternatives. Yet, when we divide respondents into clusters and assign the strategy to each cluster which explains its behavior best, the improvement from mixed over pure strategies diminishes. In scenarios where we allow four strategies to explain the observed decision-making behavior in cases with 4 alternatives and 3–5 clusters, mixed strategies do not explain more decisions than pure ones. In cases with seven alternatives, mixed strategies explain up to 6% more of the decisions than pure strategies. Therefore, if we allow for heterogenous decision-making behavior and assign different strategies to different respondents, pure strategies explain the observed behavior almost as well as mixed strategies. Thus, if we only want to explain final choices by some strategies, pure strategies seem to be sufficient. If we want to however know which decision strategy best explains the decision-making behavior which happened in reality, then we need process tracing.

3.4.2 Limitations and Future Work

The advantage of measuring the information acquisition process with eye tracking is the great level of detail it provides. However, one might criticize the artificiality of the experimental setting, decreasing the experiment's external validity. Results of the eye tracking study should therefore be compared with other process-tracing techniques such as computerized process-tracing or verbal protocols (see Meißner et al. 2010).

As Ball (1997) pointed out: "The search sequence or transitions that a decision maker uses when searching a matrix of decision information can provide important clues to the strategy guiding the processing of information." However, we are not able to clearly determine which exact strategies the respondents have used in the stages. We only concluded that in the first stages, they used strategies which use attribute-wise processing and in the second stage alternative-wise processing. Consequently, we will examine the relationship between complexity of choice tasks and the concrete decision strategy applied in the subsequent chapter.

Chapter 4
The Influence of Task and Context-Based Complexity on the Final Choice

In this chapter, we present a new approach for the design of choice task experiments that analyze the final respondent's choice but not the decision process.[1] The approach creates choice tasks with a one-to-one correspondence between decision strategies and the observed choices. Thus, a decision strategy used is unambiguously deduced from an observed choice. Furthermore, the approach systematically manipulates the characteristics of choice tasks and takes into account measurement errors concerning the preferences of the decision makers. We use this approach to generate respondent-specific choice tasks with either low or high complexity and study their influence on the use of compensatory and non-compensatory decision strategies. We provide results for the same three measurements of context-based complexity, namely the attribute range, the attractiveness difference, and the correlation of attribute vectors, which we considered in the previous study in Chap. 3. Furthermore, we study two measurements of task-based complexity, namely the number of alternatives and the number of attributes. We find that an increase in context-based complexity and number of alternatives lead to an increased use of non-compensatory strategies and a decreased use of compensatory decision strategies. In contrast, the number of attributes does not influence strategy usage. Furthermore, we observe interaction effects between the attribute range and the correlation of attribute vectors. The proposed approach does not rely on particular decision strategies or hypotheses to be tested and is immediately applicable to a wider range of decision environments. It contributes to research attempts that create designs that maximally discriminate between different models (see Sect. 2.3 and Myung and Pitt 2009).

Similarly to other outcome-based methods, our experimental study observes the alternative selected by the individuals but not the process leading to the observed choice. To be able to link the observed choice to a unique strategy used, we

[1]The experimental study was conducted in cooperation with Dejan Duzevik (Icosystem Corporation, consulting agency, USA) and Koichi Yamamoto (Dentsu Incorporated, advertising agency, Japan).

developed an optimization approach for the design of the choice tasks. Our algorithm designs choice tasks by selecting attribute levels in such a way that different decision strategies lead to different choice predictions. In this way, an individual's decision can be assigned unambiguously to one strategy (Rieskamp and Hoffrage 1999). Furthermore, to be able to study the impact of choice task characteristics on decision behavior, the proposed optimization approach systematically manipulates the three context-based measurements, which we considered in the previous study in Chap. 3, and the amount of information shown. We are thus able to create respondent-specific choice tasks of either low or high complexity, which we use to determine the strategy used from the observed choice.

In our study, we evaluate the use of four different decision strategies: WADD, MAJ, LEX and EBA. We focus on these four decision strategies for several reasons. First, we are seeking representative examples of compensatory (WADD and MAJ) and non-compensatory (LEX and EBA) decision strategies. Second, in a previous, unpublished study with about 500 respondents, we found that WADD and MAJ were among the most frequently used compensatory strategies. Similarly, LEX and EBA were among the most frequent non-compensatory strategies for explaining the behavior of decision makers. Third, considering that a higher number of decision strategies would require additional parameters and additional knowledge concerning the behavior of the decision-maker – e.g., for the satisficing heuristic (Simon 1955) – we must know the exact sequence of alternatives considered by the decision maker. The effort required to measure respondent preferences is relatively low for the four decision strategies we selected for this study. We can also determine the different parameters of these four strategies by using standard methods like questionnaires and adaptive conjoint analysis.

First, we observe that WADD, MAJ and EBA, but not LEX, explain the choices of respondents. Among all four strategies, WADD explains the majority of observed choices. Second, a low context-based complexity of choice tasks leads to an increase in the use of WADD and MAJ and a decrease in the use of EBA. Third, there are strong interaction effects between the three context-based measurements. Forth, the respondents exhibit sufficient propensities in their decision-making behavior such that we can assign them to different clusters.

4.1 Theory and Hypotheses

In Sect. 2.4.3, we have summarized studies examining the influence of the number of alternatives and attributes on the decision-making behavior. The influence of the number of alternatives on the depth and breadth of search, the search pattern, and time is quite clear while the influence of the number of attributes still is not completely understood. Furthermore, conclusions on the applied strategy are sometimes retrieved solely from search patterns, for instance researchers often conclude a compensatory strategy from alternative-wise processing (Conlon et al. 2001; Crow et al. 1980; Lee and Lee 2004; Olshavsky 1979; Payne et al. 1993).

However, as can be seen in Table A.1 in the appendix, not all decision strategies with alternative-wise processing are compensatory (i.e., CONJ, DIS, SAT), nor are all strategies with attribute-wise processing non-compensatory (i.e., ADD, MAJ, and MCD). In contrast to existing research, we analyze the influence of the amount of information on the final choice and not on the decision process. Yet, our argumentation follows the studies which used procedural approaches and we postulate that with increasing number of alternatives and attributes people use simplifying heuristics (Biggs et al. 1985; Payne et al. 1993; Timmermans 1993).

Hypothesis 1 (H1):   An increase in the number of alternatives leads to an increase in the use of LEX/EBA and a decrease in the use of WADD/MAJ.

Hypothesis 2 (H2):   An increase in the number of attributes leads to an increase in the use of LEX/EBA and a decrease in the use of WADD/MAJ.

The difficulty of a choice task not only depends on the amount of information displayed, which is determined by the number of alternatives and attributes, but also on the context-based complexity of a choice task. We operationalize context-based complexity with the same three measurements which we used in Chap. 3: the attribute range (see (3.2)), the attractiveness difference (see (3.3)) and the correlation of attribute vectors (see (3.4)), where high complexity is defined by low attribute range, low attractiveness difference and low correlation of attribute vectors.

It was found that decision makers spend more time on the decision and consider more attribute levels in case of high complexity (Böckenholt et al. 1991; Payne et al. 1988). The same studies show that the lower the attribute range and the lower the correlation of attribute vectors, the more consistent is the search (Bettman et al. 1993; Biggs et al. 1985; Payne et al. 1988). In sum, research using procedural approaches shows that in choice tasks with high context-based complexity, decision makers tend to search for more information and acquire information more consistently. Most strategies with these characteristics are compensatory (see Table A.1 in the appendix).

Process tracing approaches that study the amount of information and consistency with which people search for information suggest that individuals use a more compensatory strategy in choice tasks with high context-based complexity. Several process tracing studies also measure the search pattern, though the findings are unclear. Payne et al. (1988) and Bettman et al. (1993) found that in choice tasks with low attribute range (high complexity), people tend to search alternative-wise. Fasolo et al. (2003) and Bettman et al. (1993) recorded a more alternative-wise search in choice tasks with low correlation of attribute vectors (high complexity). In contrast to that, with high context-based complexity, we recorded a more attribute-wise search pattern in our previous study (see Chap. 3). We argued that in case of high complexity respondents spend more time on the first stage of the decision process where they eliminate inferior alternatives by attribute-wise search. However, since there are both compensatory and non-compensatory strategies with both kinds of patterns, in general, these analyses do not help identify what kind of influence context-based complexity has on the use of either compensatory or non-compensatory strategies.

Bettman et al. (1993) study the decision-making process with procedural approaches and determine the relative accuracy of the chosen alternative. The relative accuracy is the deviation from the choice with maximal expected value (EV). This normative choice is equivalent to the WADD strategy. Since Bettman et al. (1993) presented gambles and not products as alternatives to their respondents, the EV, and thus the relative accuracy, could be computed without measuring or estimating the respondents' preferences. Their results indicate that less accurate choices are made when attribute range is low, which contradicts the results from the procedural analysis that find a more compensatory and thus a more accurate decision. To explain this effect, Bettman et al. (1993) suggest that "individuals may intend to attain high accuracy but may not be able to actually implement the required mental calculations" [p. 944].

There are only a few outcome-based approaches that study the influence of context-based complexity on choice behavior (for exceptions, see Dellaert et al. 1999; Swait and Adamowicz 2001). These studies are limited since they use a compensatory model which mimics non-compensatory strategies (Swait and Adamowicz 2001). With increasing complexity, they observe an increased variance of the error term and/or part-worths of a standard utility model. They interpret this finding as an increased use of simplifying strategies because decision makers focus on only a few attributes (Swait and Adamowicz 2001) and choose the expected alternative less consistently (Dellaert et al. 1999).[2]

In sum, while process-tracing studies suggest a more compensatory decision process with increasing context-based complexity, outcome-based approaches argue that in fact people might use more simplifying strategies. None of the studies examined which specific decision strategies best explain people's choices in tasks of low and high complexity.

We follow the argument by Bettman et al. (1993) and postulate that with an increasing context-based complexity respondents search for more information and search more consistently and thus try to follow a more compensatory decision strategy like WADD or MAJ. Yet respondents may not succeed in their attempt and eventually choose an alternative that can be best explained by a non-compensatory strategy like EBA or LEX. Therefore, in contrast to the conclusions drawn from studies that used procedural approaches, but in-line with the results from Chap. 3 that indicated a longer phase of non-compensatory strategies in cases of high complexity, we formulate our hypotheses as:

Hypothesis 3 (H3):   A decrease of attribute ranges leads to an increase in the use of LEX/EBA and a decrease in the use of WADD/MAJ.

---

[2]Dellaert et al. (1999) define choice consistency as "the variance of the random error component in the consumer utility function: the smaller this variance, the higher choice consistency" [p. 1]. Thus, the higher the consistency is, the better WADD explains the choice.

Hypothesis 4 (H4):   A decrease of attractiveness difference leads to an increase in the use of LEX/EBA and a decrease in the use of WADD/MAJ.

Hypothesis 5 (H5):   A decrease of the correlation of attribute vectors leads to an increase in the use of LEX/EBA and a decrease in the use of WADD/MAJ.

4.2 Method

4.2.1 Formulation of the Experimental Design as Optimization Problem

In our study, we use a two-step approach: in the first step, we determine a respondent's preferences through an adaptive conjoint analysis (ACA) and a questionnaire. In the second step, we use optimization techniques to create individual and preference-specific choice tasks where each decision strategy leads to the choice of a different alternative. This approach is similar to comparative model fitting, but overcomes the problem that multiple strategies lead to the same choice by ensuring that each decision strategy leads to a unique choice.

To be able to link the respondent's choice with a decision strategy, we need data concerning the respondent's preferences: the attribute values (necessary for WADD, MAJ, and LEX), the attribute weights (WADD, LEX, and EBA), and the aspiration levels (for EBA). We measure the attribute values and attribute weights using ACA for fifteen attributes that define cell phones. For the aspiration levels, we use a questionnaire asking the respondents which attribute levels they find unacceptable. Table 4.1 lists the attributes and attribute levels that are used in the

Table 4.1 Attributes and attribute levels used in the experiment

Attribute	Attribute levels				
Sales rank	#1	#3	#5	#10	#20
Camera resolution	10 Mpx	8 Mpx	5 Mpx	3 Mpx	2 Mpx
Display	3.4″	3.2″	3″	2.8″	2.7″
Brand	NEC	Panasonic	Sharp	Fujitsu	
Weight	100 g	110 g	120 g	130 g	140 g
Form	Folding	Slide	Straight		
Thickness	10 mm	15 mm	20 mm		
iMode	iMode phone	Non iMode	iMode smart-phone		
Memory	500 MB	100 MB	50 MB		
Continued use	300 min	240 min	180 min		
Wallet function	Yes	No			
GPS	Yes	No			
Touch-panel	Yes	No			
Waterproof	Yes	No			
One seg TV	Yes	No			

study. Our collaborator, an advertising agency, specified the attributes and attribute levels which were the most relevant to their customers.

In the experiment, we manipulate the five variables (#attributes, #alternatives, attribute range, attractiveness difference and correlation of attribute vectors). While it is straightforward to generate choice tasks with a low vs. high number of alternatives or attributes (H1 and H2), it is difficult to systematically generate choice tasks with low vs. high attribute ranges, attractiveness differences and correlation of attribute vectors (H3, H4, and H5). This is because they depend on the individual preferences of the customers and, for the same choice task, are perceived differently by each respondent (see (3.2)–(3.4)). Consequently, in order to systematically manipulate the three context-based variables, we have to create individual sets of choice tasks for each respondent.

In addition, we want to create choice tasks where observing the respondent's choice allows us to determine the decision strategy used. Therefore, we want to achieve an injective mapping from the decision strategies used by the respondents to the alternatives. Figure 4.1 shows two different repondent-specific choice tasks, which differ in terms of their attribute levels. The respondent-specific choice task A is designed in such a way that the respondent will select phone A if and only if he or she follows a WADD strategy. Similarly, if the respondent follows a MAJ, EBA, or LEX strategy, he or she will select phone B, phone C, or phone D, respectively. If a respondent selects phone E, the respondent isn't following either one of the four strategies and we denote this case as NONE. Thus, choice task A is designed in such a way that we have an injective mapping from the used decision strategies to the selected alternatives.

Choice task B is an example of a non-injective (and non-surjective) mapping from the decision strategies to the alternatives. Here, two or more strategies can

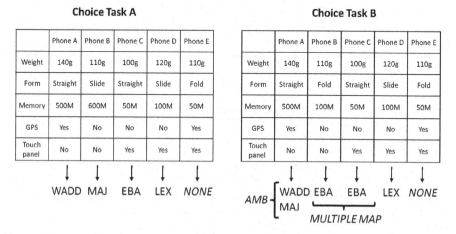

Fig. 4.1 Two mappings of alternatives to decision strategies. The GA minimizes ambiguous (*AMB*) and multiple mappings (*MULTIPLE MAP*) mappings

map to the same alternative (denoted as ambiguous mapping (AMB)) and a decision strategy can lead not only to one but several alternatives (denoted as multiple mapping). In the example, the respondent will select phone A if he or she follows WADD or MAJ. Following EBA leaves the respondent with phones B or C.

Keeping in mind that the choice of different attribute levels leads to different mappings, we want to denote all choice tasks (like choice task A above) that lead to a minimum number of ambiguous and multiple mappings as *choice tasks with optimal mapping*.

In summary, we want to consider several objectives when creating individual choice tasks for the different respondents:

1. We want to create choice tasks with optimal mapping. If the mapping is optimal, we can deduce the used strategy from the observed choice.
2. We want to manipulate the attribute range of a choice task. By systematically creating choice tasks with a low vs. high attribute range, we can test H3.
3. We want to manipulate the attractiveness difference of a choice task. By systematically creating choice tasks with a low vs. high attractiveness difference, we can test H4.
4. We want to manipulate the average correlation of attribute vectors of a choice task. By systematically creating choice tasks with a low vs. high correlation of attribute vectors, we can test H5.

Respondent-specific choice tasks with optimal mapping and manipulated context-based complexity depend on the preferences of the respondents. However, when measuring respondents' preferences with an ACA in the first step of our experiments, measurement error is inevitable. To reduce the effects of errors, we ensure that our choice tasks are *robust* in two ways. First, small changes in respondents' preferences should not result in a significantly different context-based complexity. Second, small changes should not significantly increase the number of ambiguous and multiple mappings. Consequently, we formulate the fifth objective:

5. We want to create robust choice tasks.

Finding robust choice tasks with optimal mapping is difficult since the number of different choice tasks is high even for simple choice tasks. For a choice task with n alternatives and m attributes, where the m attributes are chosen from a set of m_{all} attributes and each attribute has on average $|A_i|$ possible attribute levels, we have $|A_i|^{nm} \cdot \binom{m_{all}}{m}$ different choice tasks. As an example, for a choice task with $n = 5$ alternatives, $m = 5$ attributes that are chosen out of a set of $m_{all} = 15$ possible attributes and $|A_i| = 3$ attribute levels per attribute, we have 2.5×10^{15} different choice tasks. Thus, we need optimization methods to find robust choice tasks with optimal mapping.

To decrease the complexity of the experimental design, we will either optimize objectives 1,2,4,5 or objectives 1,3,4,5. This approach does not restrict our study because the interesting relationship from a theoretical perspective is between correlation of attribute vectors and attribute ranges and correlation of attribute vectors and attractiveness differences (for details see Sect. 2.4).

4.2.2 A Genetic Algorithm for Finding Robust Choice Tasks with Optimal Mapping

Genetic algorithms (GAs) (Goldberg 1989; Holland 1975; Reeves and Rowe 2003) are heuristic optimization methods that are inspired by the principles of evolution and apply recombination, mutation, and selection operators to a population of solution candidates. In contrast to exact optimization methods like linear programming or branch-and-bound approaches, heuristic optimization methods do not guarantee an optimal solution but often return high-quality solutions in a reasonable amount of time (Bäck et al. 1997; Glover and Kochenberger 2003). Heuristic optimization methods are often applied with success to $\mathcal{NP}$-hard problems or problems where the size of the search spaces increases exponentially with the problem size.

Algorithm 1 describes the basic functionality of a GA. After randomly creating and evaluating an initial set (population) of candidate solutions, the algorithm iteratively creates new populations by recombining (with probability p_c) the selected high-quality solutions and applying mutations (with probability p_m).

Algorithm 1 Genetic Algorithm

Create initial population P
Evaluate initial population
while termination criterion is not met **do**
    Select high-quality solutions from P and obtain P'
    Apply recombination to P' and obtain P''
    Apply mutation to P'' and obtain P'''
    Evaluate P'''
    $P = P'''$
end while

Each candidate solution must contain all the information necessary to construct a choice task. It must define which m attributes and corresponding nm attribute levels are shown to a particular respondent. Given a set of m_{all} possible attributes ($m_{all} \geq m$), we order the m_{all} possible attributes in a vector $Attr^w = (attr_1, \ldots, attr_{m_{all}})$ such that $w_i \geq w_{i+1}$. Similarly, for each attribute $attr_i$, we order the a_{all}^i corresponding possible attribute values in a vector $A_i^w = (a_1, \ldots, a_{a_{all}^i})$ such that $v(a_i) \geq v(a_{i+1})$. Then, a candidate solution is a string $x = x_1, \ldots, x_{m(n+1)}$ with two different types of elements. First, the elements $x_{(i-1)(n+1)+1} \in \{1, \ldots, m_{all}\}$ ($i = 1, \ldots, m$) indicate that the $x_{(i-1)(n+1)+1}$th element of the attribute vector $Attr^w$ is shown in the ith row of the choice task. To avoid multiple occurrences of the same attribute in a choice task, $x_{(i-1)(n+1)+1} \neq x_{(j-1)(n+1)+1}$ for $i \neq j$. Second, the elements $x_{(i-1)(n+1)+(1+j)} \in \{1, \ldots, a_{a_{all}^i}\}$ ($i = 1, \ldots, m$ and $j = 1, \ldots, n$) indicate that the $x_{(i-1)(n+1)+(1+j)}$th element of the attribute level vector A_i^w is used for the attribute $attr_i$ of alt_j.

Figure 4.2 gives an example. The first element x_1 of a solution specifies the attribute that is shown in the first row of the choice task. For the example, we

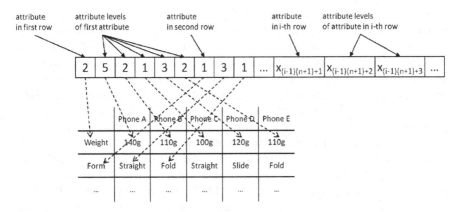

Fig. 4.2 Construction of a choice task from a solution string

assume $Attr^w = (form, weight, price, form)$, which is ordered with respect to the importance of the attributes. A value of $x_1 = 2$ indicates the attribute at the second position of $Attr^w$. The following $n = 5$ elements $x_2, \ldots, x_6$ indicate the shown attribute levels for the $n = 5$ different alternatives. Assuming $A^w_{weight} = (100\,g, 110\,g, 120\,g, 130\,g, 140\,g)$, which is ordered with respect to the respondent-dependent value function, a value of $x_2 = 5$ indicates that we use the attribute level at the fifth position of A^w_{weight} for the weight of phone A. With $n = 5$ and $m = 3$, a solution has $m(n + 1) = 18$ elements. The first, seventh and 13th element indicate the shown attributes. The other elements determine the 15 attribute levels.

This construction process ensures that the search space is fully covered and that all possible choice tasks can be represented. The construction process follows the principle of problem space search (Storer et al. 1992), where the string values select elements from a pre-ordered list. By selecting elements (attributes and attribute levels) from an ordered list, small variations of the solution string result in new solutions with similar properties (attributes have similar importance and attribute levels have similar attribute value). Such a construction process often leads to a high performance of heuristic optimization methods (Raidl and Julstrom 2000; Rothlauf 2009; Storer et al. 1992).

The GA should generate robust choice tasks with optimal mapping and manipulated attribute range, attractiveness difference and correlation of attribute vectors. We assume a maximization problem and define an additive objective function $f(c) = f_1 + f_2 + f_3$, which evaluates the quality of solution candidates. The different components of f measure the optimality of the mapping (f_1) and how well we can manipulate the attribute range (or the attractiveness difference) (f_2) and correlation of attribute vectors (f_3) of a choice task c.[3] Given the set of decision

---

[3]We will either optimize objectives 1,2,4,5 or objectives 1,3,4,5. Thus, in half of the runs f_2 measures the attribute range and in the other half it measures the attractiveness difference.

strategies $S = \{WADD, MAJ, LEX, EBA\}$, we want to create choice tasks with a minimum number of multiple and ambiguous mappings. Thus, when evaluating a solution, we consider only non-multiple strategies $s_i^n \subset S$ and calculate f_1 as $(1/2) \sum_{s_i^n \in S} 1/n_i$, where n_i denotes the number of strategies that map to the same alternative as strategy s_i^n. For the example choice task A (Fig. 4.1), we have no multiple mappings and obtain $f_1 = 2$. Example B has a multiple mapping for EBA; WADD and MAJ map to the same choice (are ambiguous). Thus, we obtain $f_1 = 1$ for example B.

Furthermore, we want to manipulate the attribute range $AR(ct)$, the attractiveness difference $AD(ct)$ and inter-attribute correlation $AC(ct)$ of a choice task ct. We do not know a priori the minimum and maximum values of AR, AD and AC. Thus, before each GA run, we generate a set of 2,000 random choice tasks. AR_{min} and AR_{max} are the minimum and maximum values of AR that occur in the 2,000 random choice tasks. Similarly, AD_{min} and AD_{max} as well as AC_{min} and AC_{max} are the minimum and maximum values of AD and AC. If we want to find a choice task ct with low AR, we define f_2 as $f_2^{low}(c) = \frac{AR_{max}-AR(c)}{AR_{max}-AR_{min}}$ and if we want to find a choice task with high AR, we define $f_2^{high}(c) = AR(c)/(AR_{max} - AR_{min})$.[4] Analogously, if we want to find choice tasks with low AC, we define $f_3^{low} = \frac{AC_{max}-AC(c)}{AC_{max}-AC_{min}}$ and if we want to find choice tasks with high AC, we define $f_3^{high} = AC(c)/(AC_{max}-AC_{min})$. If choice tasks with lower minimum or higher maximum values are created during a GA run, the corresponding values of AR_{max}, AR_{min}, AD_{max}, AD_{min}, AC_{max}, and AC_{min} are updated during the GA run. The normalization of AR, AD and AC is necessary to ensure that the GA focuses equally on both AR (AD) and AC. Overall, the contribution to the objective function is equal for f_1 and $f_2 + f_3$. Thus, finding choice tasks with optimal mapping has the same importance for the GA as manipulating correlation of attribute vectors and attribute ranges (attractiveness differences).

During initialization, the GA creates a population of 300 randomly created solutions. For each solution, the string elements that indicate the shown attributes $(x_{(i-1)(n+1)+1}, i = 1, \ldots, m)$, are randomly drawn from $\{1, \ldots, m_{all}\}$ without replacement. The elements that indicate the shown attribute levels $(x_{(i-1)(n+1)+(1+j)}, i = 1, \ldots, m$ and $j = 1, \ldots, n)$, are randomly drawn from $\{1, \ldots, a_{a_{all}^i}\}$.

After initialization, we apply standard GA operators (Bäck et al. 1997, Chap. C3). For the selection operator, we use a tournament selection of size 2. Thus, we iteratively select two random candidate solutions from P and insert the solution with higher objective value f into P' until P' is filled. Recombination then creates a new population P'' from P'. Recombination selects with probability $p_c = 1$ two random parent solutions from P' and copies them into P''. Then, with a probability of 0.5, the operator exchanges the values of all string elements that belong to the ith attribute $(x_{(i-1)(n+1)+1}, \ldots, x_{i(n+1)})$ between the two new solutions. To ensure that

---

[4]The same holds for AD in case we are manipulating AD instead of AR.

no attributes are duplicated in one solution, no exchange occurs if an attribute exists in both solutions. Finally, we copy all solutions from P'' to P''' and mutate each string element with a probability of $1/(m(n+1))$. A mutation randomly increases or decreases the value of the string element by 1. Thus, a new solution is created with either a new attribute that has similar importance or a new attribute level with similar attribute value. Mutation is not applied if it would duplicate attributes in a solution. The GA uses a population size of 300 and is stopped after 600 generations. To avoid early convergence, the GA uses duplicate elimination, which means that duplicate solutions are discarded and no identical solutions exist in a population. Furthermore, it uses an archive of size 300, which stores the best solutions observed during the GA run. The archive is updated after each generation.

At the end of a run, the GA returns to the archive that contains the 300 best solutions found. Usually, the mapping of these solutions is near-optimal or optimal and the attribute range, attractiveness difference and correlation of attribute vectors is either low or high. To address the robustness of a choice task and to reduce the effects of estimation error stemming from inaccurate measurements of the preference function, we consider all 300 solutions in the archive and examine the effects of small attribute level modifications. We take each solution c and randomly modify one of the shown attribute levels. We do this 50 times for each of the 300 choice tasks and compute the *robust objective value* $f'(c)$ as

$$f'(c) = \frac{1}{50} \sum_{i=1}^{50} f(c_i), \tag{4.1}$$

where the c_i are the 50 solutions that are created by randomly mutating one attribute level of c. We finally select the solution (choice task) that maximizes f'.

4.2.3   Evaluation of the Genetic Algorithm

The GA created 11,344 choice tasks for 709 respondents. The average running time of the GA necessary for creating a choice task was 72.6 s resulting in an overall computation time of 57.2 h on four parallel processors.

To assess the performance of the GA, we compare the choice tasks generated by the GA with a benchmark of randomly generated choice tasks. For each choice task shown to the respondents, we generated 180,000 choice tasks by randomly selecting attributes and corresponding attribute levels. Similarly to the GA, we stored the 300 best solutions (with respect to f) in an archive and selected the most robust solution (with respect to f') from this set. We denote this random generation of choice tasks as random sampling. Its computational effort is high and similar to the GA that also performs 180,000 evaluations during a run (600 generations à 300 solutions) and 15,000 evaluations at the end of the run when selecting the most robust solution (50 modifications for each of the 300 solutions in the archive).

Table 4.2 Quality of solutions found by GA versus randomly generated choice tasks (mean and standard deviation)

	Random sampling (Benchmark)	GA (Objectives 1,2,4,5)	GA (Objectives 1,3,4,5)
Robust objective value f'	2.36 (0.45)	2.37 (0.44)	2.46 (0.50)
Objective value f	2.87 (0.45)	3.26 (0.36)	3.32 (0.40)
Optimality of mapping f_1	1.75 (0.30)	1.94 (0.18)	1.98 (0.11)
Attribute range f_2	0.55 (0.17)	0.62 (0.19)	–
Attractiveness difference f_2	0.59 (0.29)	–	0.67 (0.24)
Correlation of attribute vectors f_3	0.56 (0.33)	0.70 (0.26)	0.67 (0.27)
Percentage of optimal mappings	55.8%	90.4%	94.4%

Table 4.2 compares the objective values of the solutions returned by the two versions of the GA (manipulation of the attribute range (objective 2) vs. manipulation of the attractiveness difference (objective 3)) with random sampling. For the returned choice tasks, we show the mean and standard deviation (in brackets) of the robust objective value f', the objective value f, as well as the three components of f, which are f_1, f_2, and f_3. Furthermore, we list the percentage of choice tasks with an optimal mapping.

The average objective value f of the solutions returned by the GA (3.26 and 3.32, respectively) is higher than for random sampling (2.87, $p < 0.01$). Also the partial objective values f_1, f_2, and f_3 are significantly higher for choice tasks found by the GA ($p < 0.01$). In comparison to random sampling, the GA approach yields better solutions if we assume that the measured preferences are correct. The values of the robust objective value f' indicate that a higher solution quality in the case of accurate preference measurements does not lead to a lower quality in the case of inaccurate preference measurements. The GA that optimizes objectives 1,3,4,5 even created more robust solutions than the random sampling approach.

We further analyzed the ability of the GA to successfully manipulate the three context-based complexity measures (objectives 2, 3 and 4) by comparing the distribution of complexity measure values across choice tasks with and without manipulation of the particular context-based measure. Figure 4.3 shows boxplots for the choice tasks which were generated for the high vs. the low attribute range group. We see that the attribute range differs a lot for the two groups indicating that the manipulation of the attribute range was successful and objective 3 is met. Furthermore, as intended, the correlation of attribute vectors is not affected by that manipulation: the two boxplots for the two groups do not differ. The same conclusion can be drawn for the other two complexity measures which is shown in Figs. 4.4 and 4.5. In Fig. 4.5 which displays the groups when controlling for the correlation of attribute vectors (objective 4), we have three bars per group. This is

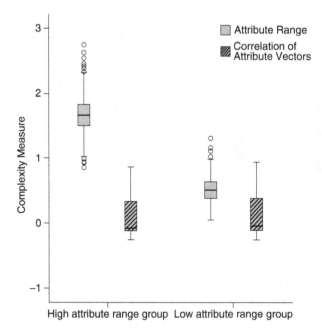

Fig. 4.3 Complexity measures when controlling for the attribute range

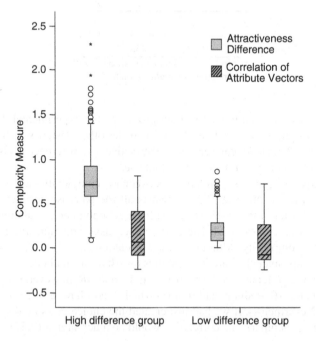

Fig. 4.4 Complexity measures when controlling for the attractiveness difference

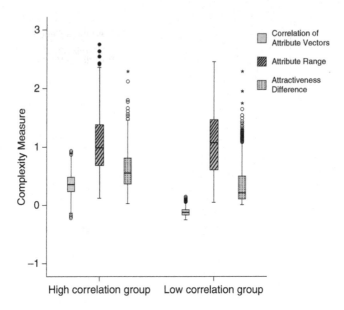

Fig. 4.5 Complexity measures when controlling for the correlation of attribute vectors

Table 4.3 Correlations of complexity measures

	AR	AD	AC
n	0.085[a]	0.183[b]	0.086[b]
m	−0.025	0.054[b]	0.192[b]
AC	0.018	0.458[b]	1

[a]Correlation is significant on 0.05 level
[b]Correlation is significant on 0.01 level

because objective 4 is optimized in both groups of the experimental design (one design which optimizes objectives 1,2,4,5 and the other design which optimizes the objectives 1,3,4,5). We can see that the attractiveness difference is also affected when manipulating the correlation of attribute vectors.

We also test for spurious correlations between the complexity measures. For the solutions returned by the GA, Table 4.3 lists all the pairwise correlations. There seems to be a tendency that choice tasks with a higher number n of alternatives have higher values of AC, AD and AR. Therefore, choice tasks with more alternatives tend to have lower complexity. Although these correlations are significant, we neglect them in our study since they are low and thus only have a small effect.

There is no significant correlation between AC and AR, however, the correlation between AD and AC is significant (0.458) which might have a larger influence on our results. Nevertheless, if we had just created the choice tasks randomly, as was done with our benchmark, the correlation would be much higher (0.57).

4.3 Experiment

4.3.1 Participants

The online-experiment was conducted in Japan with a pool of 709 participants selected by a Japanese advertising agency. All participants were between 30 and 39 years old, 49.9% of them were female and all owned a cell phone. On average, respondents took 23.84 s per choice.

4.3.2 Design and Procedure

We use a $2 \times 2 \times 2 \times 2$ factorial design ([5 vs. 8 alternatives] $\times$ [5 vs. 8 attributes] $\times$ [low vs. high correlation of attribute vectors] $\times$ [low vs. high attractiveness difference/attribute range]). We manipulate the factors in-between subjects in order to control for respondent-specific effects.

The experiment consists of three stages:

Stage 1: An ACA and a short questionnaire which determine the attribute values, the attribute weights and the aspiration levels as well as demographics.

Stage 2: The GA which generates 16 choice tasks per respondent based on the respondents' preferences from stage 1.

Stage 3: The main experiment, where each respondent is shown the 16 choice tasks. The attributes and the alternatives of each choice task as well as the 16 choice tasks were shown in random order. In this stage 609 out of the 709 respondents took part.

The approach makes two main assumptions: (1) the data gathered in the ACA and the questionnaire is a good representation of respondents' true preferences, (2) these preferences did not change before the respondents participated in the choice experiment (there was a 10-day lag between Stage 1 and Stage 3).

We removed all choice tasks with AMB mapping. This step facilitates the interpretation of our statistical analysis because when we report the frequency with which any strategy explained the observed choices, we can be sure that no other of the three strategies also explained the same choice. Deleting all AMB mappings caused as side-effect that also no multiple mappings remained in the sample, because multiple maps happened to appear in choice tasks which also had AMB mappings. Thus, we were only left with choice tasks with an optimal mapping. After the data cleansing, 9,086 choices were left in the sample. From these 9,086, 4,408 were created with objective 2, thus for the analysis of attribute ranges we could only analyze these choice tasks, and 4,678 were created with objective 3, thus only for these ones we could analyze attractiveness differences.

Table 4.4 Observed versus expected usage of strategies

Strategy	Observed	Baseline	Ratio
EBA	20.6%	16.2%	1.32
LEX	17.1%	16.2%	1.09
MAJ	19.3%	16.2%	1.23
WADD	27.1%	16.2%	1.73

4.3.3 Empirical Results

Table 4.4 lists the relative frequencies with which the strategies explained the respondents' choices. Respondents apply WADD in most choice tasks (27.1%), followed by EBA, MAJ, and LEX. We compare the observed relative frequencies with the baseline case, which is a model that randomly predicts choices. For example, for choice tasks with five alternatives, the baseline model would predict the choices with a relative frequency of 20%. In our case, where choice tasks have five or eight alternatives, the relative frequency of the baseline model is 16.2%. With $ratio = \frac{observed}{baseline}$, WADD explains 1.73 times as many choices than the baseline model; in contrast, LEX (ratio = 1.09) is only slightly better than a prediction model that guesses randomly.

In order to test the hypotheses, we want to make sure that for each respondent we evaluate an approximately equal number of choice tasks in which the independent variables n, m, AR, AD and AC have either high or low values. However, due to the removal of choice tasks with multiple or ambiguous mappings, this is not the case for every respondent. Thus, for each of the five independent variables, we do not consider respondents if the ratio between the number of choice tasks with a high independent variable value and the number of choice tasks with a low independent variable value is greater than 2 or smaller than 0.5. This happened to three respondents for n, 13 respondents for m, 13 for AR, four for AD and 37 for AC.

Figure 4.6 plots the relative frequency of the observed strategies over the values of the independent variables. We show the results for the number of alternatives n (Fig. 4.6a), the number of attributes m (Fig. 4.6b), attribute range AR (Fig. 4.6c), attractiveness difference AD (Fig. 4.6d) and the correlation of attribute vectors AC (Fig. 4.6e). We expect that an increase in the complexity of a choice task (higher value of m or n; lower value of AR, AD, or AC) will lead to an increased use of low-effort strategies (LEX and EBA) and a decreased use of high-effort strategies (WADD and MAJ).

To evaluate the association between the measures of complexity and the frequencies of strategies used, we apply the Wilcoxon signed-rank test. We use this non-parametric t-test for dependent samples used when the result data cannot be assumed to be normally distributed. We had to apply a test for dependent samples because of the in-between subjects manipulation of the complexity measurements.

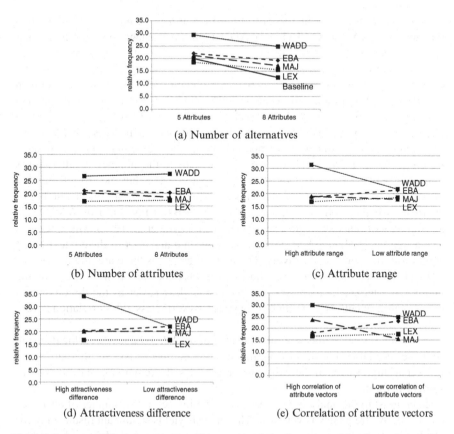

Fig. 4.6 Influence of the independent variables on the relative frequency of the observed strategies

The effect size of each test is defined as $r = \frac{Z}{\sqrt{N}}$, where Z is the signed rank statistic and N is the number of observations. Values of $r = 0.1$ determine a small effect, $r = 0.3$ a medium effect, and $r = 0.5$ a large effect (Cohen 1988, 1992).

An increase of n from $n = 5$ to $n = 8$ (Fig. 4.6a) has a significant effect on all strategies. For all four strategies EBA, LEX, MAJ and WADD, the relative frequency decreases with increasing n. The effects are small. At the same time, the number of NONE strategies significantly increases from 8.80% ($n = 5$) to 23.25% ($n = 8$) with a medium effect ($r = 0.44$).

H1 states that with increasing n the use of LEX and EBA increases, while the use of WADD and MAJ decreases. As expected, WADD and MAJ decreases; however, the use of LEX and EBA also decreases, which is in contrast to hypothesis H1. How can we explain this observation? First, our experiment is designed in such a way that an increase of n goes along with an increase of alternatives that map to NONE strategies. In small choice tasks with $n = 5$, only one alternative maps to a NONE strategy. In larger choice tasks with $n = 8$, the number of alternatives that map to NONE strategies increases to four. In contrast, the number of alternatives that map to EBA, LEX, MAJ or WADD remains constant (one alternative per strategy). Since choice tasks with a higher number of alternatives are more complex, respondents might be less able to follow a particular strategy. They are either not able to execute that strategy properly or they might mix different strategies (Bettman and Park 1980; Gilbride and Allenby 2004, 2006; Luce et al. 1997; Russo and Leclerc 1994). Since half of the alternatives in choice tasks with $n = 8$ map to a NONE strategy, the probability increases that respondents will choose an alternative indicating a NONE strategy in comparison to an alternative that can be explained by either EBA, LEX, MAJ, or WADD. Second, ff the number of alternatives indicating EBA, LEX, MAJ or WADD is kept constant but the overall number of alternatives is increased, respondents can choose between a greater number of alternatives if they follow a strategy other than EBA, LEX, MAJ or WADD (for an overview of other strategies, see for instance Payne et al. 1993). Third, there is also a significant, though low, correlation between n and each of the context-based complexity measures, respectively. The more alternatives there are, the higher AR, AD and AC (see Table 4.3) are. Thus, choice tasks become more difficult as the number of alternatives increases, but become slightly easier as the three context-based measurements AR, AD, and AC increase. Nevertheless, this correlation is very low.

Since the further analysis of the influence of m, AR, AD and AC on the decision strategies used does not suffer from the different number of NONE alternatives for low versus high values of the independent variables, the remaining analysis is more straightforward.

In contrast to the analysis of alternatives, the impact of the number of attributes on the relative frequency is very low. The analysis yields significant results only for MAJ ($p < 0.05$), but with a small effect ($r = 0.06$) (see Table 4.5 and Fig. 4.6b). While the decreasing usage of MAJ in choice tasks with fewer attributes supports H2, the insignificant results for the other three strategies lead us to reject H2.

The analysis of attribute ranges on relative frequency is statistically significant for WADD and EBA, while the results for MAJ and LEX are not significant (see Table 4.6 and Fig. 4.6c). The effect size on WADD is close to medium ($r = -0.26$) and the effect size is small for EBA. The trends of each strategy follows H3. With decreasing AR, respondents use less compensatory strategies and more non-compensatory strategies. This finding corroborates H3.

The change in the relative frequency when we manipulated attractiveness difference is statistically significant for WADD with a medium effect ($r = -0.33$) (see Fig. 4.6d and Table 4.6). We have anticipated such a strong influence on WADD, because the attractiveness difference is closely related to the definition of the WADD strategy and it measures in how far the overall utility values of products differ from each other. In summary, H4 can only be supported for the WADD strategy but with the largest effect we could find for any of our measures of complexity.

The analysis of the correlation of attribute vectors was statistically significant for EBA, MAJ, and WADD with an effect close to medium for MAJ ($r = -0.28$) and a small to medium effect for EBA and WADD (see Table 4.6 and Fig. 4.6e). Thus, in

Table 4.5 Wilcoxon tests on the relative frequencies for the strategy frequency (M = Mean) for the two task-based complexity measurements

Strategy	Z	M(5 alt.)	M(8 alt.)	Sign. (one-tailed)	Effect Size
Number of alternatives (H1)					
EBA	−3.674	22.01%	19.25%	<0.001	0.11
LEX	−4.022	18.53%	15.59%	<0.001	0.12
MAJ	−5.523	21.23%	17.19%	<0.001	0.16
WADD	−5.403	29.44%	24.72%	<0.001	0.16
NONE	−15.164	8.80%	23.25%	<0.001	0.44
Number of attributes (H2)		M(5 attr.)	M(8 attr.)		
EBA	−0.929	20.95%	20.13%	0.18	0.03
LEX	−0.749	16.82%	17.20%	0.23	0.02
MAJ	−2.197	20.17%	18.41%	0.01	0.06
WADD	−1.252	26.61%	27.44%	0.11	0.04
NONE	−1.723	15.46%	16.83%	0.04	0.05

Table 4.6 Wilcoxon tests on the relative frequency for the strategy frequency (M = Mean) for the three context-based complexity measurements

Strategy	Z	M(high range)	M(low range)	Sign. (One-tailed)	Effect Size
Attribute range (H3)					
EBA	−1.900	18.55%	21.34%	0.01	0.08
LEX	−1.221	16.77%	18.37%	0.14	0.05
MAJ	−1.560	18.84%	17.74%	0.09	0.06
WADD	−6.239	31.38%	21.72%	<0.001	0.26
NONE	−3.756	14.46%	20.83%	<0.001	0.16
Attractiveness difference (H4)		M(high diff.)	M(low diff.)		
EBA	−1.696	20.20%	22.02%	0.05	0.07
LEX	−0.163	16.59%	16.61%	0.44	0.01
MAJ	−0.190	20.01%	20.15%	0.42	0.01
WADD	−8.012	33.97%	22.01%	<0.001	0.33
NONE	−8.106	9.23%	19.20%	<0.001	0.33
Correlation of attribute vectors (H5)		M(high corr.)	M(low corr.)		
EBA	−4.697	18.01%	23.01%	0.00	0.14
LEX	−0.290	16.61%	17.53%	0.27	0.01
MAJ	−9.350	23.59%	15.50%	<0.001	0.28
WADD	−5.857	29.84%	24.72%	<0.001	0.17
NONE	−8.567	11.95%	19.24%	<0.001	0.26

Table 4.7 Binary logit models testing interaction effects between AR and AC, AD and AC, respectively

$AR*AC$	B	Std. error	Wald Chi-Square	Significance
EBA	−0.069	0.0332	4.281	0.039
LEX	−0.050	0.0347	2.058	0.151
MAJ	0.147	0.0287	26.412	< 0.001
WADD	0.049	0.0289	2.906	0.088
$AD*AC$				
EBA	−0.059	0.0361	2.693	0.101
LEX	0.004	0.0353	0.012	0.912
MAJ	0.014	0.0331	0.179	0.673
WADD	−0.026	0.0321	0.673	0.412

choice tasks with high correlation of attribute vectors (few trade-offs), significantly more compensatory strategies were applied than in cases of low correlation of attribute vectors. The complementary result is observed for EBA. In summary, H5 can for the most part be supported.

In line with previous work (see Sect. 4.1), we argue that AR (AD) and AC are different types of context-based complexity. While AR and AD measure how similar alternatives are, AC measures the extent to which decision makers have to trade-off attribute levels. To understand the influence of these two context-based complexities in more detail, we analyze the interactions between the standardized AC and AR (AD) using binary logit models. Each model includes three variables: $AR(AD)$, AC and $AR*AC$ ($AD*AC$). Similarly to the statistics for the main effects, the models take into account the dependency of choices (in-between subject design). Table 4.7 presents the results for the interaction term $AR*AC$ ($AD*AC$). We find significant interaction effects for EBA and MAJ for AR and AC.

To further clarify the findings, we plot the interaction effects for MAJ (Fig. 4.7) and EBA (Fig. 4.8). For both strategies, AR has a higher impact if AC is high. With a low correlation of attribute vectors, more respondents are influenced by the attribute range when deciding for or against the use of MAJ and EBA. Furthermore, for both strategies, AC has a higher impact if AR is high. With less similar alternatives, more respondents consider AC when deciding for or against the use of MAJ and EBA. In sum, the influence of AR, respectively AC, increases if the choice task is easy with respect to the other complexity measure.

Finally, Table 4.8 shows the relative frequencies for different combinations of AC and AR.[5] In the most difficult choice tasks (low AC and low AR), the non-compensatory EBA strategy explains most choices (22.67%). In easier choice tasks (either AR or AC are high), the compensatory WADD strategy explains the highest percentage of choices. In the easiest choice tasks, WADD explains more than a third

---

[5]Since we did not find any significant interactions for AC and AD, we refrain from reporting equivalent numbers for this combination.

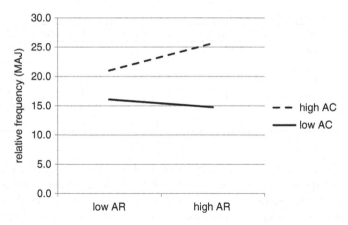

Fig. 4.7 Interaction effects for MAJ

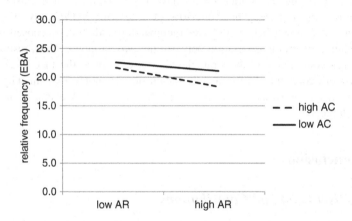

Fig. 4.8 Interaction effects for EBA

Table 4.8 Relative frequencies of the observed strategies for different combinations of *AR* and *AC*

AC	AR	EBA	LEX	MAJ	WADD
Low	Low	22.67%	18.09%	16.08%	20.34%
Low	High	21.15%	17.00%	14.75%	28.26%
High	Low	21.76%	18.30%	20.99%	23.66%
High	High	18.41%	17.54%	25.64%	35.79%

of all choices (35.79%) which is 2.2 times more than the baseline model would explain.

In an additional analysis, we clustered respondents using a K-Means algorithm into five groups according to the strategy they used most often. We allowed for a fifth cluster to capture unexplained decision-making behavior (*NONE*).

Table 4.9 Results of cluster analysis

	WADD-Cluster	EBA-Cluster	LEX-Cluster	MAJ-Cluster	NONE-Cluster
WADD	**0.40**	0.17	0.15	0.18	0.16
EBA	0.15	**0.40**	0.11	0.13	0.14
LEX	0.12	0.10	**0.42**	0.10	0.13
MAJ	0.14	0.12	0.10	**0.39**	0.13
NONE	0.14	0.12	0.11	0.14	**0.30**
Cluster size	255	150	111	142	88

Table 4.9 shows the average number of strategies used by each cluster. For instance, the respondents that fit into the WADD-cluster chose the alternative that mapped to the WADD strategy in 40% of their 16 choices. The distribution of respondents in clusters is not uniform. The WADD-cluster is the largest with 255 respondents. The *NONE*-cluster is the smallest cluster with 88 respondents. Table 4.9 shows that respondents who have been classified in a cluster chose the given dominant strategy in about 40% of cases (for *NONE* only 30%). The contingency coefficient between cluster membership and strategy chosen is 0.51, which indicates a strong association between the two variables. Thus, respondents show a high consistency in the strategies they use, even in the face of changing choice task environments. Unfortunately, the clusters cannot be explained by any of the personality traits which we recorded (gender, income, risk-aversion, and early vs. late-adopters).

4.4   Conclusions

4.4.1   Discussion and Contributions

The contribution of this work is twofold: first, it contributes to the design of choice task experiments and second, it studies how context-based complexity affects decision behavior. The proposed approach for designing choice task experiments, which is based on a genetic algorithm, allows us to systematically manipulate the context-based complexity of choice tasks and to identify the decision strategies used from the observed choices. This becomes possible since choice tasks are designed in such a way that following a particular decision strategy leads to a unique final choice. In addition, the approach creates robust choice tasks where errors in attribute level measurements do not strongly modify the characteristics of the choice task. The presented design approach does not rely on particular decision strategies or hypotheses to be tested and is immediately applicable to a wider variety of product categories, product settings, and consumer groups.

To study decision behavior in choice tasks, outcome-based approaches usually search for well-defined mathematical choice models but rarely consider adaptive decision-making or the effects of choice task characteristics. Furthermore, in choice tasks where different strategies predict the same choices, outcome-based approaches are not able to discriminate between different decision strategies. This is also true for process tracing approaches, which have difficulty discriminating between decision strategies whose processes are similar to the measurement techniques.

Since our approach systematically manipulates choice task characteristics and links observed choices to the decision strategies used, we are able to provide a solution to the problem of discriminating between strategies (Myung and Pitt 2009; Rieskamp and Hoffrage 1999). Outcome-based approaches can benefit from the ability to better manipulate the choice environment. Procedural approaches can be more accurate and respondent-specific since the observed choice can be linked to the decision strategy used.

With the ability to systematically manipulate the characteristics of choice tasks, we are also able to examine how context-based complexity affects choice behavior. For a choice experiment with cell phones, we systematically manipulate the following independent variables: the attribute range of the choice tasks, the attractiveness difference and the correlation of attribute vectors as well as the number of alternatives and the number of attributes The dependant variables are the frequencies with which each of the four strategies EBA, LEX, MAJ and WADD, are used.

Supporting previous results (Bettman et al. 1993; Swait and Adamowicz 2001) and our own study in Chap. 3, decision-making behavior is not only influenced by the amount of information presented to the respondents, but also by the context in which the information is presented. In low-complexity choice tasks with high attribute range, high attractiveness difference and a high correlation of attribute vectors, respondents more often use compensatory strategies like WADD and MAJ. More complex choice tasks with low attribute range, low attractiveness difference and a low correlation of attribute vectors lead to a higher use of non-compensatory strategies like EBA. The results are in accordance with Bettman et al. (1993) who observed that with increasing complexity, individuals make less accurate decisions and are unable to follow the more demanding compensatory strategies and switch to less demanding non-compensatory strategies. Furthermore, we observe interaction effects between the attribute range and the correlation of attribute vectors for the EBA and MAJ strategy. If a choice task is easy with respect to one of the two complexity measures, the influence of the other complexity measure increases.

Our findings suggest that choice tasks with many similar products where respondents have to trade off a lot of product features against each other are very difficult for customers. Although procedural process-tracing approaches suggest that people try to follow a compensatory decision process in complex tasks, they often do not succeed in this attempt, and end up using a strategy that can best be described as non-compensatory.

4.4.2 Limitations and Future Work

In our experiment, we tested four different strategies. WADD and MAJ are examples of compensatory strategies. EBA and LEX are examples of non-compensatory strategies. While WADD, MAJ, and EBA explain a high percentage of choice decisions, LEX is only slightly more often used in comparison to random choice. In future work, we want to consider more strategies and replace LEX. Furthermore, we want to consider the possibility that decision makers do not follow pure strategies but mix strategies (Bettman and Park 1980; Gilbride and Allenby 2004, 2006; Luce et al. 1997; Reisen et al. 2008; Russo and Leclerc 1994). Considering mixed strategies makes the creation of optimal mappings more difficult as a high number of different strategy combinations exists, but this would allow us to represent decision behavior more accurately.

In our experiment, we do not keep the ratio between the numbers of observed and NONE strategies constant, but rather, by increasing the number of alternatives we allow a higher number of NONE strategies. This increase of NONE strategies modifies the choice situation for the respondents and makes the interpretation of the strategies used more difficult. A possible way to overcome this problem would be to increase the number of strategies. However, then the respondents would be able to choose from a larger number of alternatives, which would make the interpretation of the use of single decision strategies more difficult. Another approach would be to design the NONE alternatives in such a way that they do not map to other, non-observed strategies but are only chosen if the respondents do not follow a reasonable decision strategy. This would reduce the observed choices of NONE strategies and allow a better interpretation of the observed strategies.

Our approach is limited by the assumption that the respondent's preferences are accurately derived from the ACA that precedes the experiment. The proposed approach anticipates inaccurate preferences by creating choice tasks where small modifications of a choice task have only low impact on its characteristics. We must keep in mind that the characteristics depend on the respondent's preferences. Another way to address the issue of inaccurate measurements is to directly assume some variations in the preferences. In this case, we would have to make assumptions about the type and extent of errors that occur in the preference measurement. Furthermore, such an approach would increase the computational effort since each choice task generated would have to be evaluated for a variety of different preferences. Both approaches, assuming variations either for the attribute levels or directly in the preferences, are closely related since the complexity of a choice task is calculated using respondent's preferences *and* attribute levels.

Furthermore, the design of the proposed GA approach can be improved to generate more robust solutions. At the moment, the robustness of choice tasks is only considered for the 300 best solutions at the end of a run. If we want to emphasize robustness and find more robust solutions, robustness must be considered throughout the GA run and for each solution generated. In this case, solutions in the archive would not be chosen with respect to their objective value f but with respect to their robust objective value f'. Such a procedure would allow us to find more robust solutions but strongly increase the computational effort. For example, calculating the robust objective value f' for each solution generated during a GA run would increase the number of evaluations from 195,000 to 9×10^7.

Finally, we assume that the careful generation of choice tasks in our experiment increases internal validity. However, as Rieskamp and Hoffrage (1999) pointed out, "selecting alternatives to minimize the overlap of the strategies' predictions often makes the item set unrepresentative and the results difficult to generalize" (p. 156). One could thus raise doubts about external validity and ask for a representative design (Brunswick 1955) since the choice tasks generated by the GA might not well reflect choice tasks that people find in their daily environments. From our perspective, this dilemma can hardly be solved. Both approaches, those that try to achieve high internal validity and those that try to achieve high external validity, are necessary to better understand the influence and relationship between different complexity measures and final choices.

Part II
Decision Support with Interactive Decision Aids

Part II

Chapter 5
Interactive Decision Aids

Decision support systems assist people in making a decision or choosing a course of action in a nonroutine situation that requires judgment (Häubl and Trifts 2000; Kasper 1996). In online webstores, vendors can easily offer highly interactive types of decision support. These co-called *interactive decision aids* (IDA) "help consumers in making informed purchase decisions amidst the vast availability of online product offerings" (Wang and Benbasat 2009, p. 3). However, the application of IDA is not restricted to purchase decisions. They are general enough to be of use in any kind of choice task where alternatives are known.

In general, decision aids are techniques for helping decision makers to overcome cognitive shortcomings and avoid systematic processing errors (Beach 1997). The phrasing *interactive* describes the situation where consumers can access and exchange information on demand, can customize content, and receive and give real-time feedback (Ariely 2000; Joseph et al. 1997; Zack 1993). Central to our work is the ability to access information interactively in an online database, so-called machine interactivity (Häubl and Trifts 2000; Hoffman and Novak 1996).

IDA assist several sub-processes. They elicit consumers' preferences, carry out a set of search and comparison operations, and produce a product recommendation (Maes et al. 1999). There are two different types of IDA, each of which puts a different emphasis on the sub-processes. *Recommendation systems* focus on eliciting preferences and providing recommendations. *Interactive information management tools* (IIMT) focus on comparing product information.

In the following section, we distinguish between these two types and point out that so far research on information systems has focused on recommendation agents (RA), which are a type of recommendation systems. However, as we will show empirically, customers prefer IIMT to RA. In summary, this chapter not only classifies and describes different types of IDA (see Sect. 5.2) but also examines IIMT in detail in order to address the lack of research in this field and stimulate continued research on the subject.

J. Pfeiffer, *Interactive Decision Aids in E-Commerce*, Contributions to Management Science, DOI 10.1007/978-3-7908-2769-9_5, © Springer-Verlag Berlin Heidelberg 2012

5.1 Types

5.1.1 Recommendation Systems

Recommendation systems rate products for a specific user and recommend the ones with the highest ratings (Adomavicius and Tuzhilin 2005). They can be subdivided into systems that require users to explicitly reveal information on their preferences (e.g., attribute rankings or ratings), and others that learn preferences implicitly (e.g., from click-stream search data or purchase histories) (Adomavicius and Tuzhilin 2005; Montaner et al. 2003; Murray and Häubl 2008).

In current literature, the terms RA, recommender systems, recommendation systems, shopping agents, shopping bots, and comparison shopping agents have been used interchangeably (Wang and Benbasat 2009). However, we see RA as a subcategory of recommendation systems. In line with other researchers (Häubl and Murray 2003; Häubl and Trifts 2000; Spiekermann and Paraschiv 2002), we define RA as recommender systems that are query-based, rely on the explicit revelation of user's preferences, and make recommendations to the user in the form of a sorted list of alternatives based on its understanding of the individual's preference (e.g., personalogic.com was one of the first RA). Hence, RA explicitly ask consumers for their preferences, for example in form of attribute weights, and estimate the user's utility functions (for an example see Fig. 5.1). Afterwards, the product(s) which maximize(s) the estimated preference function are (is) recommended to the customer. Although there is still some ongoing research on these kinds of query-based recommendation systems (Xiao and Benbasat 2007), they are quite scarce in the Internet.

Other types of recommendation systems do not ask users to explicitly reveal information on their preferences but are based on context-based or collaborative filtering approaches (see Fig. 5.2). In context-based systems, the rating of a new product is predicted by considering past ratings or purchases of a consumer. For instance, in order to recommend a movie, the system gives a high rating to new movies with similar characteristics (e.g., actors, genres, directors) to movies the same customer purchased or rated positively in the past. In contrast, collaborative systems estimate the rating by considering the ratings of similar users. Thus, similar products have to be found in context-based systems, whereas similar customers have to be found in collaborative-based systems. An example of the latter approach is the recommender system used by www.amazon.com, which suggests products that other customers have bought as well. Amazon thus assumes that customers are similar if they buy the same products.

Bayesian classifiers, clustering, decision trees and artificial neural networks have been used for recommendation systems (Adomavicius and Tuzhilin 2005). For more details on recommendation systems and an overview of hybrid recommendation systems, the reader is referred to Montaner et al. (2003) and Murray and Häubl (2008).

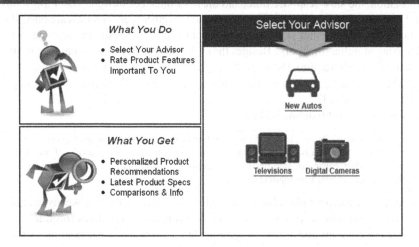

Fig. 5.1 One of the few examples of recommendation agents which still are available in the Internet (www.myproductadvisor.com)

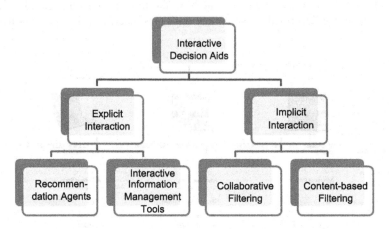

Fig. 5.2 Types of interactive decision aids. Recommendation agents and filtering techniques are recommendation systems

5.1.2   Interactive Information Management Tools (IIMT)

According to a study by Montgomery et al. (2004), RA are adopted by only 10% of online shoppers because of the lack of awareness, the lack of benefits, the lack of information, the slow response time, and the poor interface design. Also Fitzsimons and Lehmann (2004) argue that RA are rejected by customers and thus are basically unsuccessful. What other IDA with explicit interaction does the Internet currently offer to assist online shoppers? Besides the collaborative and context-based systems, neither of which require the user to explicitly enter information, and next to RA, which explicitly communicate with the user in a question-and-answer dialog, webstores offer IIMT.

Gupta et al. (2009) define IIMT as

> Tools which enable buyers to sort through and/or compare available product alternatives. For example, these tools allow buyers to limit and sort choices on levels of various attributes and/or engage in side-by-side comparisons of products in dynamically created tables [product-comparison matrix] (p. 163).

A product-comparison matrix has the same format as the choice task we investigated in previous experiments (see Chaps. 3 and 4). Typically, alternatives (products) are organized in columns and attributes (product features) in rows. An example of such a product-comparison matrix is shown in Fig. 5.3.

IIMT are the predominant form of IDA we currently see in the Internet. They support both phases of the two-stage decision-making behavior which we examined in Sect. 3. Simple filter and sort tools help consumers to screen the available products and to narrow down their search on the most promising ones. To allow this, products are described by some key attributes, such as price, product-name,

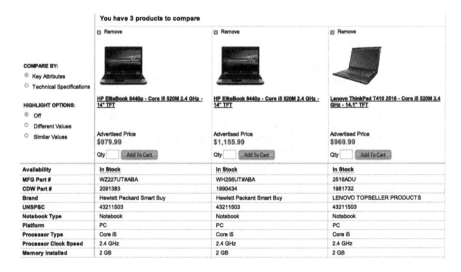

Fig. 5.3 Product-comparison matrix (www.cdw.com)

Fig. 5.4 Screening phase with filters and the possibility to sort and choose products, which can then be compared in-depth in a product-comparison matrix (www.cdw.com)

Fig. 5.5 Screening phase without any additional interactive information management tools (www. panasonic.com)

etc. (see Figs. 5.4 and 5.5). The user can then select several products and compare them in-depth in a product-comparison matrix in another screen.

In line with Gupta et al. (2009), but in contrast to Häubl and Trifts (2000), we do not consider the product-comparison matrix as a whole as IIMT, but single tools which enable the consumer to interactively manipulate a product-comparison matrix to their needs. Hence, consumers are able to remove products from the matrix, sort them and evaluate them. An example of removing a product from the matrix by clicking on the link called "remove" is shown in Fig. 5.3. So far – except for the study by Gupta et al. (2009) – IIMT for manipulating the product-comparison matrix are hardly discussed in the literature.

Spiekermann and Paraschiv (2002) examined what impedes customers from interacting with IDA. They analyzed four different kinds of recommendation systems empirically; among them, RA, collaborative systems such as the one used by Amazon, and two systems which were based on simple filter techniques (product configuration machines and shopbots & softbots). They concluded that the systems failed to motivate users and argued that insights from research on consumer behavior should be further incorporated into the design approach of such systems. They mentioned four arguments which might be responsible for the lack of user motivation: (1) limited communication, (2) no adjustment to the level of user expertise, (3) access to limited product databases for calculating recommendations, and (4) no display of the logic behind the process. We think that newer versions of recommendation systems might be able to overcome some of these deficits. They are more flexible than the earlier versions considered by Spiekermann and Paraschiv (2002) and allow the customer to reveal incomplete preferences or to state preferences in form of aspiration levels (see Wang and Benbasat 2009 or www. myproductadvisor.com).

Recently, Murray and Häubl (2008) compared different IDA. They point out that recommendation systems are too slow and thus unable to fulfill the trade-off between effective work in realtime and a deep understanding of users' preferences. Hence, they stress the need to address IDA which can quickly react to user interaction. IIMT represent such IDA.

In fact, recommendation systems can be seen as an alternative to IIMT in the screening phase because just as filters they often recommend not just one product but a whole set of them. Thus, recommendation systems might display the consideration set in a product-comparison matrix with IIMT support. The RA on www.myproductadvisor.com, for example, displays the scored products in a product-comparison matrix in the corresponding preference order (see Fig. 5.6). In the context of RA, Faltings et al. (2004) determined analytically the number or alternatives which have to be presented in the product-comparison matrix such that the optimal alternative is included. If the RA asks for five preferences, for instance, then 5–20 alternatives should be shown depending on the accuracy of the measured preference function (the rougher the estimate, the more products have to be included).

5.1.2.1   IIMT for Product-Comparison Matrices

In the following two studies, we analyze the relevance of IDA which explicitly communicate with the user and hence, do neither consider collaborative nor content-based filtering (see Fig. 5.2). The first study is descriptive and shows that only few IIMT are actually offered on real-world e-commerce websites. Furthermore, IIMT are available only in the screening phase and are rarely offered additionally for

Fig. 5.6 Another example of a product-comparison matrix (www.myproductadvisor.com)

product-comparison matrices. RA do not occur at all in the sample.[1] In a second laboratory study, we compare IIMT with RA and confirm that users prefer IIMT.

5.1.2.2 Distribution of IIMT

We analyzed the top 100 e-commerce websites, according to the Google PageRank.[2] The page rank measures the number and the importance of links linking to the respective website. Four web pages had to be excluded from the analysis since they did not have an own webstore.[3] As replacement, we added positions 101 to 104. Table C.1 in the appendix displays a complete list of all pages which were part of the study.[4]

Neither of the 100 websites offered an RA, which supports the statement by Fitzsimons and Lehmann (2004) that they can hardly be found in the Internet. Concerning the IIMT, in the first step, we analyzed the screening phase. In this phase, two different IIMT occurred, which we denote *FILTER* and *SORT*. *FILTER* allows consumers to eliminate products which do not meet an aspiration level on

---

[1] The product advisor was not part of the sample (see Fig. 5.1).

[2] see http://www.variablemarkup.com/top-ecommerce-sites/.

[3] www.audible.com,   www.safeway.com,   thesharperimage.com,   www.jockey.com,   www. blockbusters.com.

[4] This study was conducted in January 2009 together with René Riedl (University Linz).

a particular attribute (see Fig. 5.4). *FILTER* appeared in all 100 webstores. *SORT* allows user to sort products. It was offered in only 70 cases, and in its simplest form. Usually, costumers could only sort according to one criterion, such as price or past customer ratings. Furthermore, customers could not specify their own preference order so that sorting of nominal values was only possible in, for instance, alphabetic order and not the preference order (e.g., the alphabetical order of colors). In many cases, customers were not even able to switch between ascending or descending order. The possibilities for *FILTER* were more comprehensive than for *SORT*. In most cases, *FILTER* was offered for all attributes, independent of whether they had nominal (e.g., color) or metric (e.g., price) scales.

In sum, *FILTER* and *SORT* were both distributed widely. In addition, we find that the design and features of *FILTER* are quite advanced. In contrast to that, *SORT* should offer more flexibility and allow sorting all attributes in the preferred order (for instance ascending or descending order for ordinal values) and sorting according to several criteria (e.g., first according to price and then according to color). While *FILTER* and *SORT* were apparently quite frequently offered, other IIMT, for instance removing alternatives or evaluating them, were not available at all.

In the second step, we examined the IIMT offered to manipulate the product-comparison matrix. Out of the 100 web pages, only 27 offered a product-comparison matrix at all. In all other 73 cases, detailed information on products could only be considered for each product individually in a new screen. The customer usually reached the product-comparison matrix by clicking on "compare" checkboxes (see the top of Fig. 5.4 for an example). In the few cases where a product-comparison matrix was offered at all, they allowed a large amount of products in the product-comparison matrix (see Table 5.1). In more than half of the cases (15 out of 27), the number of products which could be included in the matrix was unlimited. This result is surprising, as very few IIMT were offered to deal with this large amount of product information which might lead to information overload. The only prevalent IIMT in product-comparison matrices was deleting alternatives (*REMOVE* occurred in 21 out of the 27 product-comparison matrices). In addition to deleting alternatives, two webstores offered to delete single attributes and to sort the products (www.bhphotovideo.com and www.sony.com), one offered to highlight differences/similarities and to hide product details (www.cdw.com).

Table 5.1 Results from the descriptive study. Number of products allowed in the product-comparison matrices

# of products for comparison	Frequency
No comparison possible	73
3–5	6
10–12	5
30	1
Unlimited	15
SUM	27

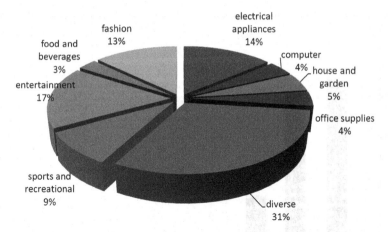

Fig. 5.7 Classification of the surveyed websites according to industries

Product-comparison matrices help to display products by means of many attributes. Yet, not all products are as complex and information-intensive that displaying many details is necessary (e.g., clothing). The results of the descriptive study reflect this observation. IIMT were offered in many industries, but a classification of the 100 websites into different industries shows that only for information-intense products was a product-comparison matrix offered (see Figs. 5.7 and 5.8). In 79% of the webstores offering electrical appliances and 75% offering computers, customers could compare products in product-comparison matrices (see Fig. 5.8). In other sectors, such as fashion and food&beverages no product-comparison matrix was offered at all.

In summary, this study has shown that the screening phase is widely supported with *FILTER* and *SORT*. Few websites support the second phase of in-depth comparison (27%). The few which offer product-comparison matrices do hardly assist the consumer with IIMT to manipulate the matrix. It seems that e-commerce companies have focused their efforts onto DSS in the screening phase and neglected assisting the comparison phase. Besides the *REMOVE* for eliminating an alternative from the matrix, basically no IIMT are offered.[5] Therefore, we address specifically the lack of IIMT for product-comparison matrices. Furthermore, as the analysis of industries has shown, product-comparison matrices are mostly offered in the electrical appliances and computer industry. We think that this might be because the products sold in these industries are rather information-intense and can be described by a great many technical details.

Our results support recent studies which criticized that as a rule only filters are offered in the web (Pu and Chen 2008). Silverman et al. (2001) suggest that consumers need more aids to compare products. Furthermore, several works point

---

[5] *FILTER* and *SORT* were mainly available for the screening phase.

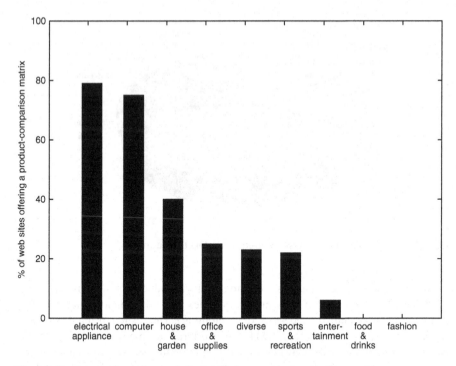

Fig. 5.8 Percentage of websites per industry offering a product-comparison matrix

out that IDA structuring the decision process into multiple stages would create a better fit between the user's behavior and the DSS (Goodhue 1995, 1998; Kamis and Davern 2005; Yuan 2003).

5.2 Comparison of Recommendation Systems & IIMT

In the previous study, we found that RA disappeared from the Internet, whereas IIMT are often offered to consumers in the screening phase. In the literature though, we found that the opposite is true: while research focuses on RA, it neglects IIMT. Xiao and Benbasat (2007) provide a detailed description of research on IDA which clearly shows the strong focus on RA in the literature so far. The following sections study how well IIMT are accepted by users compared to RA.

5.2.1 Theory and Hypotheses

We encountered four studies on IIMT for product-comparison matrices in the literature (Gupta et al. 2009; Häubl and Trifts 2000; Kamis and Davern 2005; Todd and Benbasat 2000), which we explain in this section. For a detailed overview of research on recommendation systems in information systems, the reader is referred to the excellent overview by Xiao and Benbasat (2007).

Häubl and Trifts (2000) analyzed both RA and product-comparison matrices where alternatives can be sorted by any attribute. Both IDA had a positive effect on user satisfaction and the efficiency of the purchase decisions since they increased decision quality and decreased effort. Unfortunately, the authors did not compare these two types to test which one had the larger impact.

Todd and Benbasat (2000) tested whether respondents would apply a utility maximization strategy (WADD) or an EBA strategy dependent on the IIMT they were provided with. Their IIMT were implemented in form of commands prompted to a command window for manipulating a product-comparison matrix. Entering the commands CREATE, GLOBAL, ROW TOTAL, for instance, assisted the respondents in using a WADD strategy. With the command CREATE one could assign attribute weights which were multiplied with attribute values by the command GLOBAL.[6] Finally, the command ROW TOTAL sums up the weighted scores for each alternative. The results show that respondents applied WADD more often when only decision aids supporting WADD were provided. There was no empirical evidence for the hypothesis that the same holds for EBA. Providing only decision aids supporting EBA (*REMOVE* and *FILTER*) did not increase the usage of EBA.

Kamis and Davern (2005) analyzed the effect of offering multiple IDA in a multi-stage decision process. They considered one aid for supporting CONJ, one for supporting EBA, and one simple product-comparison matrix with no additional features. Their results show that the sequence and the amount (2 vs. 3) of IDA offered to the respondent had no effects on the three dependent variables: perceived ease of use, perceived usefulness and decision quality. For all combinations of decision aids, they found that product knowledge, purchase involvement, and available time had a positive effect on the three dependent variables.

Gupta et al. (2009) examined the impact of tools which provide and explain product information and IIMT on consumers' trust in the online retailer. Furthermore, they analyzed whether trust depends on the respondents' product knowledge. In contrast to other work, they explicitly allowed some basic operations for manipulation of product-comparison matrices, namely hierarchical sorting and removing attributes and alternatives. Their results show that respondents perceived that sellers intend to help them with the buying decision if they offer IIMT. In turn, they ascribed trustworthiness to the seller when supported by IIMT. The ascribed trustworthiness was mediated by the consumer's product knowledge.

In sum, two out of the four studies do not consider IIMT for product-comparison matrices at all. Todd and Benbasat (2000) consider different IIMT for manipulating

---

[6]Attribute levels are presented on a ten point rating scale where the attribute level 1 represents the lowest attribute value of 1 and level 10 a value of 10. Hence, the authors make the simplifying and unrealistic assumption that attribute levels are equal to attribute values (see Sect. 2.1).

product-comparison matrices, but these are not implemented with a graphical user interface but must be typed in manually in form of user commands. Hence, the external validity of such a study is very limited due to the limited user prompting. This might also be the reason why the authors could only support part of their hypotheses. Gupta et al. (2009) have implemented some IIMT with graphical user interface. However, they neither compare their tool to other recommendation systems nor do they address other variables than trust for measuring user evaluation. In addition to that, their set of studied IIMT, namely *SORT* and *REMOVE*, is very limited.

In order to test whether users prefer IIMT to RA, we need to know the main criteria which are relevant for users when evaluating IDA. In a meta-study of 45 studies, Xiao and Benbasat (2007) isolated four factors important for users' evaluation: two constructs of the well-known technology acceptance model (perceived usefulness and perceived ease of use, see Davis 1989; Davis et al. 1989) as well as satisfaction (Wixom and Todd 2005) and confidence (trust) (Wang and Benbasat 2005). Hence, we compare RA and IIMT along these four factors.

The perceived ease of use is the extent to which the IDA will be free of effort, while the perceived usefulness is the extent to which one's performance is improved (Davis 1989). There are several reasons which speak in favor of both an increased perceived ease of use and an increased perceived usefulness for IIMT when compared to RA. First, people have difficulties to explicitly express their preferences. As the literature review on the influence of complexity on decision making revealed (see Sect. 2.4), preferences are constructed on the spot and contingent on environmental factors such as complexity. People find it easier to construct a model when considering examples of actual options (Payne et al. 1999). RA only show concrete alternatives after a question-and-answer dialog has finished. Consequently, users have to reveal their preferences before they actually see alternatives. In contrast, IIMT display alternatives right from the beginning of the decision process. Second, RA require more user input in form of answers to preference elicitation questions. This cannot only cause higher effort but also decrease perceived usefulness because of the imposed preference elicitation of unstable preferences. Third, due to the higher distribution of IIMT, users might have more experience with them than with RA, this might also have a positive influence on ease of use and usefulness. Taking all these aspects together, we therefore suggest the following two hypotheses.

Hypothesis 1:   The perceived ease of use is higher for IIMT than for RA.
Hypothesis 2:   The perceived usefulness is higher for IIMT than for RA.

Wang and Benbasat (2009) study the influence of strategy restrictiveness. Perceived strategy restrictiveness is defined as "decision makers' perceptions of the extent to which their preferred decision processes are constrained by the functionalities and support provided by a decision aid" (Silver 1988). They compare an RA which estimated a linear additive utility function (see the WADD strategy in Sect. 2.2.2), a purely filter-based tool (EBA), and a hybrid version of the RA and the EBA aid. As two of their decision aids implement a pure strategy (WADD or EBA), users should feel restricted to apply only the decision strategy that is supported by the aid. Their results show that customers do only feel restricted in case of the EBA aid but not in the condition with the hybrid aid or the RA. We pick up on this idea and suggest that users feel less restricted when using IIMT than when using RA since IIMT support several decision strategies. RA restrict more as they usually assume one specific preference function, estimate its parameters, and maximize the utility, as for example WADD. A user who does not want to use WADD would experience a restriction and is probably less satisfied with the decision process. Therefore, people should be more satisfied with IIMT due to less perceived restrictiveness.

Other studies examine the transparency of IDA. IIMT are more transparent as users can easily follow the consequences of their actions, while the calculation of the utility function by the RA is hidden from the user and thus not transparent. Consequently, IIMT are more transparent than RA, which is believed to increase the perceived value and confidence (Gretzel and Fesenmaier 2006; Kwak 2001; Sinha and Swearingen 2002).

Hypothesis 3: User satisfaction is higher for IIMT than for RA.
Hypothesis 4: Confidence in IDA is higher for IIMT than for RA.

As a result of increased perceived ease of use, usefulness, satisfaction, and confidence, we suppose that in the experiment participants will use the IIMT more frequently than the RA.

Hypothesis 5: User apply IIMT more frequently than RA.

5.2.2 Experiment

5.2.2.1 Participants

Thirty-two information-systems students from the Johannes Gutenberg – University participated in the experiment: 17 male and 15 female and 93.8% under 30 years old. Almost all stated that they use the Internet several times per day (93.8%). More than 2/3 had carried out more than ten online purchases in their life so far and 25% between two and ten. Thus, the participants were experienced in purchasing products online. As the web pages were available in English only, we made sure that all participants had sufficient English skills – 93.8% indicated good and very good skills and 90.6% said that they had understood the study well. The students' participation was part of a regular class and every participant automatically entered a drawing for a €20 voucher for a webstore. Therefore, they were all highly motivated ($M = 5.15, SD = 1$ at a 7-point Likert scale [1: I strongly disagree, 7: I strongly agree]).[7]

---

[7] MD: median, SD: standard deviation.

5.2.2.2 Design and Procedure

The experiment was conducted under controlled conditions in a computer laboratory and took 30 min. Participants were randomly assigned to one of the two conditions (RA or IIMT) in which they had to select a laptop. For the comparison, we chose two websites which, from our viewpoint, are among the best ones currently available in the web: www.myproductadvisor.com and www.cdw.com.

The RA www.myproductadvisor is very flexible as it allows users to reveal as many preferences as they want in form of attribute weights, attribute values (see Fig. 5.9) and aspiration levels (see Fig. 5.10). At any time during the process, they

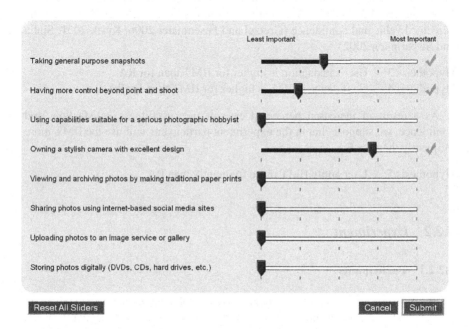

Fig. 5.9 Attribute importance dialog (www.myproductadvisor.com)

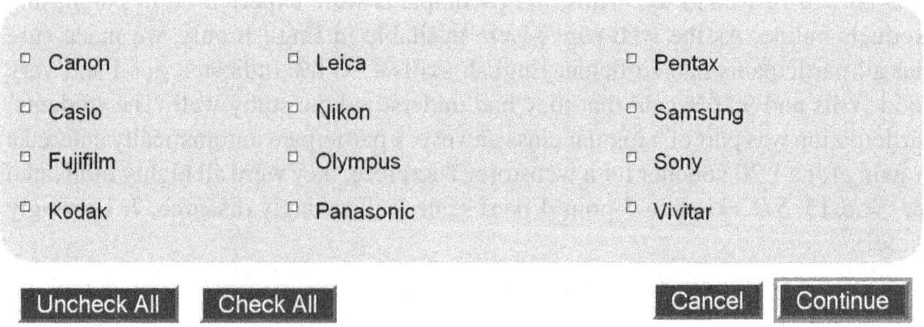

Fig. 5.10 Filter (www.myproductadvisor.com)

Fig. 5.11 User navigation on www.myproductadvisor.com

can ask for recommendations (see Fig. 5.11). The product advisor then recommends the ten products with highest score in form of a product-comparison matrix (see Fig. 5.6), separated in two screens (five products are displayed per screen). The product-comparison matrix only offers to remove alternatives. In summary, respondents who used the product advisor had good support in form of a utility-based agent with additional filter mechanisms and state-of-the-art support in the in-depth comparison phase.

While one half of the respondents were assigned to the product advisor, the other half was assigned to the IIMT (www.cdw.com). On www.cdw.com, users can first narrow down their search onto few products with *FILTER* and *SORT*. The filters are comfortable as they allow filtering all attributes, allow for specifying intervals (e.g., for prices) and show already specified filter criteria to the user (see Fig. 5.4). Afterwards, the product-comparison matrix allows to compare up to ten products which can be determined by the checkboxes "compare products". As additional IIMT, the product-comparison matrix offers highlighting rows where the products differ and removing alternatives. Furthermore, the user can choose whether the matrix should include all technical details or only key attributes (see Fig. 5.3). In summary, respondents who used www.cdw.com had comfortable filters for the screening phase, some sort aids (by price and best match) and additional IIMT such as removal and highlighting of differences for the product-comparison matrix.

Respondents got a detailed description of how to use the respective web pages. As cover story, they were told that the information systems faculty was interested in which laptops are the students' favorites. After all students had used one of the IDA to select a laptop, they answered a questionnaire with questions to their person, demographics and measures for testing the hypotheses.

We developed the questionnaire based on well tested questions from the literature on a 7-point Likert scale [1: I strongly disagree to 7: I strongly agree] (Kamis and Davern 2005; Pereira 2000; Wang and Benbasat 2009). Cronbach's Alpha showed adequate reliability of the items with levels above 0.7 for all constructs as recommended by Nunnally (1967). Hence, all answers were taken to test the hypotheses. In the appendix, we can find a detailed list of items and corresponding constructs (see Tables C.2 and C.3).

5.2.2.3 Empirical Results

A Kolmogorov–Smirnov test indicated that we can assume normal distribution for three of the five dependent variables, namely confidence, perceived ease of use, and perceived usefulness and therefore can use t-tests. Furthermore, for these three variables, we report the effect sizes as measure for the strength of the relation of the independent and dependent variables with the same approach we used in Sect. 3.3.4. The effect size, in our case the r-value, ranges between 0 and 1. An r of 0.1 is interpreted as small, 0.3 as medium, and 0.5 as large effect (Cohen 1988, 1992). For the remaining two dependent variables, satisfaction and user's frequency of applying the IDA, we use the non-parametric Mann–Whitney U test as the Kolmogorov–Smirnov test showed that these two variables might not be normally distributed.

Perceived ease of use is higher when using IIMT ($M(IIMT) = 5.72, SE(IIMT) = 0.15$) than when using an RA ($M(RA) = 4.77, SE(RA) = 0.27$). Since this difference is highly significant ($t(30) = 25, p < 0.01$), hypothesis 1 is fully supported. The effect is large since $r = 0.5$, suggesting that there is a strong relation between the independent variables (RA vs. IIMT) and perceived ease of use. The boxplot in Fig. 5.12 shows that students in the IIMT group perceived the decision aid much easier to use than in the RA group.

Perceived usefulness is higher when using IIMT ($M(IIMT) = 5.54, SE(IIMT) = 0.16$) than when using an RA ($M(RA) = 4.8, SE(RA) = 0.21$). According to hypothesis 2 the results show that users perceive IIMT to be significantly more useful than RA ($t(30) = 2.88, p < 0.01$). This effect is medium to large ($r = 0.47$).

Satisfaction for the IIMT was not significantly higher ($MD(IIMT) = 5.13$) than for the RA ($MD(RA) = 4$), $U = 86.5, z = -1.55, p = 0.062$ (one-tailed), $r = -0.27$. Hypothesis 3 can only be supported on a 0.1 significance level. Therefore, there is a tendency that users are more satisfied when using IIMT, but this tendency cannot completely be verified statistically.

Hypothesis 4 focuses on users' confidence. The test shows that users have significantly more confidence in the IIMT than in the RA ($t(30) = 2.5, p < 0.01, M(IIMT) = 5.2, SE(IIMT) = 0.21, M(RA) = 4.18, SE(RA) = 0.24$) and this effect is large ($r = 0.5$).

In the experiment, more participants in the IIMT-condition reported to have applied the decision aid ($MD(IIMT) = 6.5$) than in the RA-condition $MD(RA) = 4$). This difference is highly significant and the effect is large ($U = 47.5, z = -3.05, p < 0.01$), $r = -0.54$). Thus, hypothesis 5 is supported by the Mann–Whitney U Test.

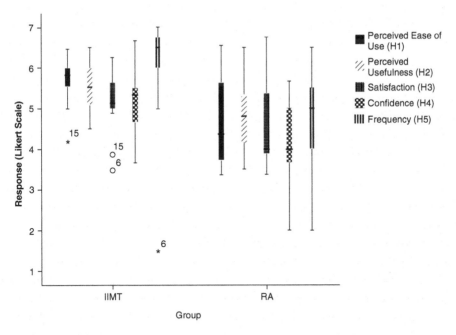

Fig. 5.12 Results of the study on IIMT vs. RA. All five hypotheses are supported

5.3 Conclusions

In this chapter, we pointed out the imbalance between the IDA present in the literature, i.e. RA, and the prevalent IDA used in current webstores, i.e. IIMT. We found that two IIMT, i.e. *FILTER* and *SORT*, are offered frequently in the screening phase. In the second study, a laboratory experiment, we measured respondents' evaluation of RA vs. IIMT. The results indicate that customers perceive IIMT to be easier to use, more useful, and that IIMT create more confidence. Moreover, IIMT were used more intensely in the study, indicating a higher users' acceptance. However, as users still are not significantly more satisfied with IIMT than with RA, more advanced IIMT should be developed. In the next chapter, we will present our design and implementation of IIMT with the aim of enhancing users' evaluation of IIMT even further.

Chapter 6
INTACMATO: An IIMT-Prototype

In the previous chapter, we pointed out that although users evaluate IIMT very positively, only a limited number of IIMT are offered. We assume that the main reason for this is that online sellers do not know which IIMT they should offer and what they should exactly look like. We address these two aspects in this chapter. Firstly, we review literature on IDA in the field of human interaction. We discuss several drawbacks of current approaches as well as the resulting requirements for the design of IIMT. Secondly, we break down observed decision-making behavior into typical steps decision makers apply in their decision processes. These steps indicate which IIMT would offer appropriate decision support. Based on these findings, we implement an IIMT-prototype, called INTACMATO in an iterative approach where two qualitative usability studies and implementation phases alternate.

From a methodological viewpoint, in this chapter we exemplify how research rigor can be ensured when designing a new prototype. Our design of the prototype is theory driven and connects results from behavioral research on decision making with the process of designing new IT artifacts (for details see Sect. 1.3 and Hevner et al. 2004).

6.1 Requirements from Information Systems Research

In line with a recent review on IDA by Murray and Häubl (2008), we have observed that RA have disappeared. Instead, the current focus lies on personalization and price search (for instance www.pricegrabber.com or www.shopzilla.com). Murray and Häubl (2008) point out several barriers which have to be overcome for a successful adoption of IDA. First, they conclude that new tools for managing information through a consistent interface are needed. Second, recommendations often contradict users' preferences. This is because a certain preference model or notion of what constitutes a high-quality decision is assumed by the system, which does not correspond to the users' conception. Third, predictions on the consumers' purchase behavior and preferences are unreliable because of the constructive nature

J. Pfeiffer, *Interactive Decision Aids in E-Commerce*, Contributions to Management Science, DOI 10.1007/978-3-7908-2769-9_6, © Springer-Verlag Berlin Heidelberg 2012

of preferences (Bettman et al. 1998; Simonson 2005). Preferences are believed to be constructed rather than stable and well known. Since, first, they are commonly constructed only when users are asked for their actual evaluations and, second, the construction process is shaped by the users' information processing and the properties of the choice task (Payne et al. 1999). Third, consumers have privacy concerns to reveal their preferences to the systems. Fourth, the consumers might feel that the costs of using the IDA outweigh the benefits when IDA are difficult to use. Fifth, even if web pages offered more IDA to the user, a new problem would arise. Offering a number of IDA adds a higher complexity level to the choice since users have to decide not only for a product but also which decision aid to apply.

We retrieve several design requirements from this review. First, IIMT should have a consistent design. Furthermore, IIMT should be flexible in that they support several preference models and allow for changes in the model. One approach to achieve this goal is to offer IIMT which support the application of a diverse set of different decision strategies relying on different preference models. Flexibility also incorporates the idea that the consumer can stop revealing preference information any time during the process. This approach also prevents privacy issues as decision makers only need to reveal as much information as they like. Moreover, preferences should be elicited when the information on the actual products is already known because of the constructive nature of preferences. People find it easier to construct a model of their preferences when considering examples of actual alternatives (Payne et al. 1999). This speaks in favor of letting decision makers choose the product out of the product-comparison matrix where all information on alternatives can be displayed and compared easily. Further, IIMT should be easy to use and intuitive in order to minimize the effort for using the aid itself. For instance, a web page can adapt to consumers and the environment and only offer those aids which are needed for the decision, in order to reduce the cognitive burden to choose one of many offered IIMT.

From other studies, similar design requirements can be retrieved. In an empirical study, Ariely (2000) verified the notion which was stated earlier by Alba and Hutchsinon (1987); Einhorn and Hogarth (1981); Payne et al. (1993) that "information control is beneficial because having an interactive and dynamic information system can maximize the fit between heterogeneous and dynamic needs for information and the information available" (p. 234). Letting the consumers control content, order, and duration of product relevant information results in higher value and increases usability. Furthermore, subjects like the interface more and feel more confident. However, when the cognitive load is high, too much control might be harmful. As recommended by Ariely's study we retrieve that IIMT should have a high degree of control. Nevertheless, as mentioned above, in complex situations, control and interaction should be reduced, for instance by offering only those aids which best support users in the particular situation.

Similar conclusions come from Pereira (2000), who studies the influence of subject's product knowledge on affective reactions. He analyzes four different IDA: an RA, an IDA asking for aspiration levels (EBA aid), a collaborative filter, and a simple product list with some product information. One could argue that simple product lists do not fall under the category of IDA at all. Yet, for now, we stay with the classification the author uses in his paper. The author subsumes several constructs to measure affective reactions. These are satisfaction, confidence in the decision, trust in the recommendation, propensity to purchase, perceived cost savings, and perceived cognitive effort. He shows that in comparison to novices, experts have stronger positive reactions towards EBA-based IDA, RA and simple product lists. One reason might be that they can process information on attributes better than novices with low product knowledge. Accordingly, novices prefer collaborative filter techniques. However, taking both groups together, they have more negative reactions towards simple product lists than towards the other three, more advanced, recommendation systems. In a second experiment, the author increases the control subjects have over the IDA. For instance, they can skip answers, jump back and forth, and express their degree of confidence. The experimental results show that these measures increase positive reactions towards aids. Pereira (2000) concludes that "optimizing the cognitive fit between agent search strategy and consumers' product class knowledge significantly increases consumer satisfaction with the decision process" (p. 41). In summary, this study recommends high user control and a system that adapts to the consumer's product class knowledge.

Spiekermann and Paraschiv (2002) propose a number of design principles which help to motivate users by integrating more insights from research on consumer behavior. They state that current systems lack communication in that the user is only allowed to reveal limited preference information, such as attribute weights. Second, the systems do not adapt to the users' levels of expertise. We think that offering the flexibility to support several decision strategies will reduce both problems as consumers can apply the decision aid that fits to their preferred decision strategy. Then, the authors point out that current systems use a limited product database to calculate recommendations. While this might still be a valid disadvantage of current systems, we will assume that product information is available and will not focus on search for data in our work. Finally, the authors criticize that the user cannot see the logic behind the system. Again, we think that the transparency of the process is increased by directly seeing the effects of the applied IIMT on the matrix. Thus, the problem of hidden logic is circumvented.

In their model, Gretzel and Fesenmaier (2006) examine the influence of three factors (relevance, transparency, and effort) on the perceived value and enjoyment of the decision process for RA. Their results show that transparency and effort have the highest influence on the perceived value, while the relevance of questions asked to the users (product-related vs. non product-related) has low impact. Furthermore, neither transparency nor relevance have any significant influence on the perceived enjoyment. However, in contrast to the stated hypothesis, low effort seems to increase the perceived value but decreases the enjoyment of the decision process. Therefore, the authors suggest that when designing IDA the conflictive impact of effort should be taken into account. From our viewpoint, this can be achieved by allowing the user to fully control how they interact with the DSS in order to control how much effort they want to invest in the decision. RA, for instance, often do not allow the user to control the interaction since most follow a pre-specified question-and-answer dialog.

In sum, we can retrieve six requirements for designing IIMT from literature:

1. **Adaptivity**: Adapt the interface to the environment and users' needs and characteristics such as expert vs. novice users.
2. **Consistency**: Provide the results of users' interaction through a consistent interface.
3. **Control**: Let the user control the interaction.
4. **Flexibility**: Allow users to stop the interaction at any time. Modularize the offered IIMT such that users can mix different IIMT and switch between different strategies easily.
5. **Low Effort**: Make the interface intuitive and minimize the cognitive effort.
6. **Transparency**: Make the actions of the IIMT transparent and comprehensible. Immediately show the effects of users' actions.

6.2   Requirements from Decision-Making Behavior Research

What can we learn further about a good design of IIMT from theory on decision-making behavior research and from our own results, presented in part? In part, we pointed out that people might not exactly follow one particular strategy (Cook 1993; Klayman 1985; Montgomery and Svenson 1976; Svenson 1979), but sequentially apply different strategies. In particular in the eye tracking experiment, we have shown that decision makers usually start with an attribute-wise information acquisition pattern (to reduce the set of alternatives), and then shift to an alternative-wise pattern to make a final decision (Ball 1997; Billings and Marcus 1983; Gensch 1987; Johnson and Payne 1985; Olshavsky 1979; Payne 1976; Todd and Benbasat 1991). In the context of decision aids, this means that online customers would start using an IIMT that helps them to exclude alternatives (e.g., *FILTER, REMOVE*) and then continue with a decision aid that helps to compare the remaining alternatives. From one of our previous studies, we further know that people's behavior can oftentimes be explained by a switch back and forth between several strategies (Pfeiffer et al. 2009a). A sequence of up to three different strategies usually explains the observed behavior best. Therefore, online shop designers should assume that customers use different strategies during one particular shopping transaction and switch between them to screen out alternatives until the final choice is made.

We argue that this switching behavior requires a flexible system which we implement with a modular structure of IIMT. In our approach we break down different decision strategies into different steps. This approach allows people to mix several steps of different strategies and hence switch easily between strategies. The modularity will also help to deal with heterogeneous decision-making behavior as a relatively small set of IIMT can be recombined in different sequences to support different strategies. In other words, one module supports steps of several decision strategies.

A second point that we can learn from decision-making behavior research, is the influence of complexity on decision-making behavior. In the two experimental studies in Chap. 3 and Chap. 4, we have shown that decision makers use more simplifying decision strategies when the complexity increases. Apparently decision makers try to reduce cognitive effort by using strategies which, on the one hand, are easier to apply but, on the other hand, also might lead to less satisfying and less accurate decisions. Hence, IIMT should aim at reducing the cognitive effort such that people do not have to revert to simple and potentially non-satisfying and non-accurate strategies. The relationship of effort and accuracy of decision strategies and the influence of IIMT thereon should be scrutinized when designing IIMT.

Besides flexibility and low effort, a third requirement can be retrieved. The above stated facts concerning the constructive nature of decision-making behavior and the switching behavior imply an adaptive system. It should recognize the complexity of the choice task and the user profile and adapt the offered IIMT to the given situation. In its easiest form, the system should allow the users to adapt their own interface, for instance, by removing IIMT or adjusting their positions. In an advanced variant, the adaption should be done automatically by a system that is able to recognize and classify the situation.

From our analysis of both domains, information systems and decision-making behavior research, we conclude that IIMT should fulfill six requirements: consistency, control, flexibility, transparency, low effort, and adaptivity. In the present work, we address the first five requirements for our design of IIMT, but we refrain from creating an adaptive system. From our viewpoint, adaptivity can be added to IIMT, once the system is implemented and validated, and we leave it to further research.

6.3 Design of INTACMATO

In order to fulfill the requirements, we use guidelines from research on human-computer interaction. We strive for *consistency* by applying standardized terminology, abbreviations, formats, colors, fonts and capitalization (Shneiderman and Plaisant 2009; Smith and Mosier 1986). In addition, we require consistent sequences of actions by users when encountering similar situations. We ensure *transparency* by allowing the user *direct manipulation*. Direct manipulation is defined as visual representation of objects and actions, as well as rapid, reversible, and immediately observable execution of pointing actions (Shneiderman 1983). Hence, we refrain from question-and-answer dialogs or other preference elicitation processes which hide the process from the user and would make decision support non-transparent. Moreover, the set of IIMT has to provide full control of which information is displayed, how it is displayed, and how users want to compare and evaluate the products. Hence, the user should perceive a high information *control*, in contrast to other systems where products are recommended by some non-transparent evaluation steps on the system side. In order to modularize the decision support and to allow for *flexibility*, we ensure that the different IIMT support a variety of decision strategies (see Sect. 2.2.1) by allowing pairwise comparison, elimination of alternatives, setting of aspiration levels used, attribute-wise vs. alternative-wise information acquisition, compensatory vs. non-compensatory strategies etc. From our viewpoint, this approach also helps to create *low effort* on the user side because the IIMT are directly derived from empirically observed decision-making behavior and their usage should be intuitive.

In order to achieve this close fit between decision-making behavior and DSS, we break down the current decision strategies into several parts. This approach shows the basic steps decision strategies consist of that can be supported by IIMT. These steps can, for the most part, be directly retrieved from the characteristics of decision strategies (see Sect. 2.2).

IIMT should allow to compare two alternatives next to each other, as some strategies assume that alternatives are compared in pairs (ADD, MCD). Other strategies assume an attribute-wise process, hence highlighting differences and similarities of products along one attribute should be provided. FRQ counts the number of good and bad attribute levels and other strategies, such as SAT, CONJ, and DIS, check whether attribute levels are above the aspiration level, so marking of attribute levels as either positive or negative should be provided. Another characteristic is the stepwise elimination of alternatives (for instance by MCD, ADD, CONJ, DIS, etc.), thus, users should be able to remove alternatives. As two strategies (SAT, CON) remove alternatives which do not meet the aspiration level of at least one attribute, a removal of alternatives with at least one negatively marked attribute level should be possible. Moreover, EBA, for instance, eliminates alternatives which do not meet the aspiration level on an attribute. This can be supported by filters which remove all alternatives not fulfilling the filter criterion. In contrast, compensatory strategies would not remove alternatives based on one filter criteria, but they allow alternatives to compensate a low attribute value with a high one. For these strategies, calculations of assigned attribute values (EQW, WADD) or of the number of positively marked attribute levels (FRQ, MAJ) are necessary. In addition to that, some strategies take the importance of attributes into account. WADD, for instance, multiplies attribute values with weights and LEX chooses the alternative with the highest attribute values on the most important attribute. Consequently, users must be able to assign attribute weights or sort attributes/alternatives.

We have just broken down the decision strategies into the following steps that need to be supported by IIMT: comparison of pairs, highlighting differences and similarities, marking attribute levels as either positive or negative, removal of alternatives (manually), automatic removal of alternatives with at least one negatively marked attribute level, filtering, scoring attribute levels with attribute values and calculations with these assigned values, summing up positively marked attribute levels, assigning attribute weights and sorting. Several IIMT supporting some of these steps can be found in the literature or on current webstores, others are not available yet. Based on our analysis, a literature review and an examination of the 100 top-ranked shopping websites according to the Google PageRank (see Sect. 5.1.2.2), Table 6.1 provides an overview of IIMT that are needed for supporting

Table 6.1 List of IIMT implemented in INTACMATO

IIMT		Characteristic	Description
CALCU-LATE	simple[a] weighted[a] marking[b]	Compensatory, quantitative	Calculates the utility of different alternatives using the customers' preferences indicated by MARK or SCORE.
FILTER[c,d]		Aspiration levels, elimination, selective, inconsistent	Remove all alternatives that do not meet the aspiration levels for an attribute.
MARK	diff/ sim[d] manually[b]	Quantitative, aspiration levels	Highlights different, similar, or manually chosen attribute levels.
PAIRWISE COMPARISON[c,d]		Pairwise comparison	Compares two alternatives.
SCORE	attribute[a] attribute-Level[b]	Compensatory, weights, quantitative	Allows assigning weights to attributes and attribute values to attribute levels.
SORT	hierar-chically[c] drag&drop[e]	Inconsistent, selective	Changes the order in which alternatives or attributes are displayed in the comparison matrix.
REMOVE	alternative[a,d] attribute[a,d] markings[b]	Elimination, aspiration levels, selective, inconsistent	Removes an alternative. Removes an attribute. Removes marked alternatives from the comparison matrix.

[a]Adapted version from Todd and Benbasat (2000)
[b]New
[c]Gupta et al. (2009)
[d]Web (e.g., amazon.com, cdw.com, dell.com, sony.com, bhelectronics.com)
[e]Adapted version from Todd and Benbasat (1992)

the common steps of decision strategies and lists their sources (literature, web or new) and the decision strategy characteristics they support.

We describe each type of IIMT and its variants in detail. With the description we also provide concrete suggestions for the design in screen shots of available webstores and mock-ups for the new IIMT. The design was chosen according to the requirements described in the previous section.

As pointed out above, the design of an *adaptive* system must be left to future work as making the DSS adaptive to different users and environments goes beyond the scope of the present work. However, we would like to note that the modularity of the system facilitates adaptivity as the webstore can easily only show the subset of IIMT which are actually needed by the particular user and the particular decision environment.

The IIMT *PAIRWISE COMPARISON* allows a customer to directly compare all attributes of two alternatives. It can be found on a number of websites because it is a variant of a product-comparison matrix with only two products (compare both examples in Figs. 6.1 and 6.2).

There are two possible variants of the IIMT *MARK*. $MARK_{diff/sim}$ allows highlighting of either differences or similarities of attribute levels in a product-comparison matrix. Figure 6.2 gives an example. $MARK_{manually}$, in contrast, makes it possible to highlight single attribute levels manually. In principle, separate marks can be used for different properties of attribute levels. For example, attribute levels that fulfill the expectations of the customer can be captured, whereas attribute levels that do not fulfill expectations can be crossed out. For examples, see Figs. 6.3,b.

With the IIMT *REMOVE*, the user can delete alternatives and/or attributes (see the *Delete* in Fig. 6.1 for an example of $REMOVE_{alternative}$). $REMOVE_{marking}$ can remove highlighted alternatives. Figure 6.3 gives an example where alternatives can be removed if at least one attribute value is marked by the customer as not acceptable (in the example, the first alternative would be removed because the battery runtime of 1.5 h is marked negatively).

The IIMT *SCORE* allows for weighting the importance of attributes and for assigning a utility to attribute levels. $SCORE_{attribute}$ allows a user to assign a

Fig. 6.1 Product-comparison matrix (example from www.myproductsadvisor.com) with one information management tool: *REMOVE* (delete) of products from the matrix

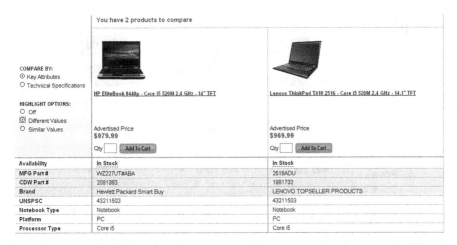

Fig. 6.2 Example from www.cdw.com where two alternatives are compared pairwise ($PAIRWISE\ COMPARISON$) and similarities are highlighted with a colored cell background ($MARK_{diff/sim}$)

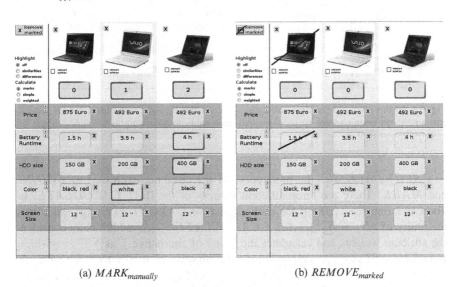

(a) $MARK_{manually}$ (b) $REMOVE_{marked}$

Fig. 6.3 This mock-up shows an example of $MARK_{manually}$. In the *left* picture, the attribute levels "4 h", "400 GB", and *white* are marked as positive by selecting the corresponding attribute levels. In the *right* picture, "1.5 h" is marked as negative. A click on the button "Remove marked" at the *top left corner*, would remove all alternatives with at least one negatively marked attribute level

weight w_i to an attribute i. $SCORE_{attributelevel}$ allows a user to assign an attribute value $v_i(a_{ij})$ to the ith attribute of alternative j. Figure 6.4 gives an example where a user can assign weights and utility values to attributes and attribute levels, respectively.

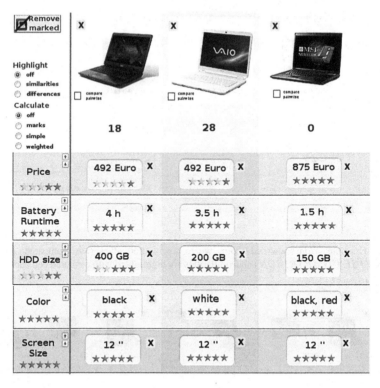

Fig. 6.4 In this mock-up for $SCORE_{attributeLevel}$, $SCORE_{attribute}$ and $CALCUATE_{weighted}$, consumers can assign scores to each attribute level and attribute weights to each attribute by coloring up to five stars

$CALCULATE$ uses the preferences of the customer expressed by $SCORE$ and $MARK$. There are three different variants of the IIMT $CALCULATE$. In Todd and Benbasat (2000), for each alternative $CALCULATE_{simple}$ calculates the utility of alt_j as $\sum_{i=1}^{m} v_i(a_{ij})$. $CALCULATE_{weighted}$ additionally considers the attribute weights and calculates the utility of alternative j as $\sum_{i=1}^{m} w_i v_i(a_{ij})$. $CALCULATE_{markings}$ simply counts the number of marks for each product. Figure 6.3 shows an example of $CALCULATE_{mar-kings}$. The first alternative has no positively marked attribute level and is assigned the score 0; for the second alternative, the user has marked "white" as positive attribute level. Thus the second alternative receives the score of 1. Figure 6.4 displays an example of $CALCULATE_{weighted}$. The first alternative gets a score of 18, since the user has assigned the price of 492 €4 stars and the HDD size "400 GB" 2 stars. Multiplying these score per star with the attribute weights of 3 for price and 3 for HDD size yields $3*4 + 2*3 = 18$ (see the linear additive utility function for the WADD strategy).

By using the IIMT $SORT$, a customer can change the order in which alternatives are displayed in the comparison matrix. $SORT_{hierarchically}$ allows several criteria, for example, prices and, if prices are equal for two alternatives, battery runtime

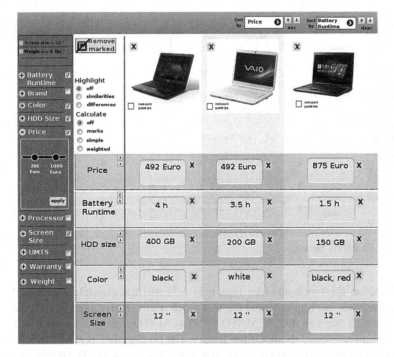

Fig. 6.5 This mock-up shows the $SORT_{hierarchically}$ according to ascending prices and descending battery runtime. Therefore, the product with the lowest price and highest battery runtime is shown in the first column. Furthermore, $FILTER$ at the *left* allows setting different kinds of filters for all attributes. Only attributes with a checked *checkbox* are actually displayed in the matrix (price, battery runtime, HDD size, color and screen size all have a checked *checkbox*)

to sort products (compare Fig. 6.5 for an example). Currently, simpler versions of $SORT$ are available on the Internet which only allow for sorting according to one attribute. If nominal attribute values (e.g. color) are used in the product-comparison matrix, the preferred order for the nominal attributes must be specified by the customer. $SORT_{drag\&drop}$ allows the user to change the order of attributes manually.

Finally, $FILTER$ allows a customer to remove alternatives from the comparison matrix where at least one attribute value does not exceed a customer-defined threshold. We have learned in Sect. 5.1.2.2 that this IIMT is available on many websites and it can be used in the screening as well as in the in-depth comparison phase. For an example, see Fig. 6.5.

To conclude, we retrieve seven different types of IIMT which are needed to support all decision strategies: $PAIRWISECOMPARISON, FILTER, MARK,$ $REMOVE, SORT, SCORE, CALCULATE.$ Since we support the basic steps decision strategies consist of, we can contribute to an efficient decision support being close to the actual needs of the users.

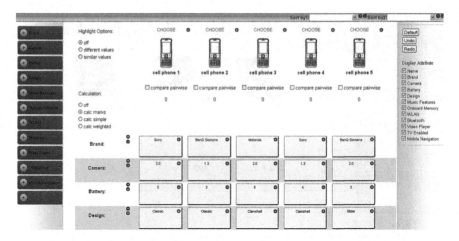

Fig. 6.6 First IIMT-prototype

Based on the mock-ups (see Figs. 6.3– 6.5) and the examples we have found in the Internet, we implemented the first version of the prototype of the proposed IIMT, which we call INTACMATO.[1] INTACMATO was programmed with the AJAX framework and the JQUERY library. The product data is stored in a mySQL database and retrieved via php. Figure 6.6 shows this prototype. The implementation of the first version of INTACMATO took about 4 months. This first version was evaluated in two qualitative usability studies.

6.4   Qualitative Evaluation of INTACMATO

6.4.1   Study 1: Brainstorming with Experts

We conducted one usability study with experts and one with both experts and non-experts. For the first study with experts, we took a brainstorming approach and followed a three-step process: (1) fact finding, (2) idea finding and (3) solution finding (Osborn 1963). The study started with an introduction to the overall software project. The experts were five faculty members who had knowledge in the field of IDA and software development. In phase 1, the experts had the opportunity to explore the IIMT. No introduction of the IIMT functionality was provided in order to observe in how far it is self-explaining. In phase 2, the experts answered a short questionnaire with openly formulated questions on their first impression and their ideas for improvement. Furthermore, we asked for evaluations of the five design

---

[1]The implementation was joint work with Felix Vogel (KIT, University Karlsruhe).

criteria: consistency, control, flexibility, low effort, and transparency. In phase 3, the results of the first two phases were recapitulated and the group discussed possible solutions. The main points of critique were:

1. Overcrowded and confusing design which overstrained the users
2. Uncertainty about the functionality of some IIMT and their actions when using them

Experts stated things like "What happens when I mark an attribute level red?", "It was unclear what to do with all the stars.", or "I am overstrained.", and "Too much stuff!". In the third phase, the following solutions were suggested for addressing these problems:

1. Redesign the filter to improve clarity and consistency: remove apply button, add unities, use less dominant colors, unify font type, show already filtered attribute levels at the top of filter.
2. Change the way the attribute levels are displayed in the table: make rows more cohesive, improve the readability of attribute levels, remove the vertical lines.
3. Replace parts of IIMT with symbols already known from well-known operation systems, such as "+" and "−" for maximizing and minimizing menus.
4. Add help functionality to explain IIMT.

Based on the results of this first usability study, the design of IIMT was improved in a further three weeks of programming and tested in a second study, which is described in the following section.

6.4.2   Study 2: Thinking Aloud

Having received enough input from the round of experts in the first study, the revisited INTACMATO was also tested with non-expert users. As method, we chose thinking aloud protocols (Ericsson and Simon 1993; Shapiro 1994). Thinking aloud requires users to verbalize their thought processes as they perform a certain task with the system (Jorgensen 1990; Woods 1993). It is thought to be one of the most valuable usability engineering methods since it is a close approximation to the individual usage. Moreover, the data can be collected from a fairly small number of users (Nielsen 1994). We followed the five guidelines by Buber and Holzmüller (2007), which state that instructions should be formalized, an appropriate experimental setting must be established, means for keeping up the think-aloud process must be undertaken, the users should talk about their experiences, and technical problems should be kept to a minimum. The usability test was conducted with seven test users, among them four women and three men. According to the users' self-reports, two of them had little technical experience, and one of them stated never to have purchased a product online before. Two of the users were computer scientists and therefore experienced in dealing with interfaces. To all subjects, we read aloud an introduction at the beginning of the study. The study was conducted in a comfortable, calm room of the university which was familiar to the subjects. The subjects had to imagine that they were shopping for cell phones online and had already chosen five cell phones of highest interest to them. They were instructed to test the functionality of the IIMT first, before they were going to actually choose one of the products. This approach helped us to observe users' interaction with all different kinds of IIMT. During the actual study, no further assistance was provided by the conductor. The subjects' statements as well as their clicking behavior were recorded with Camtasia Version 6 by TechSmith and an additional audio recorder. After the subjects had used all IIMT, recording was stopped and they had to answer a questionnaire asking for evaluations of the three constructs: consistency, control, and transparency. The questionnaire was designed with 3–5 items known from literature for each of the constructs (Ariely 2000; Kamis and Davern 2005; Pereira 2000; Wang and Benbasat 2009). We did not ask yet for the evaluation of the two constructs low effort and flexibility as we wanted the subjects to evaluate these two aspects only after they had actually chosen a product. Hence, after having answered the questionnaires, we recorded again subjects' thoughts while they actually chose a product and handed out a second questionnaire with questions concerning low effort and flexibility.

In total, 23 errors or missing functionalities were found by the users:

- Three logical errors of the system: for instance the same attribute level can be evaluated with different scores
- Five programming bugs: for instance distorted display if certain IIMT were used in sequence

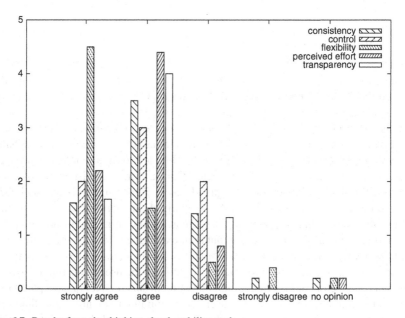

Fig. 6.7 Results from the thinking aloud usability study

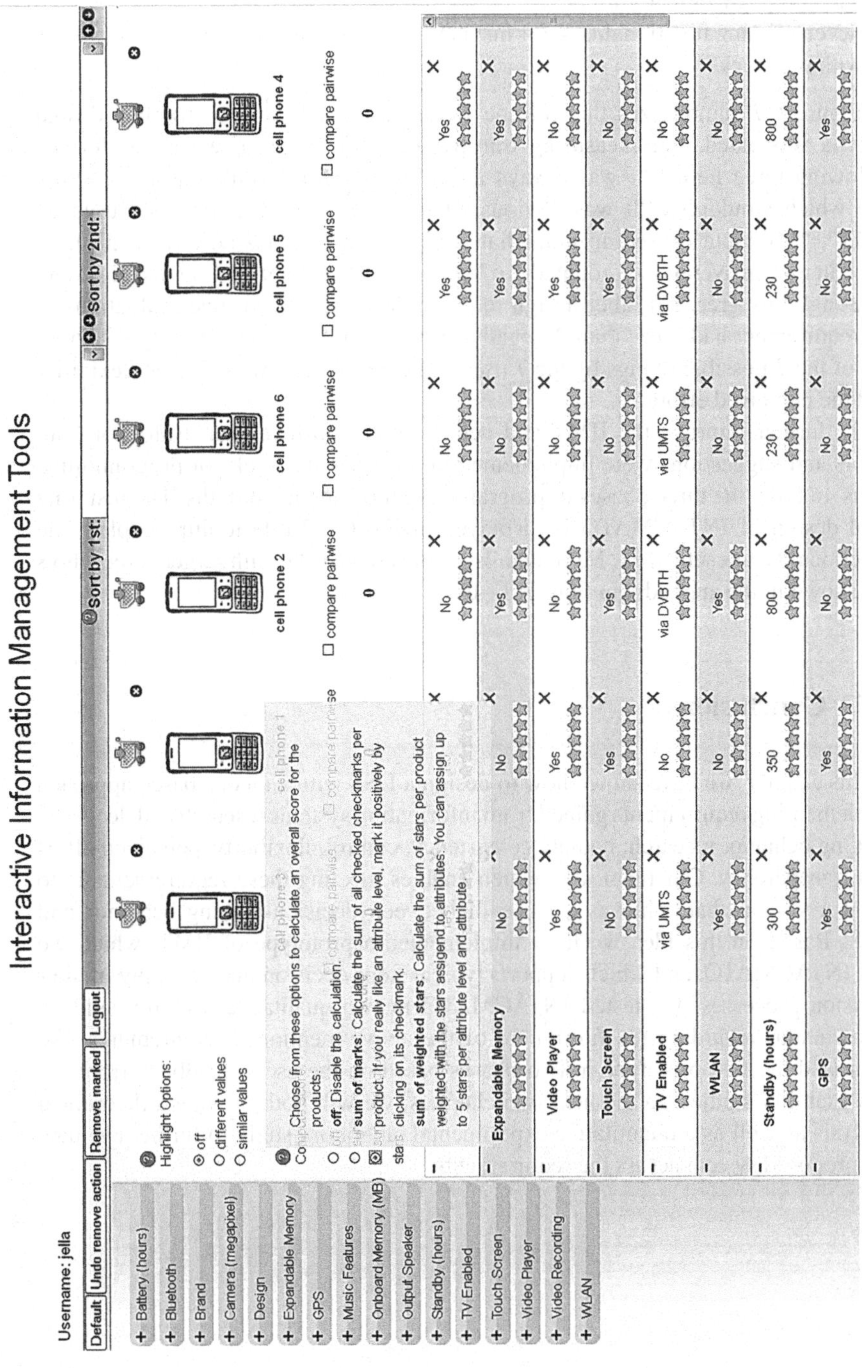

Fig. 6.8 Final design of INTACMATO. The tooltip explains the IIMT functionality

- Eight weaknesses of the design: for instance, sliders in the filter were too small and unrecognizable for users
- Seven missing functionalities: for instance, minimize and maximize all attributes with one click

Figure 6.7 summarizes the average frequencies each item of the five design criteria was rated. For measuring transparency, for instance, we asked for the following three items: "I was always aware which IIMT would cause an action and which wouldn't", "It was obvious what would happen, after I had used an IIMT", "My input caused an immediate reaction on the website". Over all these three items, on average we counted 1.67 strongly agree, 4 agree, 1.33 disagree, and 0 strongly disagree. All other design requirements also got positive evaluations as no requirement had more than 2 negative ratings (disagree and strongly disagree) out of the 7 possible ratings by the 7 users. The best ratings were for the flexibility and the perceived effort.

To further improve the IIMT and achieve more positive user evaluations, all errors and suggestions were implemented in a further six weeks of programming. Thus, in total, the three phases of programming took about 6 months. The resulting final design of INTACMATO is displayed in Fig. 6.8. Little tooltips explain the functionality of each IIMT. More details on different IIMT with larger screenshots are shown in the appendix in Figs. B.1–B.7.

6.5   Conclusions

In this chapter, we have shown how to design a DSS with a theory-based approach implementing requirements gained from information systems research and decision-making behavior research, namely consistency, control, flexibility, perceived effort and transparency. Our main idea which enables meeting these requirements is to build a system that achieves a close fit between decision-making behavior and DSS. Based on this idea we have implemented a prototype of IIMT, which we call INTACMATO, and which supports typical steps decision makers apply in their decision processes. We tested INTACMATO in two qualitative usability studies, in particular regarding the fulfillment of the above mentioned requirements. We improved the first prototype in two phases based on the users' feedback from the two usability studies. In the next two chapters, we will both provide a theoretical analysis as well as a quantitative experimental laboratory study to further evaluate the proposed system across the requirements.

Chapter 7
An Effort-Accuracy Framework for IIMT

In this chapter, we analyze to what extent INTACMATO meets the requirement of low effort. We take an existing effort-accuracy model, adapt and extend it to INTACMATO and show analytically the savings of effort achieved.

7.1 The Effort-Accuracy Framework by Johnson and Payne (1985)

In part , we found that decision makers are highly adaptive in selecting decision strategies. Based on this knowledge, several authors have suggested an effort-accuracy framework which postulates that decision makers trade off benefits gained from an accurate decision (i.e., one with high decision quality) with the effort (cost) of deciding for or against the application of a decision strategy (Hogarth 1987). In its original and more general version this framework was called cost-benefit framework (Beach and Mitchell 1978). A large body of research has yielded results consistent with this framework (Bettman et al. 1990; Creyer et al. 1990; Johnson and Payne 1985; Payne et al. 1993; Stone and Schkade 1994).

Todd and Benbasat (1992) noted that:

> Given two strategies that are expected to require the same effort, the one that is expected to produce a more accurate outcome will be preferred, and given two strategies that produce equivalent outcomes, the one that is expected to require less effort will be preferred (p. 375).

Another, often stated consequence of the effort-accuracy framework is that decision makers choose the strategy with lowest effort that provides acceptable quality (Böckenholt et al. 1991; Payne et al. 1993; Shugan 1980; Todd and Benbasat 1994a).

J. Pfeiffer, *Interactive Decision Aids in E-Commerce*, Contributions to Management Science, DOI 10.1007/978-3-7908-2769-9_7, © Springer-Verlag Berlin Heidelberg 2012

7.1.1   Measurements for Effort and Accuracy

In 1985, Johnson and Payne specified the effort-accuracy framework by suggesting measurements for both, effort and accuracy. Their framework takes into account the influence of task-based complexity because they measure effort depending on the number of alternatives and attributes displayed. However, they do not include the notion of context-based complexity in their model.

The aim of decision making is to make good decisions; in other words decisions with high quality. The accuracy of a decision strategy is supposed to reflect decision quality; but how can we measure accuracy? According to Payne et al. (1993), "a good decision is seen as one that follows a good decision process" (p. 89). Further, a good decision process is characterized by a complete search of the available information and consideration of the subjective preferences. Consequently, the WADD strategy is usually employed as benchmark for good decisions (Chu and Spires 2000) as it fulfills these requirements. It assumes a standard linear additive utility function, and it chooses the alternative with highest utility. In contrast, choosing the alternative with worst utility, in terms of EV (expected value), is represented by a random choice (RAN) by Johnson and Payne (1985). Thus, the authors assume that RAN is always worse than any other strategy. Hence, according to Johnson and Payne (1985), accuracy of a strategy falls between the two extremes (WADD and RAN):

$$\text{relative accuracy}(strategy) = \frac{EV(strategy) - EV(RAN)}{EV(WADD) - EV(RAN)}, \qquad (7.1)$$

where $EV(strategy)$ stands for expected value and represents the total utility of an alternative chosen by a *strategy*. Thus, EV(WADD) is identical to the utility of the alternative chosen by the linear additive utility function.

For measuring effort, Johnson and Payne (1985) suggest using elementary information processes (EIP), which are based upon work by Johnson (1979) and Huber (1980). EIP subdivide decision making into a sequence of basic units of thought in which information is processed and memorized (Newell and Simon 1972; Sternberg 1966), such as reading two attribute levels and comparing them. Each strategy can be described by a sequence of such EIP. As most researchers assume that each EIP takes equal cognitive effort, the sum of all EIP used in a strategy determines its overall effort (Payne et al. 1993; Todd and Benbasat 1994a; Zhang and Pu 2006).

7.1.2   Elementary Information Processes

Johnson and Payne (1985) propose the following EIP: *READ, MOVE, COMPARE, DIFFERENCE, ADD, PRODUCT, ELIMINATE,* and *CHOOSE.*

1. *READ* describes reading an attribute level into the short-term-memory (STM). Payne and Bettman (1994) also list a *MOVE* EIP for describing the effort of the eye-movement: "Go to next element". However, as *MOVE* and *READ* are always used in the sequence MOVE then READ in all strategies, we subsume MOVE and READ to one single EIP. From our viewpoint this approach also circumvents the otherwise artificial assumption that MOVE and other EIP, for instance *PRODUCT* and *DIFFERENCE*, cost each one unit of EIP, although, in reality, *MOVE* and *READ* cost supposedly much less effort.
2. *COMPARE* compares two levels/values with another, for instance two attribute levels.
3. *DIFFERENCE* computes the differences of two attribute levels/values.
4. *ADD* adds a value to the STM.
5. *PRODUCT* multiplies an attribute weight with an attribute level/value.
6. *ELIMINATE* eliminates an alternative from consideration
7. *CHOOSE* chooses the preferred alternative and finishes the process.

We see several deficits in the definition of EIP and hence add three more EIP to the framework. First, the authors do not distinguish between attribute levels and attribute values (see Sect. 2.2.2). Hence, they assume that evaluating an attribute level with an attribute value has no costs. Moreover, the effort for recalling aspiration levels and attribute weights from long-term-memory (LTM) is not reflected by any EIP. Thus, we introduce the EIP *EVALUATE* for describing the effort of assigning attribute values, attribute weights, and aspiration levels. This idea is partly in line with work by Todd and Benbasat (1994a) who, however, neglect the effort of assigning attribute values.

Second, storing the status of alternatives (e.g., whether they have already been eliminated) is not reflected by any EIP of Johnson and Payne. Todd and Benbasat (1994a) refer to this effort as tracking effort. Tracking effort comprehends the notion of storing the status of alternatives, assigned scores, etc. and is represented by the additional EIP *STORE*.

Third, while *EVALUATE* encompasses the notion of assigning values from the LTM and can potentially be quite effortful, we need an EIP for retrieving information from STM which, potentially, costs less effort than *EVALUATE*. In other words, we add the EIP *RETRIEVE* to quantify the effort for retrieving any value stored by a previous *STORE* during this choice task, such as an assigned score. In Table 7.1 an overview of the original seven EIP and the three new ones is displayed.

Figure 7.1 shows an example of six strategies and their positions in the effort-accuracy framework taken from Payne et al. (1993, p. 93). Both effort and accuracy depend on parameters of the particular choice task such as the number of alternatives and attributes, the shown attribute levels and the preference function. Only the positions on the y-axis of WADD and RAN are fixed. By definition WADD will always provide a relative accuracy of 100% and RAN of 0% (see equation 7.1). The number of EIP for RAN is always 0 but the number of EIP for WADD and all other strategies depends on the number of alternatives and attributes. Unfortunately,

Table 7.1 EIP as used in our extension. Adapted from Payne et al. (1993) and Todd and Benbasat (1994a)

EIP	Description
READ	One attribute level is read into the STM.
COMPARE	Two values are compared.
DIFFERENCE	The difference of two values is calculated.
ADD	Add an attribute value to another value in STM.
PRODUCT	An attribute value is multiplied with an attribute weight.
ELIMINATE	Remove an alternative or an attribute from consideration.
CHOOSE	The preferred alternative is chosen and the decision process ends.
EVALUATE	Assign a value, weight or aspiration level to an attribute from the LTM.
STORE	Store information in the STM.
RETRIEVE	Recall information from the STM, such as assigned scores or the status of alternatives.

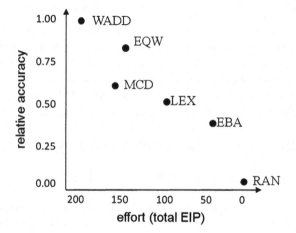

Fig. 7.1 Example of positions of decision strategies in the effort-accuracy space for some choice task (see Payne et al. 1993)

Payne et al. (1993) do not give any further details on the parameters of this example. Yet, this example depicts the idea of the effort-accuracy framework well.

7.2   Extended Effort-Accuracy Framework

We focus on the effort-reduction which can be achieved by offering IIMT to users. We emphasize the effort-reduction more than the potential increase of accuracy, because the findings of several studies by Todd and Benbasat (1991, 1992, 1993, 1994a,b, 2000) indicate that decision makers tend to adapt their strategy selection to the type of decision aids available in such a way as to maintain a low level of effort expenditure. Furthermore, several studies have argued for the general tendency that consumers put more emphasis on reducing effort than on increasing accuracy (Bettman and Kakkar 1977; Horrigan 2008; Johnson and Payne 1985; Russo and Dosher 1983). One reason for this might be that "feedback on effort expenditure is relatively immediate, while feedback on accuracy is subject to both delay and ambiguity" (Todd and Benbasat 1992, p. 375). Todd and Benbasat (1992) conclude further, "it might be fruitful to adopt an effort-perspective in trying to understand the behavior of decision makers using DSS" (p. 375).

We incorporate the effort-reduction achieved by IIMT in the effort-accuracy framework. Hence, our approach explicitly analyzes influences stemming from the technical environment in form of IIMT and extends the three influence factors on decision making (see Payne et al. 1993), problem, person and social context, by the fourth factor "technical environment" (see Fig. 7.2).

Following the term EIP for describing the cognitive effort in the decision makers' minds, we introduce the term *elementary communication processes* (ECP) for describing the decision makers' effort for using an IIMT. The extended framework is able to (1) describe for each strategy which IIMT make which EIP unnecessary, (2) the ECP this replacement costs and (3) the saving of effort when comparing the traditional way of decision making (original framework with only EIP) and the IIMT-supported way of decision making (extended framework with EIP and ECP). We define the net and the relative saving of effort as follows:

$$\text{net saving of effort} = EIP_{noIIMT} - EIP_{withIIMT} - ECP, \qquad (7.2)$$

$$\text{relative saving of effort} = 100\% - \left(\frac{(EIP_{withIIMT} + ECP)}{EIP_{noIIMT}}\right), \qquad (7.3)$$

where EIP_{noIIMT} is the sum of EIP for a strategy when not supported with IIMT and $EIP_{withIIMT}$ when supported by IIMT.

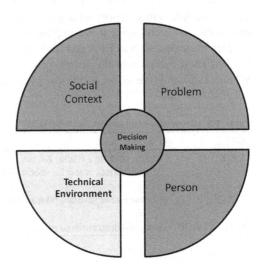

Fig. 7.2 The technical environment as additional factor influencing decision making

7.2.1   Elementary Communication Processes

For using the IIMT which are suggested in Sect. 6, we need the following ECP. First, CLICK describes one click action, such as using radio buttons for choosing among IIMT, clicking on a button, or clicking on a star for using the IIMT *SCORE*. SELECT describes the action of choosing an option from a list, for instance, choosing the criterion for *SORT* from the drop-down menu or selecting the filter criteria. This can incorporate moving the start and end of a slider for numerical values (for instance a filter on the price range) or clicking on several checkboxes. Finally, DRAG&DROP describes reordering rows for the IIMT $SORT_{drag\&drop}$.

Table 7.2 summarizes these three ECP and shows to which IIMT they belong to. Table 7.2 also reflects that we have followed the guidelines *consistency* and *low effort* (see Sect. 6.3), since the number of different ECP is kept small (consistency), and most IIMT require only a simple CLICK (low effort).

7.2.2   Model Assumptions

Before we start computing the saving of effort for the different strategies, we lay out the assumptions of our analysis. First, the exact amount of EIP and ECP depend on the particular scenario. While when using EBA, for instance, in some scenarios a decision maker might exclude all except one alternative just because of one attribute, in another scenario the decision maker might have to compare the products across several attributes to be able to narrow down the choice task to only one alternative. In the subsequent analysis, we assume the worst-case scenario. Thus, regarding EBA, for example, we assume that a decision maker has to consider all attributes. This assumption provides a clear criterion for the analysis and permits the comparison of net savings of effort among all strategies. However, it biases the analysis towards more effortful, compensatory strategies. WADD, for instance, has the same best and worst-case effort since it is complete (see Fig. A.1 in the appendix), while for simpler strategies, such as EBA and LEX, the effort of worst and best case behavior differ a lot if early on in the search process many alternatives can be excluded. When calculating the effort in the pseudo-code notation, we label sequences of

Table 7.2 Elementary communication processes

ECP	Description	IIMT
CLICK	Mouse click on a (radio) button, checkboxes, a star for scoring, etc.	*MARK, REMOVE, SCORE, CALCULATE, PAIRWISE COMPARISON*
SELECT	Choose one or several options from a set.	*SORT, FILTER*
DRAG & DROP	Drag and drop attribute rows.	*SORT*

the decision-making process which assume worst-case behavior correspondingly to make this point transparent.

Second, following other researchers, we assume that each EIP and ECP costs one unit of effort (Payne et al. 1993; Todd and Benbasat 2000). Thus, there is no difference between more complicated EIP such as PRODUCT and easy EIP such as ELIMINATE.

Although our IIMT-prototype could easily integrate attributes with nominal attribute values (such as color), we will assume ordinal values for the analysis. This assumption only affects the cost of *SORT*.

7.2.3   Related Work

Against the background of the effort-accuracy framework, the goal of IDA is to reduce effort and increase accuracy. There has been some, although inconsistent, empirical evidence that RA reduce the effort by reducing the decision time and the extent of product search (Häubl and Murray 2006; Häubl and Trifts 2000; Hostler et al. 2005; Pedersen 2000; Xiao and Benbasat 2007). Further research has found evidence for improved decision accuracy (Häubl and Murray 2006; Häubl and Trifts 2000; Hostler et al. 2005; Pereira 2000; Xiao and Benbasat 2007).

Todd and Benbasat (1992) find evidence for a reduction of effort for IIMT, but not for an increased accuracy. This mixed result is probably due to the implementation of their IIMT: there was no graphical interface for using decision aids, but consumers had to type in commands like "DROP", "SORT", etc. in the console. Later, Häubl and Trifts (2000) find the empirical evidence that a product-comparison matrix can increase accuracy and decrease effort but they do not consider single IIMT rather they consider the whole product-comparison matrix to be one IIMT. Todd and Benbasat (2000) propose a decomposition approach where they use EIP for measuring effort-reduction achieved by an IDA. However, they do not take into account the effort for using the IIMT and only analyze how many EIP become unnecessary in case of IDA-support. Their empirical results are mixed. WADD is used more often when supported by IDA, which might have been caused by a reduced effort induced by the IDA. However, EBA is not used more often when respondents are given IDA which support EBA strategies. Therefore, there does not seem to be a reduction in effort. To sum up, Todd and Benbasat showed some evidence that IDA can reduce effort and increase accuracy for WADD but not for EBA.

Zhang and Pu (2006) examine the influence of IDA on effort and accuracy and also take into account the effort for expressing user preferences (similar to our notion of ECP). In a computer simulation, they compare the performance of IDA which support exactly one strategy (e.g. WADD, EQW, MCD) with hybrid strategies which are composed out of EBA, MCD, LEX, or FRQ to eliminate alternatives and WADD to then choose the best alternative from the remaining ones. Zhang and Pu (2006) conclude from their simulations that hybrid decision aids have the potential to increase accuracy and increase the net saving of effort.

As Zhang and Pu (2006) is the only work which we found that also presents some notion of incorporating ECP into the effort-accuracy framework, we would like to comment further on the difference between our approach and theirs. First, they assume that one single or – in the hybrid version – two decision strategies are supported by decision aids. Thus, their approach is restrictive and there is no notion of modularization or flexibility. With the IIMT which we propose, decision makers can apply single steps or whole decision strategies in any order.

Second, their results are only based on computer simulation. They do not implement the IDA in some kind of user interface, as we do, but rather list what kind of input parameters are generally needed for supporting different strategies. Hence, they assume that the simulated agents reveal these kinds of parameters directly to the system without concretizing with which kind of interface this happens (e.g. filters, etc.). For instance, WADD needs a value function and attribute weights as parameter, while SAT needs aspiration levels; but the authors do not explain how these parameters are prompted into the system.

Third, in their environment, they assume that each value function can be determined by three midvalue points, thus each value function requires only three ECP. As we have seen in Sect. 2.1, this is a rather simplifying approach. Usually a value function requires that the value of each attribute level is determined, thus requiring k ECP if k attribute levels are displayed per attribute. Thus, in their environment, EQW costs $3m$ ECP for determining each value function of each of the m attributes, instead of km.

Hence, we conclude that their notion of costs for expressing user preferences is in general similar to ours but due to their simplifying assumptions, the missing implementation of a user interface, and only a computer-based empirical validation, no conclusions for real-world scenarios can be drawn from their simulations. In contrast, since we suggest a concrete prototype, we can be more specific when determining effort. To sum up, we are the first to analyze and quantify in detail the effort of decision strategies when supported by IIMT. With a pseudo-code like notation, our analysis is very transparent and more exact in quantifying effort than other work.

7.2.4 Application to IIMT-Prototype

In order to compute both the net as well as the relative saving of effort for a strategy, we need to analyze which EIP are needed when users have no support by IIMT and how the effort changes when they are supported. We discuss three prominent strategies: WADD, LEX, EBA in detail. The analysis of the other strategies is in the appendix in Figs. A.2–A.25.

Before we start with the exact calculation of EIP and ECP, we would like to point out that different researchers assume slightly different decision processes, which results in different assignments of EIP. Thus, assigning EIP to decision strategies is not clearly defined. Nevertheless, the results we retrieve from our analysis are quite robust, because different definitions only result in minor differences in the terms in the EIP equations. Thus, the order of magnitude should be affected only slightly and valid results can still be concluded. Furthermore, due to our transparent and detailed description of each decision process, our analysis can be easily adapted to changes in the decision process. Moreover, we discuss the results of the complete analysis of the computed savings of effort in detail at the end of this chapter.

7.2.4.1 WADD

From Sect. 2.2.2, we know that WADD is the normative rule which chooses the utility maximizing alternative, $\max_{j=1,...,n}[u(alt_j) = \sum_{i=1}^{m} w_i v_i(a_{ij})]$, where n is the number of alternatives, m the number of attributes, $v_i(a_{ij})$ the attribute values, and w_i the weights. The typical choice process when applying WADD is that, first, decision makers assign attribute weights, then they start with the first alternative and compute its overall utility. This utility is stored in STM and the second alternative is evaluated accordingly. Then, decision makers eliminate the inferior alternative and proceed with the next one until all alternatives have been considered.

We use pseudo-code notation to note the sequence of EIP for WADD. Figure 7.3 shows the analysis and also indicates the costs measured in EIP. $3m$ EIP (m-times the three EIP: READ, EVALUATE, and STORE) are needed for assigning attribute weights, $(3m + 3(m - 1) + 1 + m)n$ for assigning the attribute values and computing the utility of alternatives, $3(n - 1)$ for determining the alternative with highest utility, and 1 for choosing the remaining alternative. Thus, in total, we need $7mn + 3m + n - 2$ EIP when executing WADD without any decision support. Note that for WADD there is no difference between worst and best-case analysis because when applying WADD, decision makers always consider all information, independent of their preference functions.

When the decision makers can profit from IIMT, the effort reduces to $3m + 3mn + 2$. For calculating this effort, we again use the pseudo-code notation, as is displayed in Fig. 7.4. While the effort for assigning attribute weights still remains $3m$, storing, retrieving and calculating information is completed by the DSS. Hence, the step of assigning attribute values and computing the utility of alternatives reduces to $3mn$, since the three IIMT: $SCORE_{attributeLevel}$, $SCORE_{attribute}$, and $CALCULATE_{weighted}$ make the four EIP RETRIEVE, PRODUCT, ADD, and STORE unnecessary. $3nm$ is an upper bound for the effort (worst-case) under the assumption that each attribute level is shown at most once. In case attribute levels are shown several times, for instance, if several products have the same size, the users only have to assign their attribute value for this attribute level once because the system will automatically assign this attribute value to all other equivalent attribute levels of other products. In addition to reducing the effort for assigning and calculating the utility of alternatives, determining and choosing the alternative with highest utility is

---

Algorithm   WADD without support of IIMT

// Assign attribute weights.
for $i = 1$ to m **do**
   READ $attr_i$
   EVALUATE $attr_i$ with weight w_i } **3m**
   STORE w_i
end for
// Compute utility of each alternative.
for $j = 1$ to n **do**
   for $i = 1$ to m **do**
     READ a_{ij}
     EVALUATE a_{ij} with $v_i(a_{ij})$ } **3m**
     RETRIEVE w_i
     if $i \neq 1$ **then**
       PRODUCT $prod = w_i * v_i(a_{ij})$
       RETRIEVE $utility_j$ } **3(m-1)**
       ADD $utility_j + = prod$
     else
       PRODUCT $utility_j = w_i * v_i(a_{ij})$ } **1**
     end if
     STORE $utility_j$ } **m**
   end for
   // Eliminate alternative with lower utility.
   if $j > 1$ **then**
     RETRIEVE $utility_{j-1}$
     COMPARE $utility_{j-1}$ and $utility_j$ } **3(n-1)**
     ELIMINATE alt with lower $utility$
   end if
end for
CHOOSE remaining alt } **1**

(bracket spanning inner loop: } **n**)

Fig. 7.3 Effort for WADD without support of IIMT

reduced to 2, as the decision makers can use the IIMT *CALCULATE* for comparing the different utility values.[1] It reduces the effort for finding the alternative with highest utility by highlighting the product with the highest utility. In summary, the application of IIMT reduces the effort by $4mn + n - 4$ which is larger than 0, $\forall m, n >= 2$.

---

[1]The IIMT *CALCULATE* must be activated at the beginning of the decision process because only then are the appropriate stars for *SCORE* visible on the screen. The score is automatically updated by the interface as soon as a new attribute value or attribute weight is assigned.

Algorithm WADD with support of IIMT	

// Activate the possibility to assign stars.
CLICK $CALCULATE_{weighted}$
// Assign attribute weights.
	$\Big\}1$

for $i = 1$ **to** m **do**
    READ $attr_i$
    EVALUATE $attr_i$ with weight w_i
    CLICK assign w_i with $SCORE_{attribute}$
end for
	$\Big\}3m$

// Compute utility of each alternative.
for $j = 1$ **to** n **do**
    for $i = 1$ **to** m **do**
        READ a_{ij}
        EVALUATE a_{ij} with $v_i(a_{ij})$
        CLICK assign $v_i(a_{ij})$ with $SCORE_{attributeLevel}$
    end for
	$\Big\}3nm$
	(worst case
	scenario)

end for CHOOSE alt with highest utility	$\Big\}1$

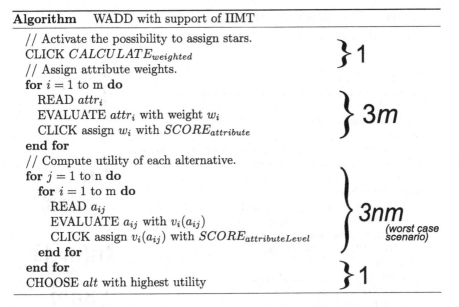

Fig. 7.4 Effort for WADD with support of IIMT

7.2.4.2   EBA

In the deterministic version, EBA considers attributes according to decreasing attribute weights. It eliminates an alternative j if it does not meet the aspiration level for the considered attribute i: $asp(a_{ij}) = 1$. The elimination process stops when the alternative set has been narrowed down to a single remaining alternative. As we assume the worst-case for our calculations, we consider the case that all m attributes have to be taken into account until only one candidate remains. We assume that the decision maker first assigns weights and aspiration levels to all attributes.[2] This costs 5 EIP for reading, evaluating, sorting and storing. Overall, the evaluation of attributes must be repeated m times (see Fig. 7.5). Afterwards, the decision maker chooses the attribute to consider next. We assume that this only costs 1 EIP and in total m EIP (once for each attribute). In case the decision makers are already comparing the remaining products across the second most important attribute, they have to retrieve which product has already been eliminated ($n(m - 1)$). Each attribute level is then compared to the aspiration level with up to five operations: READ attribute level, RETRIEVE aspiration level, COMPARE attribute level with aspiration level, and, in case the aspiration level was not met, ELIMINATE the alternative and STORE the new status. In the worst-case scenario, all elimination

---

[2]Although only the order of attributes and not exact attribute weights are important, we follow the common analysis by Todd and Benbasat (1994a) and others and put assigning attribute weights on the same level with ordering them according to the importance.

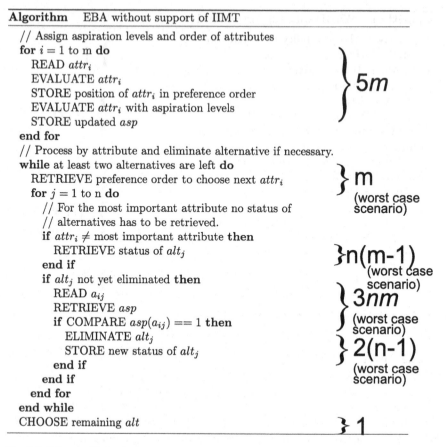

Algorithm   EBA without support of IIMT

// Assign aspiration levels and order of attributes
for $i = 1$ to m **do**
    READ $attr_i$
    EVALUATE $attr_i$
    STORE position of $attr_i$ in preference order $\left.\vphantom{\begin{array}{c}1\\1\\1\\1\\1\end{array}}\right\}$ **5m**
    EVALUATE $attr_i$ with aspiration levels
    STORE updated asp
end for
// Process by attribute and eliminate alternative if necessary.
while at least two alternatives are left **do**
    RETRIEVE preference order to choose next $attr_i$ $\left.\vphantom{\begin{array}{c}1\\1\end{array}}\right\}$ **m**
    for $j = 1$ to n **do**   (worst case scenario)
        // For the most important attribute no status of
        // alternatives has to be retrieved.
        if $attr_i \neq$ most important attribute **then**
            RETRIEVE status of alt_j $\left.\vphantom{\begin{array}{c}1\\1\\1\end{array}}\right\}$ **n(m-1)**
        end if   (worst case scenario)
        if alt_j not yet eliminated **then**
            READ a_{ij}
            RETRIEVE asp $\left.\vphantom{\begin{array}{c}1\\1\\1\end{array}}\right\}$ **3nm**
            if COMPARE $asp(a_{ij}) == 1$ **then**   (worst case scenario)
                ELIMINATE alt_j
                STORE new status of alt_j $\left.\vphantom{\begin{array}{c}1\\1\end{array}}\right\}$ **2(n-1)**
            end if
        end if   (worst case scenario)
    end for
end while
CHOOSE remaining alt $\left.\vphantom{1}\right\}$ **1**

Fig. 7.5 Effort for EBA without support of IIMT

steps occur for the least important attribute. The effort in the best and average-case is lower, as all except one alternative would be excluded already when considering only the most important (best–case) or some proportion of attributes (average–case).

In the scenario with IIMT, several EIP are replaced by the IIMT *FILTER* (see Fig. 7.6). Instead of comparing all attribute levels for an attribute with the aspiration level, the aspiration level is communicated to the *FILTER* with the ECP SELECT and all alternatives which do not meet the aspiration level are deleted automatically from the matrix. This also saves effort in terms of the storage and retrieval of the alternatives' status since the choice task no longer includes these alternatives. The decision maker can continue with the subsequent decision process without being weighed down by previously eliminated alternatives. In sum, while the effort of $5m$ for assigning weights and aspiration levels remains the same, the remaining effort is reduced to $2m + 1$. $2m$ for retrieving the aspiration level for the next attribute to be considered as well as the ECP SELECT for the IIMT *FILTER*, and one for

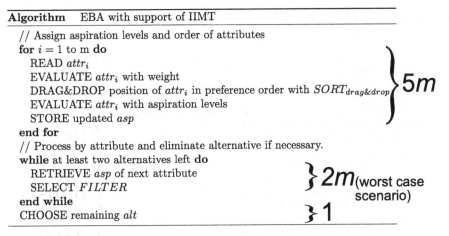

Algorithm   EBA with support of IIMT

// Assign aspiration levels and order of attributes
for $i = 1$ to m **do**
    READ $attr_i$
    EVALUATE $attr_i$ with weight
    DRAG&DROP position of $attr_i$ in preference order with $SORT_{drag\&drop}$ $\Big\}$ 5m
    EVALUATE $attr_i$ with aspiration levels
    STORE updated asp
end for
// Process by attribute and eliminate alternative if necessary.
while at least two alternatives left **do**
    RETRIEVE asp of next attribute
    SELECT $FILTER$ $\Big\}$ 2m (worst case scenario)
end while
CHOOSE remaining alt $\}$ 1

Fig. 7.6 Effort for EBA with support of IIMT

choosing the final alternative. The decision makers also save the effort for retrieving the next attribute from the preference order (m EIP) because they have already sorted attributes with $SORT_{drag\&drop}$ in the right preference order in one of the first steps. In sum, the net saving of effort is: $4mn - 3m + n - 2 > 0, \ \forall m, n >= 2$.

7.2.4.3   LEX

LEX compares products attribute-wise by considering the attributes according to decreasing attribute weights. It chooses the alternative(s) with the most valuable attribute level: $v_i(a_{ij}) = 1$ for the most important attribute.[3] If there is more than one alternative with $v_i(a_{ij}) = 1$, these alternatives are compared on the second most important attribute, etc.

In the worst-case scenario, LEX is very expensive when not supported by IIMT because we have to assume that alternatives are eliminated only for the least important attribute. Thus, for all attributes, decision makers have to determine the preference order of attributes and retrieve the attributes with effort of $4m$ ($2m$ for reading and evaluating attributes and $2m$ for storing and retrieving the preference order). They then have to retrieve the previously eliminated alternatives $n(m - 1)$ times. Afterwards, they evaluate the attribute levels ($2mn$) and compare them $m + 2(n - 1)m$. If there is an attribute level which is better than all other levels for that attribute, alternatives are eliminated with effort of $3(n - 1)$ and the remaining alternative is chosen.

Apparently in the worst-case scenario, LEX sounds quite complicated and has high effort. However, the worst-case scenario for LEX is quite unrealistic, as it

---

[3]We assume that attribute values range from 0 to 1.

Fig. 7.7 Effort for LEX without support of IIMT

assumes that only the least important attribute is used to eliminate alternatives. For all other attributes, the alternatives would all have the same attribute values. The fact that the cost for applying LEX depends on the particular situation is indicated in Fig. 7.7, where we can see that many lines in the pseudo-code are labeled as *worst-case scenario*. In a best-case scenario, the effort would be reduced dramatically. While $3m$ for finding the most important attributes stays the same, retrieving the preference order has only to be done once, for the most important attribute (1 EIP). Then, all attribute values for the most important attribute have to be assigned and compared ($4n - 1$) and the alternatives with lower attribute values are eliminated

Algorithm   LEX with support of IIMT

```
// Assign aspiration levels and order of attributes        ⎫
for i = 1 to m do                                          ⎪
   READ attr_i                                             ⎬ 3m
   EVALUATE attr_i                                         ⎪
   STORE position of attr_i in preference order            ⎪
end for                                                    ⎭
// Process by attribute and eliminate alternative if necessary.
repeat
   RETRIEVE preference order to choose next attr_i   ⎫ 1        ⎫
   for j = 1 to n do                                 ⎫          ⎪
      READ a_ij                                      ⎬ 2n       ⎬ m
      EVALUATE v_i(a_ij)                             ⎪          ⎪ (worst-case
   end for                                           ⎭          ⎪  scenario)
   SELECT SORT_hierarchically for attr_i             ⎬ 1        ⎭
until no alternatives are equivalent on considered attributes
CHOOSE most left alt                                 ⎬ 1
```

Fig. 7.8 Effort for LEX with support of IIMT

$(2(n-1))$. Finally the remaining alternative is chosen (1 EIP). The effort reduces to $3m + 6n - 1$ for the best-case instead of $5mn + 3m + 2n - 2$ for the worst-case.

When LEX is supported with IIMT, the decision process becomes much easier (see Fig. 7.8). The $4m$ for finding the preference order of attributes and retrieving it later again (m), as well as evaluating attribute levels $(2mn)$, is still needed. However, the rest is replayed by $SORT_{hierarchically}$. In the worst-case, the decision makers sort the products according to all attributes, before they can choose the one which is at the left-most position in the matrix. This is possible as the IIMT-prototype allows for sorting products hierarchically, according to several criteria.[4] In total, we get an effort of $2mn + 5m + 1$ and achieve a net saving of effort of $3mn - 2m + 2n - 3 > 0$, $\forall m, n >= 2$.

For all other strategies, the pseudo-code and details on their respective effort can be found in the appendix (Figs. A.2–A.25). The results of the analysis for all strategies are summarized in Table 7.3 and discussed in the following section.

7.2.5   Results and Evaluation

Table 7.3 indicates that IIMT are able to reduce the effort. For all strategies, the effort without IIMT support is larger or equal than with IIMT support. In the last two columns in Table 7.3, we show the effort in the worst-case of two exemplary

---

[4]Our current prototype only allows to sort for two criteria at one time, but it is easily extendable to allow for more attributes.

Table 7.3 Effort-reduction when using IIMT and the relative saving of effort in % in the worst-case

Strategy	Effort	$m, n = 2$	$m = 16$ $n = 6$
ADD no IIMT	$10mn - 4m + 2n$	36	908
ADD with IIMT	$3mn + 3m + n + 3$	23 (36%)	345 (62%)
COM no IIMT	$6mn + 3m + n - 1$	31	629
COM with IIMT	$4mn + 3m + n + 1$	25 (19%)	439 (30%)
CONJ no IIMT	$2mn + 3m + 2n - 1$	17	251
CONJ with IIMT	$2mn + 3m + n + 1$	17 (0%)	247 (2%)
DIS no IIMT	$6mn + 3m + n - 1$	31	629
DIS with IIMT	$4mn + 3m + n + 1$	25 (19%)	439 (30%)
DOM no IIMT	$6mn - 3m + 3$	21	531
DOM with IIMT	$5mn - 2m + 4$	20 (5%)	452 (15%)
EBA no IIMT	$4mn + 6m + n - 1$	29	485
EBA with IIMT	$7m + 1$	15 (48%)	113 (76%)
EQW no IIMT	$5mn + n - 2$	20	484
EQW with IIMT	$3mn + 2$	14 (30%)	290 (40%)
FRQ no IIMT	$6mn + 3m - 2n - 1$	25	611
FRQ with IIMT	$4mn + 3m - n + 3$	23 (8%)	429 (30%)
LEX no IIMT	$5mn + 3m + 2n - 2$	28	538
LEX with IIMT	$2mn + 5m + 1$	19 (68%)	273 (49%)
LED no IIMT	$7mn + 3m + 2n - 2$	36	730
LED with IIMT	$2mn + 8m + 1$	25 (31%)	321 (56%)
MAJ no IIMT	$5mn + m + 4n - 1$	29	519
MAJ with IIMT	$5mn - m + 3$	21 (28%)	467 (10%)
MCD no IIMT	$7mn - 4m + 2n - 1$	23	619
MCD with IIMT	$6mn - 6m + 2n + 2$	18 (22%)	494 (20%)
SAT no IIMT	$2mn + 3m + 2n - 1$	17	251
SAT with IIMT	$2mn + 3m + n + 1$	17 (0%)	247 (2%)
SAT+ no IIMT	$2m^*n + 3m^* + 2n - 1$	17	251
SAT+ with IIMT	$2m^*n + 3m^* + n + 1$	17 (0%)	247 (2%)
WADD no IIMT	$7mn + 3m + n - 2$	34	724
WADD with IIMT	$3mn + 3m + 2$	20 (41%)	338 (53%)

scenarios with their net saving of effort and the relative saving of effort displayed in parenthesis. The first scenario is with the minimum case of 2 alternatives and 2 attributes ($m = n = 2$) and the second one is with 6 alternatives and 16 attributes.[5] For this second scenario, the normative strategy WADD has 53% of relative saving of effort, so more than half of the effort can be saved when applying IIMT. For ADD, the relative saving of effort is 62%. For EBA the relative saving of effort is the largest. Users who apply EBA can save 76% of effort. In contrast, CONJ, SAT,

---

[5]This is the same number of alternatives and attributes which we will use in the experimental study in Chap. 8.

and SAT+ only achieve a very low relative saving of effort (2%) and even no saving for the small scenario with $m = n = 2$.

Three different effects of IIMT contribute to the good results for the saving of effort:

1. **Omission of EIP STORE**: Whenever the user communicates preferences to the system, for instance in form of evaluations by stars or negatively marked attribute levels, the system will store this information for the user. Costly sequences of EIP operations with STORE, and RETRIEVE can hence be replaced by applying the IIMT *SCORE* or *MARK*.

2. **Omission of EIP CALCULATE**: Based on the user's preferences, IIMT calculate sums, or products of attribute values or markings. Users do not have to do any calculations themselves and thus the EIP ADD, DIFFERENCE, and PRODUCT are replaced by the IIMT *CALCULATE*. In particular, compensatory strategies can profit from that effect because they usually require a lot of calculations.

3. **Omission of EIP ELIMINATE and COMPARE**: The combination of the IIMT *SCORE* plus *SORT*, *FILTER*, and CALCULATE automates long sequences of comparisons on attribute levels and eliminations of alternatives which are needed for non-compensatory strategies. Since sequences of such comparison and elimination steps are very long for a large number of attributes and alternatives, non-compensatory strategies such as LEX and EBA profit most from that fact. A remarkable fact is that the effort for EBA does no longer depend on the number of alternatives, n, once it is supported by IIMT. In other words, increasing the number of alternatives has no negative effects on its effort. This in turn, is the main reason for the great effort-reduction for EBA. The omission of ELIMINATE and COMPARE also helps to reduce effort of all strategies that use *SCORE* to evaluate alternatives, such as WADD and FRQ. The IIMT presents not only the total scores to the user but also highlights the maximum value. The user no longer has to compare the total scores but can easily choose the winning alternative.

Recall that for the analysis worst-case behavior is assumed. The formula for the effort for EBA in Table 7.3, for instance, assumes that the users have to compare the alternatives along all attributes until, finally, all alternatives except one are eliminated. Consequently, the number of iterations for certain sequences of operations depends on the particular scenario. There are several of such scenarios and the one with the most effort will be the worst-case. Hence, such sequences of operations are labeled with the phrase *worst-case scenario* in the pseudo-code notation (see for instance Fig. 7.5). For the WADD strategy, the effort is constantly $7mn + 3m + n - 2$ when no IIMT support is offered. However, in case of IIMT support, the amount of effort of $3mn + 3m + 2$ might even decrease further, since the term $3mn$ only holds for the worst-case. As pointed out above, $3mn$, stands for assigning attribute values for attribute levels with the IIMT *SCORE*. As soon as one attribute level is assigned a score, all other alternatives which have the same attribute level will be assigned the same score automatically. Assuming that in the scenario with six alternatives, four other products also have the same attribute level, instead of executing the three EIP/ECP (READ, EVALUATE, CLICK) six times, they only need to be executed twice. Thus, the effort-reduction for WADD when supported by IIMT is even larger in the average or best case. The same holds for other strategies which make use of SCORE, such as EQW and FRQ.

Finally, let us compare the effort of the normative WADD strategy which yields by definition 100% relative accuracy with other, simpler strategies. As soon as WADD is supported by IIMT we get an effort of 20 for the small scenario and an effort of 338 for the larger scenario (see Table 7.3). While WADD, and its pairwise variant, ADD, are among the most effortful strategies for the cases without IIMT support, in the case with IIMT support, they become less effortful than simpler strategies with less accuracy. For the small scenario, WADD is less effortful than ADD, COM, DIS, FRQ, LED, and MAJ and for the larger scenario WADD beats in addition MCD and DOM but no longer LED. If we now compare WADD with IIMT support with simpler strategies without IIMT support, WADD beats all strategies except CONJ, SAT, and SAT+. Consequently, when we support WADD with IIMT and leave other strategies unsupported, in larger scenarios we can achieve that the application of WADD is both more accurate and less effortful than all other strategies except CONJ, SAT, SAT+. Assuming that users are willing to spend a fixed amount of effort in the decision making process, higher accuracy might be reached if they are offered IIMT. Indeed, the IIMT might further improve the accuracy of decisions since they process preference information correctly and do exact calculations. Whilst human beings are prone to errors when they are computing, for example, the total utility of alternatives, IIMT present exact solutions.

In sum, in line with Chu and Spires (2000) and Todd and Benbasat (1994b), we argue that decision aids not only reduce the effort for applying strategies, but might also increase the accuracy of executing a strategy. Hence, due to the decision support offered by IDA, the cost-benefit relationship can shift in favor of the higher quality and more effortful strategies. Todd and Benbasat (1994b) assume that this leads to a shift to other strategies only if a strategy becomes dominant. In other words, the decision aids change the cost-benefit framework such that another, more accurate strategy dominates all others. Chu and Spires (2000) analyze this concept in more detail. Based on work by Payne et al. (1993) they consider the decision makers' preferences regarding the trade-off between effort and accuracy. Hence, they do not only assume a shift of strategies in case of changing dominance structures, but show how different iso-preference lines in this framework might lead to a shift of strategies. An example is drawn in Fig. 7.9 for the scenario with $n = 6$ and $m = 16$ assuming the same accuracy as in Fig. 7.1. We can see that all strategies with IIMT support are translated parallel, since effort decreases but accuracy is assumed to stay constant in this example. Furthermore, an example of a preference function for trading-off effort against accuracy is provided in the figure. We can see that in this example, WADD is the preferred strategy chosen in case of IIMT support, and EQW in case of no IIMT support. This is because, in our example – coming from the upper right corner in the picture – WADD in the IIMT and EQW in the non-IIMT case are the first strategies to touch the iso-preference lines. From our viewpoint it would be interesting to further analyze decision makers' preferences regarding the trade-off of effort and accuracy as well as the potential infuence of IDA and in particular IIMT.

Fig. 7.9 The extended
effort-accuracy framework. In
case of IIMT support, the
decision maker would choose
WADD, in case without EQW

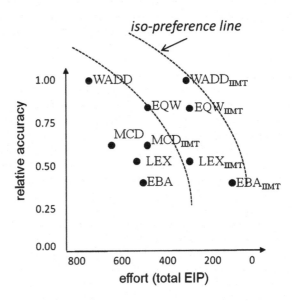

7.3 Conclusions

In summary, IIMT are able to reduce effort for all strategies. For most strategies, the relative saving of effort is larger, the larger the amount of information displayed. Furthermore, LEX and EBA, as well as compensatory strategies such as WADD and ADD can profit most from the IIMT support. In the case of IIMT support, WADD achieves lower effort than much less accurate strategies without IIMT support. Hence, offering IIMT for WADD might improve decision quality as it becomes the dominant strategy of choice, having low effort but yielding best quality.

Chapter 8
Quantitative Evaluation of INTACMATO

The main purpose of the empirical study which we present in this chapter is to evaluate the IIMT-prototype (INTACMATO). INTACMATO is evaluated across the criteria: perceived ease of use (effort), perceived usefulness, shopping enjoyment, confidence, and satisfaction. The results show that – compared to a control group of more than 30 students who just saw a product-comparison matrix without any IIMTs – the web store with INTACMATO was evaluated more positively across all five evaluation criteria.

Furthermore, we determined decision strategies which respondents used in the experiment with two different approaches: process tracing and observing final choices. A click stream analysis was used a process tracing method which records which IIMT respondents use in the experiment. Since we know which IIMTs should be applied in which sequence when a particular decision strategy is used, we are able to learn about people's decision behavior based on the click stream data. In addition to process tracing, we observe the final choices. For that purpose, in a separate part of the experiment, we determine people's preferences with pairwise-comparison-based preference measurement (PCPM, Scholz et al. 2010) and directly ask them for their aspiration levels. Consequently, we are able to determine decision strategies both through analyzing the decision process and final choices.

Both the clickstream and the final choice analyses show that EBA is applied most often. We also attempted to influence decision-making behavior by only presenting a subset of IIMT to one third of respondents in the group *few IIMT*. The presented IIMT only support a WADD and EQW strategy. Our conjecture cannot be supported with the analysis of final choices. From the perspective of final choices, only EBA is used significantly less often in the group *few IIMT*, but there is no increase in the use of WADD or EQW. When we do the same analysis with the clickstream data, however, we find that people apply significantly more often WADD and EQW. However, they do not necessarily apply these two strategies in their pure form but also mix them with other strategies. The latter would be a possible explanation why we cannot find the same effect with the analysis of final choices, which is unable to detect mixed behavior.

J. Pfeiffer, *Interactive Decision Aids in E-Commerce*, Contributions to Management Science, DOI 10.1007/978-3-7908-2769-9_8, © Springer-Verlag Berlin Heidelberg 2012

The click stream analysis reveals that the most used IIMTs are SCORE and FILTER, followed by MARK and PAIRWISE COMPARISON. The IIMTs SORT and REMOVE were applied least often.

The final empirical study of the dissertation addresses three aspects which we have captured hitherto:

1. The main goal of this study is to measure users' evaluation of the IIMT-prototype (INTACMATO).
2. We count how often each IIMT is used.
3. We observe which decision strategies respondents have used and analyze whether they apply only one or whether they mix several strategies.
4. We try to influence decision-making behavior by showing only part of INTAC-MATO. We conjecture that people will apply the strategies for which an IIMT is offered more often than strategies for which no decision support is offered.
5. Finally, we introduce a new measure of complexity.

We evaluate INTACMATO across the criteria: perceived ease of use (effort), perceived usefulness, shopping enjoyment, confidence, and satisfaction. Our results show that compared to a control group which just saw a product-comparison matrix without any IIMT, the webstore with the complete INTACMATO is evaluated more positively across all five evaluation criteria.

In addition to these five criteria, we once more let users evaluate the design criteria: adaptivity, consistency, control, effort, flexibility, and transparency. Again, the design of INTACMATO is evaluated very positively.

Second, we determine the frequency with which the different IIMT are used. The most often used IIMT are *FILTER* and $SCORE_{attributeLevel}$. The IIMT $SORT_{drag\&drop}$ and $REMOVE_{markings}$ are applied least often. Some of the IIMT which are newly proposed in the present work (such as $SCORE_{attributeLevel}$) are among the most often applied ones in our study.

Third, we aim to learn about people's decision-making behavior. Hence, we determine decision strategies which respondents used in the experiment with two different approaches: a clickstream analysis for tracing the decision process and an analysis of final choices. From our theoretical framework (see Chap. 7) we know which and in which sequence IIMT can be used to support the application of a particular decision strategy. Accordingly, we are able to learn about people's decision-making behavior based on an analysis of the applied IIMT during their decision process. In addition to process tracing, we analyze the final choices. For that purpose, as part of the experiment, we determine people's preferences with pairwise-comparison-based preference measurement (PCPM, Scholz et al. 2010) and directly ask them for their aspiration levels. Both the analysis with clickstreams and final choices reveal that EBA is used most often. Moreover, in about 80% of cases, people applied IIMT which support exactly one strategy. Thus, we assume that in these cases, people have used only one pure strategy, while in 20% of cases they use mixed strategies. In the mixed cases, the combination of EBA followed by a compensatory strategy occurs most often – supporting our results from the eye-tracking study which we presented in Chap. 3.

Our fourth point of interest is whether the offered IIMT influence the applied decision strategy. Specifically, we want to know whether showing people only such IIMT which support the two strategies $WADD$ and EQW ($SCORE_{attribute}$, $SCORE_{attributeLevel}$, $CALCULATE$) leads to an increased usage of these two compared to other strategies. We have chosen these two strategies, because $WADD$ is the normative utility maximizing strategy which yields highest accuracy (highest decision quality) and EQW is supported by the same IIMT as $WADD$, which makes it hard to analyze these two strategies separately. Our analysis of final choices shows that only EBA is significantly less often used when only IIMT for EQW and $WADD$ are shown. The usage of $WADD$ and EQW is apparently not influenced. An analysis of clickstream data further reveals that the $SCORE$ and $CALCULATE$ IIMT are used more frequently in the case where they are the only IIMT offered, in comparison with the cases where the complete IIMT-prototype is offered. Nevertheless, respondents apply the $SCORE_{attribute}$ only 6.3 times on average (for 16 different attributes) and the $SCORE_{attributeLevel}$ only 16.17 times (for on average 37 different attribute levels). This is not enough to fully support either a $WADD$ or an EQW strategy. We conjecture that people mix $WADD$ and EQW strategies with other ones in these cases.

Fifth, we control choice task complexity by introducing a new measure of the similarity of alternatives by computing how many attribute levels the alternatives have in common. We find that although respondents do not perceive this kind of complexity to influence the difficulty of the choice task, in choice tasks with low similarity, they need more time for the decision than in tasks with high similarity. However, similarity does not influence the decision strategy which explains the final choice.

All in all, INTACMATO is evaluated very positively and some of our newly proposed IIMT are applied frequently and should be considered in future webstores. Moreover, our analysis of clickstream behavior on IIMT supports findings on decision-making behavior from literature. Thus, learning from clickstream data on IIMT seems possible and might be a valuable tool for merchandisers for learning about costumer's decision-making behavior. Our attempts to influence decision-making behavior by restricting people to the usage of only certain IIMT and by manipulating complexity were of limited success.

8.1 Theory and Hypotheses

In order to test whether our prototype is evaluated positively by users, we measure satisfaction, perceived ease of use, perceived usefulness, and confidence which – according to Xiao and Benbasat (2007) – are important factors for assessing users' evaluation (see Sect. 5.2). Moreover, we choose to extend the four factors by a fifth one: shopping enjoyment. Enjoyment when using a system has been found to increase user's perceived usefulness and ease of use (Agarwal and Karahanna 2000; Moon and Kim 2001; Venkatesh 1999, 2000). Also in the field of e-commerce, it was found to have a positive influence on the intention to return to the shop (Koufaris 2002), on positive attitude and on online customer loyalty (Eighmey and McCord 1998; Hassanein and Head 2007; Jarvenpaa and Todd 1997; Lee et al. 2005; Monsuwé et al. 2004). Van der Heijden et al. (2003) found that enjoyment and perceived ease of use have almost as much influence on attitude as perceived usefulness.

The decision support process was designed to be very similar to the user's decision process. We have analyzed in detail decision strategies, have broken them down into common elements and created a modular system of IIMT which supports these different elements and allows users to easily switch between different decision strategies. Hence, we designed the system such that it yields a high fit between task and technology. This notion of *task-technology fit (TTF)* was defined by Goodhue and Thompson (1995) in their TTF model as the "degree to which a technology assists an individual in performing his or her portfolio of tasks" (p. 216). Several studies have shown that TTF is an important factor determining performance improvement of a system (Goodhue and Thompson 1995; Huang et al. 2006; Lim and Benbasat 2000; Todd and Benbasat 1993; Vessey 1991; Vessey and Galletta 1991). Higher performance is defined by a mix of improved efficiency, improved effectiveness, and/or higher quality (Goodhue and Thompson 1995). Klopping and McKinney (2004) showed that a combination of the technology acceptance model with TTF can also be extended to the field of online purchasing. They found that TTF has a significant positive effect on ease of use and perceived usefulness.

In the extended effort-accuracy framework (see Chap. 7), we found that for all decision strategies, users can save effort when applying INTACMATO compared to using a decision strategy without decision support. This finding, however, only affects users if they are aware of the net saving of effort. Chu and Spires (2003) found that this is indeed the case. Therefore, we assume that decision makers are aware of the improved ease of use when applying INTACMATO.

Furthermore, Song et al. (2007) showed that compensatory strategies are perceived by users as less effortful and more effective in cases where they are supported by a system. The authors argue that this is because some compensatory strategies, such as WADD, cannot be applied by users without without the help of a support system which would for example, allow them to take notes. Since INTACMATO automatizes the process of taking notes and supports compensatory strategies, this result should also hold for our system.

We break down our hypotheses in two parts (a and b) to distinguish that INTACMATO not only is supposed to perform better compared to a benchmark but also that it is supposed to perform better, the more IIMT are offered.

Hypothesis 1a: Compared to a product-comparison matrix with no further decision support, INTACMATO increases the perceived ease of use.

Hypothesis 1b: With the amount of IIMT offered, the perceived ease of use increases.

Hypothesis 2a: Compared to a product-comparison matrix with no further decision support, INTACMATO increases the perceived usefulness.

Hypothesis 2b: With the amount of IIMT offered, the perceived usefulness increases.

In terms of confidence, Gupta et al. (2009) provide empirical evidence that offering IIMT has a positive influence thereon. The authors demonstrate in two empirical studies that online consumers experience trust towards new or unfamiliar sellers in case they were supported by IIMT and/or comprehension tools which offer buying guides and glossaries for product-related terms. Furthermore, Ariely (2000) shows empirically that information control leads to higher confidence. Since one of our design criteria was control, we argue that the more IIMT are offered to consumers, the more control they should experience, and the more confident they should be. Finally, Swearingen and Sinha (2002) find that the more transparent recommender systems are, the more confident are the users. We think that this also holds for IIMT and therefore postulate that:

Hypothesis 3a: Compared to a product-comparison matrix with no further decision support, INTACMATO increases the user's confidence in the website.

Hypothesis 3b: With the amount of IIMT offered, the user's confidence increases.

Bechwati and Xia (2003) find that users' satisfaction is the higher, the more they perceive the effort-reduction provided by IDA. Thus, we think that the net saving of effort achieved by our prototype also increases satisfaction.

West et al. (1999) compare the customers' interaction with IDA (in their case an RA) with the interaction with traditional retailers and conclude that – like traditional retailers influence consumer's satisfaction in brick and mortar business – IDA influence satisfaction. In case of online shopping, possibilities of personalizing the web interface as well as controlling the interaction with the web interface should have a large effect on users' satisfaction. The design criteria according to which we have built the IIMT-prototype included control and flexibility. Consequently, we think that the more IIMT are offered, in other words, the more control and flexibility is provided by the system, the more satisfied the user should be.

Another important component of increasing satisfaction is perceived restrictiveness. Empirical evidence suggests that "decision makers' perceptions of the extent to which their preferred decision processes are constrained by the functionalities and support provided by a decision aid" influence their intention to use IDA (Wang and Benbasat 2009, p. 2). We think that perceived restrictiveness also influences users' satisfaction. Thus, the more IIMT are offered, the less should consumers feel restricted and the more satisfied they should be with the buying process.

Murray and Häubl (2008) argue that limiting the monotonous or menial tasks associated with making a purchase decision online can increase both satisfaction and enjoyment. Several studies in the context of RA have shown that IDA are capable of automating parts of the decision-making process that consumers prefer to avoid, because they are tedious or unpleasant (Häubl and Trifts 2000; Maes et al. 1999; West et al. 1999). This should also hold for INTACMATO, which supports effortful, tiring and error-prone tasks, such as calculating scores or filtering the product assortment. Further empirical evidence was provided that consumers enjoy the interaction with IDA (Urban and Hauser 2003). Based on their literature research, Murray and Häubl (2008) conclude that, "a well designed interactive consumer decision aid [IDA] not only improves the quality of consumer decision outcomes, but it also makes the process of deciding a more pleasurable one" (p. 14).

Hypothesis 4a: Compared to a product-comparison matrix with no further decision support, INTACMATO increases the user's shopping enjoyment.

Hypothesis 4b: With the amount of IIMT offered, the user's shopping enjoyment increases.

Hypothesis 5a: Compared to a product-comparison matrix with no further decision support, INTACMATO increases the user's satisfaction.

Hypothesis 5b: With the amount of IIMT offered, the user's satisfaction increases.

Besides testing whether INTACMATO is evaluated positively by users, we are interested in whether decision-making behavior can be influenced by offering only specific IIMT. Our idea is that users will favor those decision strategies which are supported by IIMT. This is because, IIMT will reduce the effort of the supported strategies and therefore facilitate their usage compared to strategies which are not supported (see the extended effort-accuracy framework in Chap. 7) .

This idea follows partly the notion of Wang and Benbasat (2009), who examine the influence of perceived strategy restrictiveness (see also Sect. 5.2.1). However, while they study whether greater perceived strategy restrictiveness negatively influences users' intention to use the IDA, we want to test whether we can influence the decision strategies people use. More specifically, we suppose that:

Hypothesis 6:   When only offering the IIMT $SCORE_{attributeLevel}$ and $SCORE_{attribute}$, the user will more often apply the two strategies that are supported by these two IIMT: WADD and EQW.

8.2   Operationalization

8.2.1   User Evaluation

For measuring the five constructs concerning respondents' evaluation (perceived ease of use, perceived usefulness, satisfaction, confidence, and enjoyment), we developed a questionnaire based on well-tested questions from the literature (Kamis and Davern 2005; Koufaris 2002; Pereira 2000; Venkatesh and Davis 1996; Wang and Benbasat 2009). All questions had to be answered on a 5-point Likert scale (1: I strongly disagree to 5: I strongly agree). Cronbach's alpha showed adequate reliability of the items with levels above 0.7 for all constructs as recommended by Nunnally (1967) and Kline (2000). Only for confidence, was α slightly below 0.7 (0.686). This might be because for confidence we used new items, since items from literature only fitted to RA and not to IIMT. Furthermore, Cronbach's alpha is sensitive to the number of items per scale with fewer items yielding a lower Cronbach's alpha (Cortina 1993). Since we used only three items to measure confidence, we accept a value which is slightly below the suggested threshold of 0.7. Hence, all items were taken to test the hypotheses. In the appendix in Tables C.4 and C.5, you can find a detailed list of items, corresponding constructs and their literature sources.

Perceived ease of use is the extent to which the IDA will be free of effort (Davis 1989). In addition to measuring the perceived effort with the questions in the questionnaire, we measured the time which each respondent took for each choice. Thus, we measured the perceived effort (questionnaire) and the objective time.

8.2.2 Design Criteria

Although two qualitative pre-studies evaluated if INTACMATO met the design criteria (see Sect. 6.4), we allowed the users to evaluate the prototype design once again. Because measuring the design criteria was not a focus and we did not want to impose too many questions on the subjects, we only took few (two to three) items to measure each design criteria. Hence, the Cronbach's alpha was relatively low for two of them: transparency ($\alpha = 0.501$) and consistency ($\alpha = 0.564$); but acceptable for the other two: perceived control ($\alpha = 0.681$) and flexibility ($\alpha = 0.774$). We also asked respondents to rate adaptivity. Since our design of the prototype neglects this design criteria, we assumed that respondents would not rate INTACMATO to be more adaptive than the website without any IIMT. The sixth design criteria, low effort, is already covered by our construct *perceived ease of use* in the user evaluation (see above).

In the control group, respondents did not see any IIMT. Hence, we formulated the questions so as to be as general as possible, asking them to evaluate the complete website across the design criteria and not single IIMT. All questions asked are listed in Tables C.6 and C.7 in the appendix.

8.2.3 Determination of Strategies

We are interested in which decision strategies respondents used. Thus, we measured all parameters for each respondent which were necessary to determine the applied strategy. In Chap. 3 and Chap. 4, we introduced CBC, ACA and PCPM as two methods for measuring attribute values and attribute weights (Scholz et al. 2010). We decided for the newer method, PCPM, since it was available for free. In contrast to the two other studies (see Chap. 3 and Chap. 4), in the present study, we were unable to access the Sawtooth Software to use CBC or ACA.

In addition to attribute values and attribute weights, we need consumers' aspiration levels. There are two ways of determining aspiration levels: self-reports and comparative models which estimate aspiration levels (Garbarino and Edell 1997; Gilbride and Allenby 2004, 2006; Kohli et al. 2004; Yee et al. 2007). In the latter approach, researchers determine aspiration levels for each respondent under the assumption that a particular strategy (e.g., EBA) has been used. Until now, none of these two methods has been proved to be superior to the other and there seems to be incongruence between self-reported and estimated aspiration levels (Yee et al. 2007).

Likewise to our approach in Chap. 4, we decided for a self-report because we do not assume respondents to apply the same strategy for all choices, which would make the estimation of aspiration level with comparative models very difficult. For each attribute, we asked respondents directly whether they would exclude a product only because of a particular attribute level. An example question for the TV-functionality of a cell phone is: "Would you exclude a cell phone from your consideration set only because it has or does not have a TV-functionality?".

8.2.4 Measuring the Process with Clickstream Analysis

In order to study which IIMT respondents used in which sequence, we track each respondent's clickstream when applying INTACMATO. This data can be used for two kinds of analysis. First, we can count how often each IIMT is used. Second, we can determine which decision strategies best fit to the observed clicking behavior. This analysis is based on the ideas described in Sect. 7.2, where we formalize in detail in which sequence which IIMT support which strategies (see also the pseudo-code notation in the appendix, Sect. A). This analysis will also provide insights into respondents' switching behavior. We can determine whether several strategies have been used in sequence and whether there are patterns, such as a switch from non-compensatory strategies to compensatory ones.

8.2.5 Complexity

Motivated by our findings on the strong influence of context-based complexity on decision-making behavior (see Chaps. 3 and 4), we wanted to control for complexity. We decided to show each respondent three choice tasks of different complexity: easy, medium, and hard. Two problems arise in this study which make it impossible to use any of the existing context-based measurements. First, like in the study on information acquisition in Chap. 3 and in contrast to the study in Chap. 4, users' preferences were not known before we conducted the study. The context-based measures which we presented in Chap. 2, such as attractiveness differences or the correlation of attribute vectors for determining trade-offs, however, rely on preference information such as value functions or attribute weights (see Sect. 2.4.1.2). Thus, we cannot generate choice tasks of particular context-based complexity. Second, we wanted some measurement which can be kept constant even if alternatives are eliminated during the choice process, because this is a disadvantage of the current measures of complexity. The range of attribute levels or attractiveness differences, for instance, most probably change their value when an alternative is eliminated. In consequence, we decided to test a new measurement for which no preference information is needed and which stays constant even when alternatives are eliminated. Since to the best of our knowledge no such measure yet exists, we tried a simple measure of complexity: we measured how many attribute levels alternatives have in common. Our idea was that the more attribute levels alternatives have in common, the easier the choice tasks should be. This is because of two reasons. First, fewer trade-offs can occur and, second, the amount of information which must be compared decreases. Thus, the new measure of complexity is a combination of context-based and task-based complexity, as this influences the amount of trade-offs as well as the number of attributes which must be compared.

However, note, that on the other hand, the more attribute levels alternatives have in common, the lower is the attractiveness difference. Thus, the more similar the alternatives are, the more complex the choice should be. Nevertheless, we think that the effect of fewer trade-offs and less information will be stronger than the effect of low attractiveness difference and argue that the more attribute levels alternatives have in common, the less complex the choice task is.

Mathematically, counting the number of different attribute levels for a pair of alternatives, alt_k and alt_l, is the same as computing their Hamming distance. The Hamming distance counts the number of positions where $alt_k = (a_{1k}, ..., a_{mk})$ and $alt_l = (a_{1l}, ..., a_{ml})$ differ. Table 8.1 provides an example of three alternatives, where the Hamming distance between all pairs of alternatives (PHD) is two.

In sum, for our stimuli with six alternatives and sixteen attributes, we created the following three complexity groups:

1. Low complexity: PHD of 3–5
2. Medium complexity: PHD of 8–9
3. High complexity: PHD of 11–12

We programmed an algorithm which generated random choice tasks for one of the three given complexity groups. In total, we generated two choice tasks per

Table 8.1 Example of a pairwise Hamming distance of two

Attribute	Alternative 1	Alternative 2	Alternative 3
Price	€30	€30	€40
Size	20 mm	25 mm	20 mm
Color	Yellow	Black	Black

complexity group and assigned them to different experimental sessions, with the purpose of preventing influences stemming from particular choice tasks.

8.3 Experiment

8.3.1 Participants

In total, 115 respondents (72 females, 43 males) from the Johannes Gutenberg-University Mainz participated in the experiment. The students' participation was part of a regular tutorial class and every participant took part in one of several drawings for a €20 voucher for a webstore. The experiments took place in several tutorial sessions over two weeks. On average, the experiment took 33.17 min ($SD = 7.86$).

Students were moderately motivated ($M = 3.2, SD = 0.98$ at a 5-point Likert scale [1: I strongly disagree, 5: I strongly agree]), found the experiment interesting ($M = 3.5, SD = 0.95$) and had understood the study ($M = 4.2, SD = 0.79$). Most of the students (80.5%) reported to use the Internet several times per day, 18.6% reported to use it once per day and 0.9% once per week. Besides the frequent usage of the Internet, respondents said to have experience with online shopping: 43.4% of the respondents indicated to have made more than 10 online purchases in their life and only 11.5% said never to have bought any product online.

The students were moderately interested in cell phones ($M = 3.33$), with quite high differences among students ($SD = 1.12$). The question whether they would judge themselves to be experts in the field of cell phones reached a mean value of 2.33 ($SD = 0.97$). We not only asked them for their self-assessment, but also asked them several question about cell phones to be able to judge their product knowledge from a more objective perspective. On average they said to know 17.29 of the 29 listed cell phone functions with high differences among students ($SD = 4.54$). Also they answered on average 6.35 out of 9 questions on cell phones correctly ($SD = 1.29$). In sum, the respondents' product knowledge was average to high, with a wide spread.

8.3.2 Design and Procedure

Each experimental session consisted of three parts and took between 30 and 40 min. In the first part, respondents had to answer some questions, in the second part, they had to make three choices of cell phones in the webstore, and in the third part, they had to answer some questions again (see Fig. 8.1 for an overview of the experimental design).

At the beginning of the experiment, participants were told to imagine that they had been a loyal customer of a cell phone provider which offered them to take three cell phones for free. They would encounter a webstore where they had to make

Fig. 8.1 Experimental design

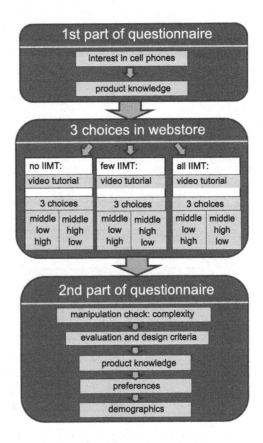

these three choice decisions. Each choice task showed six different cell phones, from which they each had to choose one.

Participants were randomly assigned to one of three groups: *all IIMT*, *few IIMT*, and *no IIMT*. Participants were not aware that there were different groups. At the beginning of the experiment, all participants were asked about their interest in cell phones and knowledge of them. In the second part, respondents were directed to one of the three versions of the webstore. The group *all IIMT* saw the complete INTACMATO (see Chap. 6 for more details and Fig. 6.8). The group *few IIMT* only saw the IIMT $SCORE_{attribute}$, $SCORE_{attributeLevel}$, and $CALCULATE_{weighted}$ (see Fig. 8.2). The third group just saw the product-comparison matrix without any further IIMT (see Fig. 8.3). Thus, the third group's only interaction with the webstore was clicking on the shopping cart for choosing one of the six cell phones.

Before respondents started with the choice task, they watched an introductory, group-specific video which in detail explained the functionality of the web page and each IIMT. This approach follows Todd and Benbasat (1994b), who also provided a tutorial to explain the mechanics of each of their IDA commands in order to familiarize subjects with the way the commands functioned.

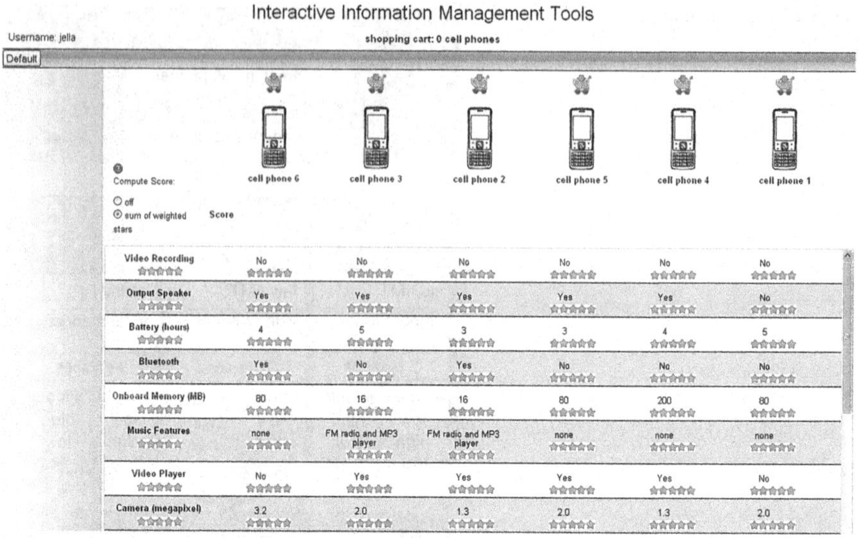

Interactive Information Management Tools

Username: jella   shopping cart: 0 cell phones

Default

	cell phone 6	cell phone 3	cell phone 2	cell phone 5	cell phone 4	cell phone 1
Video Recording ☆☆☆☆☆	No ☆☆☆☆☆	No ☆☆☆☆☆	No ☆☆☆☆☆	No ☆☆☆☆☆	No ☆☆☆☆☆	No ☆☆☆☆☆
Output Speaker ☆☆☆☆☆	Yes ☆☆☆☆☆	Yes ☆☆☆☆☆	Yes ☆☆☆☆☆	Yes ☆☆☆☆☆	Yes ☆☆☆☆☆	No ☆☆☆☆☆
Battery (hours) ☆☆☆☆☆	4 ☆☆☆☆☆	5 ☆☆☆☆☆	3 ☆☆☆☆☆	3 ☆☆☆☆☆	4 ☆☆☆☆☆	5 ☆☆☆☆☆
Bluetooth ☆☆☆☆☆	Yes ☆☆☆☆☆	No ☆☆☆☆☆	Yes ☆☆☆☆☆	No ☆☆☆☆☆	No ☆☆☆☆☆	No ☆☆☆☆☆
Onboard Memory (MB) ☆☆☆☆☆	80 ☆☆☆☆☆	16 ☆☆☆☆☆	16 ☆☆☆☆☆	80 ☆☆☆☆☆	200 ☆☆☆☆☆	80 ☆☆☆☆☆
Music Features ☆☆☆☆☆	none ☆☆☆☆☆	FM radio and MP3 player ☆☆☆☆☆	FM radio and MP3 player ☆☆☆☆☆	none ☆☆☆☆☆	none ☆☆☆☆☆	none ☆☆☆☆☆
Video Player ☆☆☆☆☆	No ☆☆☆☆☆	Yes ☆☆☆☆☆	Yes ☆☆☆☆☆	Yes ☆☆☆☆☆	Yes ☆☆☆☆☆	No ☆☆☆☆☆
Camera (megapixel) ☆☆☆☆☆	3.2 ☆☆☆☆☆	2.0 ☆☆☆☆☆	1.3 ☆☆☆☆☆	2.0 ☆☆☆☆☆	1.3 ☆☆☆☆☆	2.0 ☆☆☆☆☆

Fig. 8.2 Screenshot of webstores for group *few IIMT*

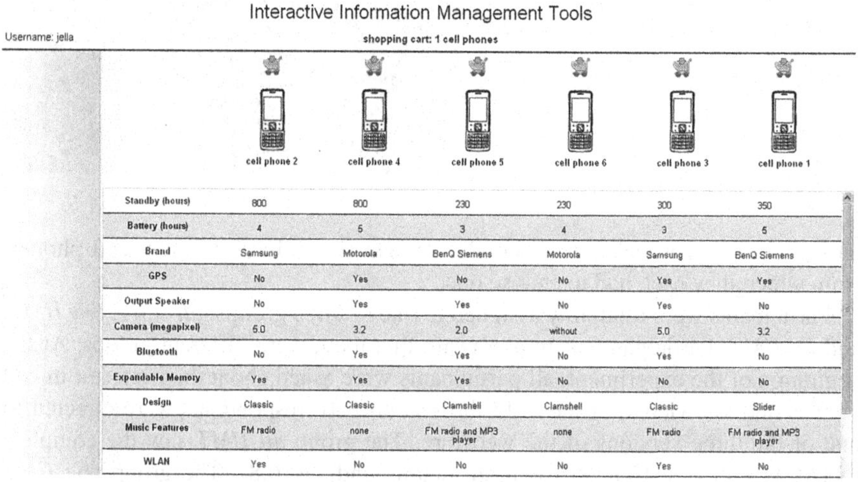

Interactive Information Management Tools

Username: jella   shopping cart: 1 cell phones

	cell phone 2	cell phone 4	cell phone 5	cell phone 6	cell phone 3	cell phone 1
Standby (hours)	800	800	230	230	300	350
Battery (hours)	4	5	3	4	3	5
Brand	Samsung	Motorola	BenQ Siemens	Motorola	Samsung	BenQ Siemens
GPS	No	Yes	No	No	Yes	Yes
Output Speaker	No	Yes	Yes	No	Yes	No
Camera (megapixel)	5.0	3.2	2.0	without	5.0	3.2
Bluetooth	No	Yes	Yes	No	Yes	No
Expandable Memory	Yes	Yes	Yes	No	No	No
Design	Classic	Classic	Clamshell	Clamshell	Classic	Slider
Music Features	FM radio	none	FM radio and MP3 player	none	FM radio	FM radio and MP3 player
WLAN	Yes	No	No	No	Yes	No

Fig. 8.3 Screenshot of webstore for group *no IIMT*

After having watched the video, respondents were confronted with the three choice tasks. They were able to choose between an English and a German version of the website. The choice tasks consisted of six cell phones each, described by sixteen attributes. These attributes were taken from the study by Scholz et al. (2010) and slightly adapted to match the technical details of up to date cell phones. Scholz et al. (2010) used think aloud and repertory grid techniques to identify these basic distinctive attributes (Kelly 1955), the laddering technique to extract the relevant attribute levels (Reynolds and Gutman 1988), and the dual questioning technique to identify the salient product attributes (Myers and Alpert 1968). Attributes and products were shown in random order to avoid any sequence effects. All participants first saw a choice task of medium complexity, then they were randomly assigned to see the hard (easy), and finally the easy (hard) version. The choice tasks were the same for each group. However, we changed the set of the three choice tasks three times during the two weeks of experiments in order to prevent influences stemming from particular choice tasks. The complete clicking behavior of respondents on the shopping carts and IIMT was tracked and stored in a database. As soon as respondents had finished the three choices, they were directed to the second part of the questionnaire.

In the second part of the questionnaire, we conducted manipulation checks concerning the perceived complexity of choice tasks and asked respondents for their evaluation. Then, some further questions regarding product knowledge followed. Afterwards, we measured respondents utility functions with the PCPM techniques (see 3.2 and Scholz et al. 2010) and asked for the participants' aspiration levels. The experiment ended with some final questions about respondents' demographics and motivation.

8.3.3   Data Cleansing

Due to different reasons, some respondents had to be either excluded completely or at least for parts from the analysis.

1. Fully excluded: we excluded all respondents who were not motivated to do the study. Hence, we excluded respondents who took too little time for the study (below 1.5 times of the interquartile range Tuckey 1995) and who indicated that they had disliked the study. This lead to the exclusion of one respondent.
2. Fully excluded: one further respondent was excluded who had reported not to have understood the study at all.
3. Excluded from manipulation check and tracking analysis: there was a system error which in a few cases led to a situation where respondents were not redirected to the second part of the questionnaire exactly after three choice tasks. In six cases, respondents only did two choice tasks and we could thus only analyze their first two choices. For the seven respondents who made more than five decisions, we did not evaluate the manipulation check concerning the choice task complexity because after having made so many choices it was too hard for these respondents to remember how difficult only the first three choices had been. Furthermore, we could not analyze tracking data for these respondents because we were unsure whether they had made their choices consciously or had just pressed the shopping cart button accidentally several times. In addition, for five respondents we could not compute the times for either the second or third choice task which, however, only affects the (objective) manipulation check.

4. Excluded from tracking analysis: because of a system error, for nine respondents we could not match the questionnaire to the tracking data. We were therefore unable to analyze the tracking behavior for these nine respondents.

8.3.4 Empirical Results

8.3.4.1 Manipulation Check: Complexity

We wanted to know whether respondents experienced the more complex choice tasks to be more difficult. Therefore, after they had visited the webstore, they had to report the perceived difficulty for each of the three choices. In addition to that, we compared the times, respondents needed for each of the choice tasks as objective measure for the complexity. We expect respondents to take longer for the more complex choice task. Since the first choice task, which was of medium complexity, was only for training purposes, we compared only the second and third choice tasks. Hence we compared only the choice tasks with low and high complexity against each other.

On average, respondents took 86.36 s to complete the easy choice task ($SE = 6.39$) and 98.3 s to complete the difficult choice task ($SE = 7.55$). A paired t-test shows that this difference is significant ($t(97) = -1.968$, $p < .05$, one-tailed).

Next, we tested the perceived complexity. A paired t-test shows that respondents did not perceive choice tasks with higher complexity as more difficult than choice tasks with lower complexity ($M(high) = 2.9$, $M(low) = 3.0$, $t(98) = .791$, $p > .05$)).

Although respondents took more time for their choices for the more complex task, they did not perceive these tasks to be more difficult. There are three possible explanations for that. First, our manipulation check may not have measured perceived complexity. This is unlikely, as respondents were asked to rate how difficult they had found each choice task immediately after they had made all three choices. Consequently, their experience was still fresh and the phrasing of our question is very close to the definition of complexity, and should be easy to understand. Second, it might be the case that the pairwise Hamming distance does not measure complexity. However, as respondents took more time for the more complex tasks, there obviously is an effect. Third, it might be that respondents are unaware of the complexity but that complexity still influences their decision. However, an analysis of the applied strategies in case of low vs. high complexity choice tasks does not show any significant difference. Thus, people do not apply different strategies depending on the complexity. We therefore conclude that people need more time for acquiring information when there is more different information to process (in case of high complexity), but taking longer for acquiring information does not affect their decision-making behavior. To sum up, our newly proposed PHD does not influence the decision strategy applied and we may ask whether PHD is a valid measure for the complexity of choice tasks.

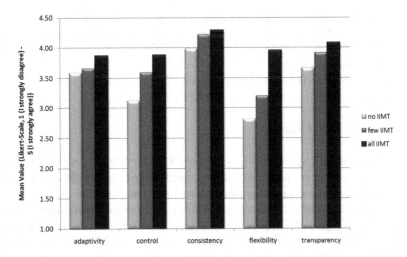

Fig. 8.4 The more IIMT respondents saw, the more positive they evaluated the design criteria

8.3.4.2 Design Criteria

We wanted to know whether respondents thought that the design criteria were met. The results were very positive and the more IIMT were shown, the more positively the design criteria were evaluated. In the group *all IIMT*, on the five point-Likert scale, consistency was rated highest ($M = 4.29, SD = 0.53$), followed by transparency ($M = 4.08, SD = 0.56$), flexibility ($M = 3.95, SD = 0.72$), control ($M = 3.88, SD = 0.77$), and adaptivity ($M = 3.86, SD = 0.81$). Figure 8.4 depicts the mean values for all design criteria for each of the three groups (*all, few,* and *no IIMT*).

For testing the differences we used an analysis of variance (ANOVA), because a Levene's test for all dependent variables was not significant and indicates that we can assume equal variances for all groups (Field 2009). Furthermore, due to the central limit theorem with more than 30 respondents per group we can assume a normal distribution (N(*no IIMT*) $= 40$, N(*few IIMT*) $= 34$, N(*all IIMT*) $= 39$) (Hays 1973). The ANOVA shows that there are significant differences ($p < 0.05$) between flexibility ($F(2, 110) = 17.77$), control ($F(2, 110) = 19.73$), and transparency ($F(2, 110) = 3.94$). There was no significant difference for adaptivity ($F(2, 110) = 1.11$) and consistency ($F(2, 110) = 2.43$).

The difference for flexibility and control can be explained because offering more IIMT should yield more flexibility (and less perceived strategy restrictiveness) in applying the preferred strategy and more control due to more possibilities to interact with the webstore. Offering many IIMT can lead to a decreased transparency in case online consumers do not understand functionalities. However, the result is the opposite: the design of the IIMT seems to be transparent and easy to understand. A more or less equal level of consistency and adaptivity is no surprise. First, we tried to design all three groups so as to be as consistent as possible, and there is no reason why more IIMT should be more consistent than no or less IIMT. Furthermore, we did not intend to design INTACMATO to be adaptive yet and thus did not expect to encounter a difference here.

In sum, INTACMATO is evaluated positively across the design criteria.

8.3.4.3 Evaluation Criteria

In this section, we test hypotheses 1–5 (see Sect. 8.1). An ANOVA only tells whether all three groups differ from another, but not which group exactly differs from which other one. Since for testing our hypotheses, we like to be as precise as possible, we calculate planned contrasts to test whether IIMT are at all evaluated higher against the control group (*few/all IIMT* vs. *no IIMT* (part a of the hypotheses)) and whether increasing the number of IIMT yields a better evaluation (*few IIMT* vs. *all IIMT* (part b of the hypotheses)).

Finally, we report effect sizes for both the ANOVA and the planned contrasts. For the ANOVA, we report $\hat{f}$ which can be computed with the "omega2" procedure in STATA/SE 10. For the planned contrasts, we report Pearson's correlation coefficient r as effect size (for more details, see Sect. 5.2.2.3). Cohen (1988) reports the following interpretations for $\hat{f}$ and r:

- Small effect: $r = 0.1$, $\hat{f} <= 0.1$
- Medium effect: $r = 0.3$, $0.1 <= \hat{f} < 0.4$
- Large effect: $r = 0.5$, $0.4 < \hat{f}$

Hypothesis 1 states that INTACMATO increases perceived ease of use of the webstore. As expected, there is a significant effect across groups ($F(2, 110) = 15.64, p < 0.01, \hat{f} = 0.48$). In support of hypothesis 1a, planned contrasts reveal that offering IIMT significantly increased the perceived ease of use compared to offering *no IIMT* at all (control group), $t(110) = 4.93, p < 0.01$ (one tailed), $r = 0.43$. In support of hypothesis 1b, we find that having more IIMT (*all IIMT*) significantly increased perceived ease of use compared to having only *few IIMT*, $t(110) = -2.43, p < 0.01$ (one tailed), $r = 0.23$. Thus, hypothesis 1 is fully supported with a medium to large effect for the difference between *no* and *few/all IIMT*. Figure 8.5 and Table 8.2 reveal more details on the mean values for the different groups.

Comparing the perceived ease of use with the actual time which the respondents took for each choice reveals an interesting phenomenon. In contrast to their perceived (subjective) ease of use, measuring the ease of use with the objective measure (time) shows that in total respondents took longest in the groups with *few IIMT*, followed by the group *all IIMT* and *no IIMT*.[1] Times for all three groups differ

---

[1] We computed the average times for the second and the third choice tasks.

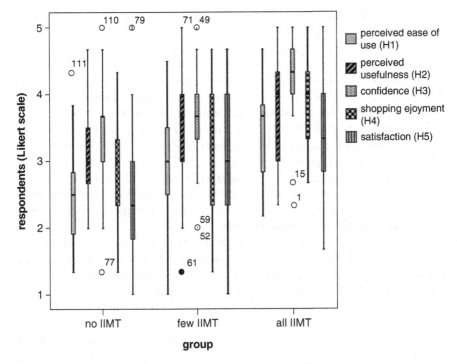

Fig. 8.5 Main Result: the more IIMT, the better the users' evaluation

Table 8.2 Mean values (and standard deviations) for our evaluation criteria

	No IIMT	*Few IIMT*	*All IIMT*
Ease of use (H1)	2.48 (0.71)	2.97 (0.78)	3.39 (0.68)
Usefulness (H2)	3.03 (0.67)	3.57 (0.86)	3.72 (0.76)
Confidence (H3)	3.41 (0.73)	3.74 (0.71)	4.25 (0.58)
Shopping enjoyment (H4)	2.82 (0.67)	3.39 (0.89)	3.79 (0.63)
Satisfaction (H5)	2.46 (0.9)	3.00 (1.02)	3.35 (0.86)

significantly ($F-Welch(2, 24.43) = 29.8, p < 0.01$). The planned contrasts show that the time spent on the choice tasks with *no IIMT* is significantly lower than the time spent on choice tasks with IIMT support, $t(78.97) = 7.02, p < 0.01, r = 0.62$. Furthermore, respondents spent significantly more time on the choice task with *few IIMT* than on the choice tasks with *all IIMT*, $t(50.69) = 2, p < 0.01, r = 0.27$. Thus, although with more IIMT offered, people perceive less effort, they take more time for making their choices. However, when respondents are restricted to use only IIMT which support the more accurate strategies, as is the case in the group *few IIMT*, they take longest. We will analyze this effect of perceived restrictiveness in detail later on.

Significant differences are also found for hypothesis 2 in which we consider perceived usefulness ($F(2, 110) = 8.72, p < 0.05, \hat{f} = 0.37$). Planned contrasts reveal that offering IIMT significantly increases the perceived usefulness compared to offering no IIMT at all, $t(110) = 4.06, p < 0.01$ (one tailed), $r = 0.36$, but that having more IIMT did not significantly increase perceived usefulness compared to having only few IIMT, $t(110) = -.83, p > 0.05$ (one tailed). Thus, hypothesis 2a can be supported and has a medium effect, while hypothesis 2b is not supported.

Hypothesis 3 states that INTACMATO increases user's confidence in the web-store. The ANOVA supports this hypothesis ($F(2, 110) = 15.37, p < 0.05, \hat{f} = 0.50$), as well as both planned contrasts (*no IIMT* vs. *few/all IIMT*: $t(110) = 4.38, p < 0.01$ (one-tailed), $r = 0.39$; *few IIMT* vs. *all IIMT*: $t(110) = -2.32, p < 0.01$ (one-tailed), $r = 0.29$). Consequently, hypothesis 3a (comparison with control group) as well as hypothesis 3b (the more IIMT, the higher the user's confidence) can be supported and have a medium effect.

Hypothesis 4 considers shopping enjoyment and we find significant differences ($F(2, 110) = 17.49, p < 0.05, \hat{f} = 0.54$) with the ANOVA and with the planned contrasts (*no IIMT* vs. *few/all IIMT*: $t(110) = 5.5, p < 0.01$ (one-tailed) $r = 0.46$; *few IIMT* vs. *all IIMT*: $t(110) = -2.3, p < 0.05$ (one-tailed), $r = 0.21$). Thus, also both parts 4a and 4b of hypothesis 4 are fully supported with a large effect for the comparison of *no* vs. *few/all IIMT*.

Finally, we test user's satisfaction (hypothesis 5). Again, we find significant differences ($F(2, 110) = 9.21, p < 0.05, \hat{f} = 0.38$). However, here for the planned contrasts we only find significant differences for the groups *no* vs. *few IIMT*, $t(110) = 3.93, p < 0.01, r = 0.35$, and no significant difference but only the supposed trend for *few* vs. *all IIMT*, $t(110) = -1.56, p < 0.1, r = 0.15$. Thus, we can support hypothesis 5a with a medium effect for the difference between *no* and *few/all IIMT* and we cannot support hypothesis 5b.

In sum, all five hypotheses are at least partly supported with mostly medium effect sizes. The largest effect is observed for ease of use, confidence and shopping enjoyment. Furthermore, for ease of use, the hypothesis is only supported when we measure the perceived ease of use and not when we measure the ease of use by the time each respondent took for making a choice. Table 8.3 summarizes the results.

Table 8.3 Results of hypotheses tests (supported vs. not supported) with effect sizes in parenthesis

	All groups	No vs. Few/all IIMT	Few vs. All IIMT
Ease of use (H1)	Supp. ($\hat{f} = 0.48$)	Supp. ($r = 0.43$)	Supp. ($r = 0.23$)
Usefulness (H2)	Supp. ($\hat{f} = 0.37$)	Supp. ($r = 0.36$)	Not supp.
Confidence (H3)	Supp. ($\hat{f} = 0.50$)	Supp. ($r = 0.39$)	Supp. ($r = 0.29$)
Shopp. enjoyment (H4)	Supp. ($\hat{f} = 0.54$)	Supp. ($r = 0.46$)	Supp. ($r = 0.21$)
Satisfaction (H5)	Supp. ($\hat{f} = 0.38$)	Supp. ($r = 0.35$)	Not supp.

8.3.4.4   Clickstream Analysis: Popularity of IIMT

In this section, we analyze the clicking behavior of respondents when using INTAC-MATO. For each respondent, we tracked each click on an IIMT or the shopping cart. The clicks on the shopping cart tell us which alternative the respondents have finally chosen. Because in the group *no IIMT* respondents were not offered any IIMT, tracking data on IIMT is available only for the group with *few* and *all IIMT*.

In the first part of the clickstream analysis, we analyze which IIMT respondents used in order to draw conclusions on how popular each IIMT is. We analyze the data from two perspectives:

1. Total number of clicks per IIMT: the number of clicks on each IIMT for each choice task.
2. IIMT which were used at least once: since some IIMT, such as $SCORE_{attributeLevel}$ must be used many times in order to support a strategy (e.g., WADD or EQW) while others, such as *FILTER* might be used only once for supporting a complete strategy (e.g., EBA), the total number of clicks must be interpreted with caution. It is biased towards IIMT which have to be used many times for supporting a strategy. Thus, it is more probable that $SCORE_{attributeLevel}$ gets a large number of clicks than *FILTER*, for instance. Therefore, we count the number of IIMT which are clicked at least once per choice task and per respondent.

In the second part of the clickstream analysis, we infer the applied strategies. This analysis is described in the next section, called strategy manipulation.

First of all, we count the total number of clicks for all three choice tasks. The SD are very high because of some respondents who made very many clicks (see the maximum values for clicks, Max). On average, respondents in the group *few IIMT* made 38.55 clicks ($SD = 20.53$, $Max = 88$) in the first choice task, in the second choice task 21.93 ($SD = 19.05$, $Max = 63$) and in the third choice task 23.31 ($SD = 18.28$, $Max = 68$). In the group *all IIMT*, we count 23.87 ($SD = 20.94$, $Max = 78$) clicks for the first, 8.95 ($SD = 8.5$, $Max = 36$) for the second, and 11.03 ($SD = 13.76$) for the last choice task.

As we had expected, in the first choice task, respondents used much more IIMT than in the following two choice tasks. That is because the first choice task has to be seen as training period. Furthermore, we were not surprised that respondents in the group *few IIMT* had on average more clicks, because they were restricted to use the *SCORE* IIMT, which has to be applied very often in order to support either the WADD or the EQW strategy.[2] In contrast, in the group *all IIMT*, respondents might not have used the *SCORE* IIMT at all but, for instance, *FILTER* and *SORT*, which support simple decision strategies like EBA and LEX with very few clicks.

In order to carry out more analysis, we had to clean the tracking data. This was because respondents could undo some of their actions during their choice process.

---

[2]As we have seen when testing hypothesis 1, they also took more time.

Thus, by cleaning the data we made sure to get a final data set with clicking behavior that was purposeful and really had an impact on the product-comparison matrix. For instance, the webstore showed an *undo* button which reset the whole matrix. In case, respondents clicked on this button, all IIMT they had used before had to be deleted from the tracking data because respondents had decided to follow a different decision strategy and start again. Therefore, this data is useless for determining both the most popular IIMT and for matching clicking behavior to decision strategies. Further steps of the cleaning process were to remove all clicking behavior on *FILTER, SORT, SCORE* or *MARK* which was afterwards reset or changed. Some respondents, for instance, clicked several times on $SCORE_{attributeLevel}$ for the same attribute level because they were rethinking their evaluation of a level. The same happened for already set *FILTER*, which were then again changed during the process, etc. In these cases, we decided to always only evaluate the latest click.

After the data cleansing, in the group *few IIMT*, respondents had clicked on all available IIMT on average 30.14 ($SD = 15.59$) in the first choice task, in the second choice task 18.34 ($SD = 16.34$), and in the third choice task 19.76 ($SD = 15.93$). For the group *all IIMT*, we have 10.65 ($SD = 13.45$) for the first, 6.31 ($SD = 7.79$) and in the third choice task 6.29 ($SD = 8.34$). As we had expected, the number of clicks for the first group decreases substantially after data cleansing. With a repeated-measure design we test whether there are still differences between the groups. Mauchly's test indicates that the assumption of sphericity is violated both for the group *few IIMT* ($\chi^2(2) = 11, p < 0.05$) and *all IIMT* ($\chi^2(2) = 10, p < 0.05$). Therefore we correct statistics by using the conservative Greenhouse-Geisser estimates of sphericity. The results show that there is a significant difference both for *few IIMT* ($F(1.5, 42) = 13.15, p < 0.05$) and for *all IIMT* ($F(1.6, 59.6) = 3.48, p < 0.05$) with a large effect size for the difference between the first and the second choice task for the group *few IIMT* ($r = 0.6$) and a medium effect for *all IIMT* ($r = 0.32$) and no significant differences between the second and third choice task. Thus, even after the data cleansing, we observe a higher number of clicks in the first compared to the other two choice tasks. Furthermore, we still observe that respondents clicked more often on IIMT in case only few IIMT were available.

We now analyze in more detail the clicking behavior of the group *all IIMT*.

To start with, we wanted to know whether there were respondents who did not use any IIMT at all. In the first choice task, all respondents used at least one IIMT. Hence, in the training phase, they were all motivated to test at least some IIMT. In the second choice task, 10.5% of the respondents did not use any IIMT, and in the third choice task 21.1%.

Most clicks were done on $SCORE_{attributeLevel}$, *FILTER*, and $SCORE_{attribute}$. The least clicks on $SORT_{drag\&drop}$, $REMOVE_{markings}$, and $CALCULATE_{mar-kings}$. Figure 8.6 displays the frequencies.

As we have pointed out before, the analysis of this total amount of clicks is biased. Users have to apply *SCORE* more often in order to get support for a strategy. The more astonishing it is, then, that *FILTER* was still used so often. Although *FILTER* can implement an EBA strategy already by only few clicks, it was among

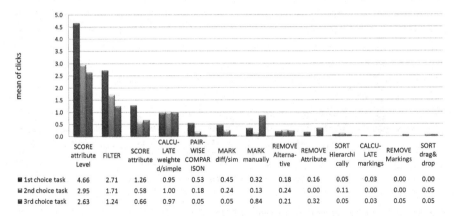

	SCORE attribute Level	FILTER	SCORE attribute	CALCULATE weighte d/simple	PAIRWISE COMPAR ISON	MARK diff/sim	MARK manually	REMOVE Alternative	REMOVE Attribute	SORT Hierarchi cally	CALCULATE markings	REMOVE Markings	SORT drag& drop
■ 1st choice task	4.66	2.71	1.26	0.95	0.53	0.45	0.32	0.18	0.16	0.05	0.03	0.00	0.00
■ 2nd choice task	2.95	1.71	0.58	1.00	0.18	0.24	0.13	0.24	0.00	0.11	0.00	0.00	0.05
■ 3rd choice task	2.63	1.24	0.66	0.97	0.05	0.05	0.84	0.21	0.32	0.05	0.03	0.05	0.05

Fig. 8.6 Mean of clicks for group *all IIMT*

the most often used IIMT. Thus, in contrast to current webstores where *FILTER* is only offered in the screening phase, *FILTER* seems to be a popular tool also for the in-depth comparison phase. Moreover, *SCORE* is not available at all in current product-comparison matrices in the Internet but was very popular in our experiment.

Next we analyze which IIMT were used at least once. Here, we had to exclude $CALCULATE_{weighted}$ from the analysis, because it was by default activated when entering the webstore. In further experiments, we should probably refrain from activating this IIMT by default in order to be able to include it in the analysis. The fact that $CALCULATE_{weighted}$ was activated by default might also have biased respondents to apply $SCORE_{attributeLevel}$, and $SCORE_{attribute}$ instead of $SCORE_{markings}$. This is because $SCORE_{markings}$ was only usable by activating the radio button for $CALCULATE_{markings}$ instead of $CALCULATE_{weighted}$. We hope that we were able to prevent part of the bias by the introduction video which had explained all IIMT directly before the first choice in detail and had explicitly explained how to activate $CALCULATE_{markings}$. Furthermore, the IIMT $CALCULATE_{weighted}$ and $CALCULATE_{simple}$ are activated by the same radio button because they implement the same score function. Thus, we distinguish between these two functions by examining whether respondents have weighted all attributes by the same weighting factor (which would mean that they use $CALCULATE_{simple}$ and the EQW strategy) or if they weight the attributes differently (which would mean that they use $CALUCLATE_{weighted}$ and a WADD strategy).[3]

In the first choice task, *FILTER* was used by 84.2% of respondents at least once, followed by $SCORE_{attributeLevel}$ with 26.3% and $MARK_{diff/sim}$ with 18.4% (see Fig. 8.7). Furthermore, 2.6% of respondents had the $CALCULATE_{markings}$ IIMT activated before making their final choice, and the same percentage had deactivated any *CALCULATE* before making their final choice.

---

[3]By default, the webstore showed the same weight of three stars for each attribute.

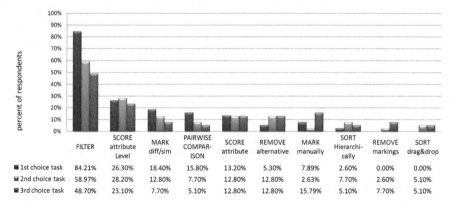

	FILTER	SCORE attribute Level	MARK diff/sim	PAIRWISE COMPAR-ISON	SCORE attribute	REMOVE alternative	MARK manually	SORT Hierarchi-cally	REMOVE markings	SORT drag&drop
1st choice task	84.21%	26.30%	18.40%	15.80%	13.20%	5.30%	7.89%	2.60%	0.00%	0.00%
2nd choice task	58.97%	28.20%	12.80%	7.70%	12.80%	12.80%	2.63%	7.70%	2.60%	5.10%
3rd choice task	48.70%	23.10%	7.70%	5.10%	12.80%	12.80%	15.79%	5.10%	7.70%	5.10%

Fig. 8.7 IIMT used at least once for group *all IIMT*

In the second choice task, the order did not change much. $REMOVE_{alternative}$ gained a bit in popularity (from 5.3% in the first choice task to 12.8% in the second choice task), $PAIRWISE\ COMPARISON$ lost from 15.8% to 7.7%. In the third choice task, respondents tended to increase the usage of IIMT such as $REMOVE_{markings}$ (7.7%), $SORT_{drag\&drop}$ (5.1%), and $MARK_{manually}$ (10.3%) and used less *FILTER*. However, *FILTER* is still the most widely used one with 48.7%.

In sum, we observe that in the first choice task *FILTER* and $SCORE_{attribute-Level}$ are dominant but with increasing familiarity with INTACMATO respondents become more diverse in their behavior and all IIMT are used at least once by over 3% of respondents. Thus, all IIMT seem to be of relevance and there is no IIMT which was not used at all. It would be interesting to see whether this trend of a more balanced usage of all different kinds of IIMT would further be observable when respondents become even more familiar with INTACMATO.

We now analyze in more detail the clicking behavior of the group *few IIMT*. In this group, the only IIMT available were $SCORE_{attribute}$, $SCORE_{attributeLevel}$ and $CALCULATE_{weighted}$ on/off.

We again want to know whether there were respondents who did not use any IIMT at all. In the first choice task, all respondents used at least one IIMT, in the second choice task, 17.2% of the respondents did not use any IIMT, and in the third choice task 10.3%. Thus, most respondents did make use of the IIMT. It is further interesting that the number of respondents not using IIMT decreased quite a lot from choice task two to choice task three. An explanation might be that respondents noticed after the second choice task that the IIMT made sense and consequently decided to use it again in the third choice task. Compared to the group *all IIMT*, more IIMT were used at least once.

Examining the total number of clicks, we found that in the first choice task, $SCORE_{attribute}$ was used 9.24 times on average, followed by 4.59 and 5.1 for the

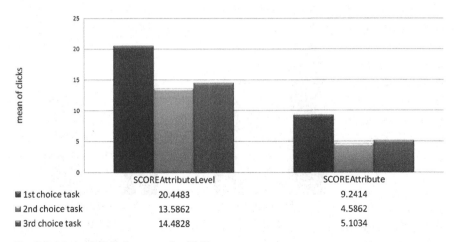

Fig. 8.8 Mean of clicks for group *few IIMT*

second and third choice task respectively (see Fig. 8.8). $SCORE_{attributeLevel}$ was used 20.45 times in the first choice task and 13.59 and 14.28 times in the second and third task, respectively. Please note that $SCORE_{attribute}$ can be executed for the 16 displayed attributes, while $SCORE_{attributeLevel}$ can be executed for each attribute level. In the case of choice tasks with low complexity, there were on average 30 different attribute levels, in case of medium complexity 37, and in case of high complexity 44. So, on average, respondents evaluated about $\frac{1}{3}$ of attributes and $\frac{1}{2} - \frac{1}{3}$ of attribute levels. However, if we count the frequency of usage for only those respondents who used the IIMT at all, we get an average number of 22.2 clicks for $SCORE_{attributeLevel}$ and 10.02 for $SCORE_{attribute}$. Thus, it seems that once respondents decided to use either EQW or WADD, they used the decision support for the most part of the decision process. We will discuss this aspect further in the following two sections.

We want to know further which IIMT were at least used once by the respondents. In the first choice task, 82.8% of respondents used $SCORE_{attributeLevel}$ at least once, 79.3% $SCORE_{attribute}$, and 19.4% deactivated the calculations before their final choice (see Fig. 8.9). Thus, about 80% of respondents used the IIMT which support either WADD or EQW. In the second choice task, the percentage declined a bit with 62.1% of respondents using $SCORE_{attributeLevel}$ at least once, 48.3% $SCORE_{attribute}$ and 19.4% who deactivated the calculation of scores. The numbers for the third choice task were comparable to the second one with 69% for $SCORE_{attributeLevel}$, 58.6% for $SCORE_{attribute}$, and 19.4% of respondents who deactivated the calculation before their final choice.

In total, we can conclude that most respondents (about 67–80%) made use of the few offered IIMT.

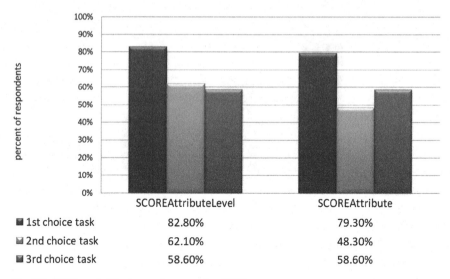

	SCOREAttributeLevel	SCOREAttribute
■ 1st choice task	82.80%	79.30%
▨ 2nd choice task	62.10%	48.30%
■ 3rd choice task	58.60%	58.60%

Fig. 8.9 IIMT used at least once for group *few IIMT*

8.3.4.5   Strategy Manipulation

In this section, we analyze whether restricting respondents in the *few* IIMT group to only use a subset of IIMT, influenced their decision-making behavior (hypothesis 6). As pointed out before, we can assign strategies to the observed choices with two methods. First, we can assign strategies to the final choices by making use of the preferences we have measured during the experiment (with PCPM and self-reports of aspiration levels). Second, we can match the clickstream on IIMT with the strategies that the IIMT support. The pseudo-code notation which lists the IIMT and EIP for each strategy facilitates this analysis (see Chap. 7). Because the latter analysis can only be done for the groups *few* and *all* IIMT and not for the group *no* IIMT (for which we obviously cannot gather clickstream data on (non-existing) IIMT), the analysis of assigning strategies to final choices is more meaningful. Thus, we start by analyzing final choices and proceed with the clickstream analysis later on.

For the analysis of the final choices, we developed an algorithm which determines for each respondent and each choice task which strategies explain the choice. The algorithm reads in respondents' preferences, the choice tasks which they encountered, and their final choices. It then assigns all strategies which explain the final choice.

Some of the strategies had to be excluded from the analysis:

1. When using SAT and SAT+, the decision maker chooses the first alternative which satisfies aspiration levels across all or m^* attributes (see Sect. 2.2). Since we do not know the order in which subjects consider alternatives, we cannot know whether a subject has applied SAT or SAT+. The same holds for MCD. We do not know the order in which alternatives are compared pairwise in case of MCD and thus exclude SAT, SAT+, and MCD from the further analysis.

2. For 70.6% of all the choice tasks in our experiment, CONJ eliminates all six alternatives because none meets all aspiration levels. Furthermore, for only 10.5% does CONJ explain exactly one choice. Thus, for in total 89.5% we cannot determine the exact alternative a respondent would choose when applying CONJ. A proper analysis with CONJ was impossible.
3. In contrast to CONJ, DIS does not eliminate any alternative at all and would always explain the choice of any of the six alternatives. This is because DIS only excludes an alternative if it violates aspiration levels on all attributes, which was not the case for any of the choice tasks in our experiment. Thus, an analysis of DIS is not meaningful.
4. We decided against measuring parameters k and Δ which are needed to determine COM and LED (see Sect. 2.2). We have several reasons for this. First, we have not found any approach in the literature how to determine these parameters. Second, we could not think of any way to ask for k in a way which would be easy for respondents to understand. Third, LED is only a variant of LEX. Thus, conclusions for LED can at least partly derived from the behavior we observe for LEX. Fourth, a Δ_i is needed for every attribute. Thus, asking for Δ_i i times would have prolonged the already long experiment.
5. There was no dominant alternative for any of the choice tasks and for any of the decision makers. Thus, DOM never explains any choice and is excluded from further analysis. This is in line with the notion that usually there is no dominant alternative in the context of purchase decisions (Fasolo et al. 2003).

In sum, we analyze the following strategies: EBA, EQW, FRQ, MAJ, LEX, and WADD. Before we can start to analyze in how many cases which strategy explains which choice, we have to address the problem of multiple mappings. Multiple mappings occur when several alternatives might be chosen by the same strategy. If, for instance, no aspiration levels at all were shown in a choice task, EBA would explain the choice of any of the alternatives because no alternative is eliminated throughout the decision process. Multiple mappings occur for 27.3% in case of EBA, for 2.1% in case of EQW, for 51% in case of FRQ, and for 28.3% in case of MAJ.[4] We see two possible approaches to address this problem. First, for every strategy, we only include choice tasks in the analysis where no multiple-mappings occur. Second, instead of taking the binary variable (1: a strategy explains the choice, 0: strategy does not explain the choice) for the statistical analysis, one can weight the variable by the multiple mappings ($\frac{1}{\#multiplemappings}$: a strategy explains a decision, 0: strategy does not explain the decision). Thus, in case FRQ has a multiple mapping of three, which means FRQ would explain the choice of three different alternatives, we would count that observed choice as $\frac{1}{3}$ instead of 1. Both

---

[4]In contrast to the study presented in Chap. 4 we were not able to measure the respondents' preferences before the actual experiment took place. Therefore, we could not optimize the choice tasks with the GA as we did in the previous experiment, which would have ensured an optimal mapping of strategies to alternatives.

approaches yielded similar results. Therefore, we report the simpler, first approach
where choice tasks with multiple mappings are excluded from the data set. Besides
these exclusions, we also had to exclude the third choice of five respondents since
the database had failed to record their final choices.

Table 8.4 shows in how many cases each strategy explains the observed choices.
In the left columns, we see the percentage of choices which were explained by
each strategy. The number of observations (N), which is in parentheses, differs
from case to case because the number of exclusions caused by multiple mapping is
different for each set. We set the numbers in relation to some strategy, RANDOM,
that randomly predicts the choices. The columns on the right display the ratio of
$\frac{explained\ choices}{expected\ under\ random\ choice}$. The value for *expected under random choice* is $\frac{1}{6} =$
16.67%, because each choice task consisted of six alternatives. Figure 8.10 displays
the percentages graphically.

In the group *no IIMT*, EBA explains 41.67% of the choices. Compared to the $\frac{1}{6}$
probability of randomly choosing among the 6 alternatives, EBA explains 2.5 times

Table 8.4 Frequencies of strategies which explain choices. Multiple mappings are excluded

	Explained choices in % (N)			Ratio of expl. choices		
	No IIMT	Few IIMT	All IIMT	No IIMT	Few IIMT	All IIMT
EBA	41.67 (72)	25.00 (64)	40.28 (72)	2.50	1.50	2.42
EQW	14.46 (83)	9.78 (92)	12.38 (105)	0.87	0.59	0.74
FRQ	39.13 (46)	28.57 (42)	40.38 (52)	2.35	1.71	2.42
LEX	20.24 (84)	17.20 (93)	12.84 (109)	1.21	1.03	0.77
MAJ	0.00 (60)	1.49 (67)	7.79 (77)	0.00	0.09	0.47
WADD	11.90 (84)	8.60 (93)	10.09 (109)	0.71	0.52	0.61

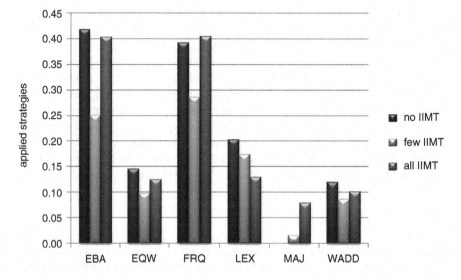

Fig. 8.10 Applied strategies (analysis of final choices)

as many choices as expected from a random strategy ($2.5 = \frac{41.67\%}{16.67\%}$). For the group *all IIMT*, the percentage is almost as high, but for the group *few IIMT*, EBA explains only 25% of choices.

For FRQ we observe a similar behavior as for EBA. In about 40% of cases, FRQ explains the choice for the groups with *no* (*all IIMT*) which is 2.35 (2.42) as much as expected under random choice. While for the group *few IIMT*, it only explains 28.57% of the choices. Thus, in sum, EBA and FRQ are the strategies which best explain the observed behavior, specifically for the groups *no* and *all IIMT*. Furthermore, EBA and FRQ show the behavior we had anticipated. In case of a restricted decision support (*few IIMT*), the strategies are applied less often than in the other two groups because these two strategies are not supported by any IIMT in the group (*few IIMT*). In case that either all decision strategies are supported by IIMT or no support is provided at all, there is no difference because no particular behavior is imposed on the respondents.

LEX and MAJ behave differently to FRQ and EBA. While with more IIMT the percentage of choices explained by LEX decreases monotonically, the percentage for MAJ increases. In case of *no IIMT*, LEX is used more often than expected under random choice (ratio is 1.21), roughly as expected in the group *few IIMT* (ratio is 1.03) and less than expected in the group *all IIMT* (0.77). MAJ, in contrast explains no choice at all in the group *no IIMT* and 7.79% of choices in the group *all IIMT*, which is only 0.47 as much as expected with a random choice. In sum, LEX explains roughly as many choices as under random choice and MAJ explains a very low percentage of choices.

The results for LEX are quite interesting. As computed in our extended effort-accuracy framework, in a worst-case scenario, IIMT support saves 81% of the effort, thus applying LEX has very little effort. Apparently, the high reduction in the effort does not outweigh the low accuracy of LEX. In case of *no IIMT* support, LEX seems to be one of the preferred strategies because of its simplicity but the more IIMT are offered, the more respondents tend to refrain from using LEX and use more effortful but also more accurate strategies, such as MAJ.

For EQW and WADD, we had expected that they would explain more decisions in the group *few IIMT* than in the other two groups because the only IIMT offered in this group support the WADD and EQW strategy. Furthermore, particularly for WADD we had expected an increased usage in case of *all IIMT* compared to *no IIMT* because INTACMATO decreases the net saving of effort for this very accurate but effortful strategy. The results show the opposite behavior. Likewise to EBA and FRQ, less users apply EQW and WADD in the group *few IIMT*. Furthermore, there is no difference in the usage of WADD between the groups *no* and *all IIMT*.

Summing up the frequencies with which all decision strategies are used in the group *few IIMT* compared to the two other groups, we note that the six strategies in total explain fewer choices under this condition (*all IIMT*: 127.40%, *few IIMT*:

90.64%, *no IIMT*: 123.76%.[5]) Consequently, in the condition *few IIMT*, subjects might have used some other strategy or some mixed strategy which we cannot explain with the analysis of final choices.

In order to test this observation in more detail, we wanted to know whether the drop of the usage under the condition *few IIMT* is significant for the two strategies, EBA and FRQ, that show the expected behavior. For this analysis, we formed two groups. Group *few IIMT* includes choices under the condition *few IIMT*, and group *no/all* includes choices under the condition *no IIMT* and *all IIMT*. Thus, for each strategy we have one categorial variable distinguishing between the two groups and a categorial variable which signifies whether the particular strategy explains the choice. To test whether there is a difference between the two groups, we compute a χ^2-test. Since the χ^2-test assumes independence of the data, we compute the statistics for each of the three choices, thus for each complexity group, separately.

The only significant association between the group and the application of a strategy was for EBA in case of high complexity $\chi^2(1) = 5.28$, $p < 0.05$, this effect is small to medium with $\Phi = -0.269$. Out of 73 choice tasks with high complexity, 45.8% respondents applied EBA in case of *no IIMT*, 32% in case of *all IIMT* and 12.5% in case of *few IIMT*. Thus, respondents use EBA much less often in the group when only IIMT supporting WADD and EQW are offered compared to the two other groups with *no* and *all IIMT*. In sum, for EBA we find the expected behavior in case of high complexity. Although the same tendency can be observed for FRQ, this result is not significant.

In addition to the analysis of final choices, the number of clicks on $SCORE_{attribute}$ and $SCORE_{attributeLevel}$ tells us whether respondents used more often EQW and WADD in the group *few IIMT* than in the group *all IIMT*. We cannot include group *no IIMT* in the analysis because there are no clicks on IIMT in this group. In total, in the group *few IIMT*, more respondents applied at least once $SCORE_{attribute}$ (*few IIMT*: 57% vs. *all IIMT*: 15%) and $SCORE_{attributeLevel}$ (*few IIMT*: 71% vs. *all IIMT*: 32%). This result indicates that respondents use more often EQW and WADD in the group *few IIMT*. We want to know further whether the respondents who presumably use EQW or WADD (who have at least on click on $SCORE_{attribute}$ and $SCORE_{attributeLevel}$ respectively), abort the decision strategy after a while or whether they use the IIMT to support the complete strategy and whether there is a difference between the two groups. An independent t-test shows that, in the group *few IIMT*, we have significantly more clicks for $SCORE_{attributeLevel}$ ($M = 22.2$, $SE = 9.72$), than in the group *all IIMT* ($M = 14.21$, $SE = 11.31$, $t(38) = 2.37$, $p < 0.05$, $r = 0.36$). Given that the average number of different levels ranges between 30 and 44, we can say that respondents in both groups mix the strategies with other ones.[6] We will analyze this switching behavior

---

[5]Values above 100% can be reached because two strategies which explain the same choice are counted twice.

[6]Note that by default each attribute level is assigned three stars. Thus, the rating of some attribute levels might already fit to the user's evaluation by default. The range between 30 and 44 is an upper bound for the amount of attribute levels that need to be evaluated with $SCORE_{attributeLevel}$.

between different strategies in the next section. For $SCORE_{attribute}$, we have $M = 10.02$, $SE = 3.77$ clicks for group *few IIMT* and $M = 8.38$, $SE = 4.91$ for group *all IIMT* which is not a significant difference ($t(28) = 0.94$, $p > 0.05$). Given the 16 different attribute levels, we conclude that WADD is only applied partly for both groups.

To sum up, we find contradictory results for hypothesis 6. While the analysis of final choices only reveals a decreased usage of EBA for the group *few IIMT* and thus does not support the hypothesis, the analysis of clickstream data shows the expected behavior and thus supports hypothesis 6. Respondents use more EQW and WADD, either in their pure form or they mix them with other strategies. We have two possible explanations for the unexpected results for the analysis of final choices. First, the measured preferences do not estimate the real respondents' preferences well enough. We therefore suggest to redo the study with other preference measurement methods to analyze this phenomenon further. Second, respondents show the expected behavior and apply more EQW and WADD. However, they do not necessarily apply these two strategies in their pure form but also mix them with other strategies. That is why we cannot find the expected behavior with an analysis of final choices because our analysis of final choices assumes that people have used one pure strategy. Unfortunately, we can also only speculate about mixed behavior for the the clickstream analysis in the group with *few IIMT*. That is because we have no further process data in this group which would indicate the usage of other strategies that were not supported by any IIMT. In future work, we should redo the experiment and include other process data, such as mouse movements and eye tracking. A more detailed analysis of mixed behavior for the group *all IIMT* will be provided in the following section.

8.3.4.6 Pure Versus Mixed Strategies

We assigned strategies to the clickstream data using our theoretical analysis from Chap. 7. The pseudo-code notation helps to assign strategies to the applied IIMT. This analysis can only be done for the group *all IIMT*. In total, we could map the tracking data to 38 respondents of the group *all IIMT*. Since in 12 choices, respondents had used no IIMT at all and in one case, because of a technical error, a respondent had made four choices, we were able to analyze the clickstream data of 102 choices.

For each clickstream, we matched the sequence of applied IIMT with the sequence of IIMT specified in the pseudo-code for each strategy. Thus, the most important criteria was that the IIMT included in the pseudo-code notation were applied in the sequence defined by the pseudo-code notation. In some choices people were mixing several decision strategies. In total we identified the application of 128 different strategies in these 102 choices. Out of these 128 strategies, in 97 cases the clicking behavior matched well with the sequence of IIMT specified in the pseudo-code notation. In eight cases, the behavior also clearly followed a strategy but respondents in addition applied a $MARK_{diff/sim}$. Apparently, in these cases, respondents wanted to double check whether they had examined all attributes across which the alternatives differed. In four cases, respondents combined $REMOVE_{attribute}$ or $REMOVE_{alternative}$ with a FILTER. We identified this still as the application of an EBA strategy, although it does not exactly match to our pseudo-code notation. In the remaining 21 cases, the applied sequence of IIMT did not clearly match to any of the IIMT patterns in the pseudo-code notation. In these cases, we assigned several strategies which might explain the clicking behavior. The most frequent combination was SAT and SAT+ for the application of only the IIMT $REMOVE_{alternative}$. In other cases, respondents used $PAIRWISE\ COMPARISON$ but did not combine this IIMT with any other IIMT. Thus, we were not able to differentiate between the application of MCD and ADD.

In the next step, we analyzed which strategies respondents had used. In 79 of the 102 choices, respondents used only one strategy. In 14 out of the remaining 23 cases of mixed behavior, they switched from a non-compensatory strategy to a compensatory strategy. The most common combination is EBA mixed with a compensatory strategy. This result confirms our eye-tracking study and common results from literature (see Chap. 3). All combinations which occurred are shown in Table 8.5.

Table 8.5 Occurrences of mixed strategies

Frequency	Phase 1	Phase 2	Phase 3
Non-compensatory $\Rightarrow$ compensatory			
1	SAT/SAT+	WADD	
2	LEX/LED	WADD	
3	EBA	EQW	
3	EBA	WADD	
3	EBA	ADD/MCD	
1	EBA	EQW/ADD	
1	EBA	LEX/LED	EQW
Compensatory $\Rightarrow$ non-compensatory			
1	EQW	CONJ	
1	EQW	LEX/LED	
1	EQW	SAT,SAT+,CONJ	
2	WADD	EBA	
Compensatory $\Rightarrow$ compensatory			
1	EQW	MCD,ADD	
Non-compensatory $\Rightarrow$ non-compensatory			
1	EBA	SAT+	
1	EBA	LEX	
Compensatory $\Rightarrow$ non-compensatory $\Rightarrow$ compensatory			
1	EQW	COM	EQW

In sum, we find that the few mixed strategies which we observe in our studies are mostly in line with results from other studies. However, five respondents started with a compensatory and finished with a non-compensatory strategy. A possible explanation might be that they start with the more effortful EQW or WADD but give up after some time to switch to a less effortful strategy. Furthermore, the question remains whether by analyzing only the clicking data on IIMT, we are able to identify all mixed behavior. It might be that people execute some decision phase in their mind without using any IIMT. As we have pointed out above, combining our analysis with eye tracking or some other process tracing technique could reveal these mental processes and contribute relevant data for analyzing mixed behavior in more detail.

8.4 Conclusions

8.4.1 Discussion and Contributions

In essence, our findings suggest that INTACMATO is evaluated very positively by users and they apply it often in their decisions. We observed large effects between the groups *all/few IIMT* vs. *no IIMT* for ease of use and shopping enjoyment and medium effect for usefulness, confidence, and satisfaction. In many studies it has been shown that these variables have a positive influence on the intention to return to a webpage, the actual usage of the webpage and online purchase behavior (Chen et al. 2002; Chuan-Chuan Lin and Hsipeng 2000; Davis 1989; Gefen et al. 2003; Klopping and McKinney 2004; Lee et al. 2001; Mun and Hwand 2003).

Some of the IIMT respondents applied most often in the study are not available in the Internet yet (such as different kinds of *SCORE*). Furthermore, *FILTER* is the predominantly used IIMT in this study. One might argue that this is because of respondent's familiarity with this IIMT. Yet, since this observation is still true after respondents have got used to new IIMT after the first two choices, we advise to also offer *FILTER* in the in-depth comparison phase in current webstores. Moreover, it seems that with increasing familiarity with INTACMATO, respondents become more diverse in their behavior, which speaks in favor of offering a variety of IIMT in webstores.

We are able to determine decision strategies based on the user's clicking behavior on different IIMT and based on analyzing final choices. Our approach of analyzing clicking behavior is new and based on our extension of the effort-accuracy framework which we presented in Chap. 7. Both the clickstream and the final choice analyses show that EBA is applied most often. We also attempted to influence decision-making behavior by only presenting a subset of IIMT to one third of respondents in the group *few IIMT*. The presented IIMT only support a WADD and EQW strategy. Our conjecture cannot be supported with the analysis of final choices. From the perspective of final choices, only EBA is used significantly less often in the group *few IIMT*, but there is no increase in the use of WADD or

EQW. When we do the same analysis with the clickstream data, however, we find that people apply significantly more often WADD and EQW. However, they do not necessarily apply these two strategies in their pure form but also mix them with other strategies. The latter would be a possible explanation why we cannot find the same effect with the analysis of final choices, which is unable to detect mixed behavior.

With our new kind of clickstream analysis, we are also able to distinguish between mixed vs. pure decision strategies. Our analysis shows that most observed decision strategies are not mixed (77% of choices). In 61% of the mixed cases, respondents applied the common form of starting with a non-compensatory and finishing with a compensatory strategies. The large percentage of pure strategies contradicts results from two of our other studies (see Chap. 3 and Pfeiffer et al. 2009a). We think that the clickstream analysis should be extended by other process tracing methods, such as eye tracking, to enable a more detailed analysis of mixed vs. pure decision-making behavior.

Finally, the newly proposed measure of complexity was not successful. The measure of complexity only influenced the time respondents needed for the decisions, but not the applied decision strategy.

8.4.2 Limitations and Future Work

We see two main limitations of our work which should be addressed in future studies. First, we evaluated INTACMATO with 115 students. Since the students use the Internet very often and we expect them to be able to deal with new elements of interfaces faster than the average Internet user, our results might be biased. A larger and more representative pool of subjects should repeat the study in order to validate our very positive results further.

Second, the analysis of decision strategies has its limits. As we have pointed out before, the current clickstream analysis might not cover the whole decision process because some parts of decision strategies might still be made mentally and without IIMT support. An additional eye-tracking analysis or another process tracing method might help to find out about these mental processes. Furthermore, the preferences measurement techniques might capture the users' preferences incompletely. This would at least be an explanation why the clickstream and the final choice analysis come to different results. Further research on how to measure preferences more accurately needs to be done.

Finally – and this is not a limit of our study, but rather a limitation of the design of INTACMATO – some IIMT were not used as much as other IIMT. We think that the design of some IIMT must be improved further. $SORT_{drag\&drop}$ was very rarely used. Probably, it was not obvious for users that this IIMT exists. Furthermore, switching between different options for scoring evaluations with the radio button was apparently not the most intuitive and easiest approach for users. We guess that some did not understand that they could evaluate attribute levels with stars or choose to mark attribute levels positively or negatively with $MARK_{manually}$. Moreover, $SORT_{hierarchically}$ is only implemented in a preliminary version in the current prototype. There is no possibility to define an own preference order. In the current version, we assume a monotonic increasing/decreasing value function on attribute levels. This might have hindered users from applying $SORT_{hierarchically}$ more often.

Chapter 9
Summary, Conclusions, and Future Work

It is good to have an end to journey toward; but it is the journey that matters in the end.

Ursula LeGuin

9.1 Summary and Discussion

In the present work, we addressed two research questions: (1) How does the complexity of a choice task influence decision-making behavior? (2) How can we consider knowledge about decision-making behavior for the design of IIMT? By answering the first research question, we contributed to current theory on decision-making behavior, while the main contribution of addressing the second research question is the development of INTACMATO, an IIMT-prototype for supporting choice decisions.

More specifically, in Chap. 2, we outlined the fundamentals of the present work. We focussed on multi-criteria preferential decision problems with a limited number of alternatives and no uncertainties. We provided a detailed overview on decision strategies which explain people's decision-making behavior. Furthermore, we retrieved several characteristics of decision-making behavior which allowed to categorize decision strategies in certain groups, such as compensatory vs. non-compensatory strategies or strategies with alternative-wise vs. attribute-wise information acquisition.

Choice behavior depends on characteristics of choice tasks such as task-based and context-based complexity. The complexity reflects how difficult decision makers experience the choice. We provided a detailed literature overview on different measures of complexity and their effect on decision-making behavior. One main result of our literature review is that the influence of context-based measures of complexity, such as (1) attractiveness differences, (2) trade-offs, and

J. Pfeiffer, *Interactive Decision Aids in E-Commerce*, Contributions to Management Science, DOI 10.1007/978-3-7908-2769-9_9, © Springer-Verlag Berlin Heidelberg 2012

(3) attribute ranges, is still unclear. That is why we focused on these three measures of complexity in the following empirical studies.

We began with an empirical study that investigated the influence of the above mentioned three context-based measures on the decision process (in Chap. 3). Our study attempted to measure both the decision process and context-based complexity as accurately as possible. First, we recorded the decision process with the latest technique for eye tracking. Second, rather than relying on less precise estimates of preferences to determine context-based complexity, we measured each subject's preferences individually with two advanced techniques from marketing research: choice-based conjoint analysis (CBC, Haaijer and Wedel 2007); and pairwise-comparison-based preference measurement (PCPM, Scholz et al. 2010). Our results showed that low context-based complexity leads to less information acquisition and more alternative-wise search. Moreover, people search information attribute-wise in the first stage of the decision process, then eliminate alternatives, and search alternative-wise in the last stage. We also found evidence that in situations of low context-based complexity, people switch earlier to alternative-wise processing.

In a second empirical study, we measured the influence of the same three context-based measures from Chap. 3 together with the influence of the number of alternatives and the number of attributes. The design of stimuli was optimized using a GA which created choice tasks of low vs. high complexity and ensured an opimal mapping between four decision strategies (EBA, LEX, MAJ, and WADD) and alternatives. Overall, the number of alternatives and the amount of trade-offs had the largest effect on decision-making behavior. Furthermore, among the four strategies considered, WADD explained the choices best, followed by EBA. In particular, we found that when alternatives are very similar and there are many trade-offs, people do not succeed in their attempt to follow a compensatory decision process and finally choose a product which can best be explained by a non-compensatory strategy such as EBA. Finally, respondents were consistent enough in their usage of one of the four decision-making strategies to be meaningfully clustered according to the predominantly used strategy.

From the two experimental studies, we conclude that a DSS for preferential choice tasks must be very flexible. First, people mix different decision strategies when making a choice. So they need different kinds of decision support tools during their choice. Furthermore, we found that people first eliminate alternatives by an attribute-wise search. This elimination process affects both the number of alternatives and the context-based measures. For instance, the elimination of inferior alternatives will decrease the attractiveness difference and the attribute range. Thus, complexity not only influences the choice process, but the complexity itself changes throughout the choice process, which makes the choice very adaptive and hard to predict. A flexible system which supports all different kinds of behavior is one solution to encounter this problem. A further argument for a flexible system stems from our cluster analysis. We found that different groups of people use very different kind of strategies but that clusters cannot be explained by personality traits. Hence, the system must be flexible enough to support very heterogenous behavior and it is hard to know in advance which user will prefer which kind of decision support.

In the second part, we aimed to design this flexible DSS. In Chap. 5, we provided a literature review on current DSS for the domain of online purchase decisions, so-called IDA. IIMT are one kind of IDA which enable buyers to sort through and/or compare available product alternatives. We dissociated IIMT from related IDA such as recommendation systems. With a descriptive and an empirical study, we showed that only few IIMT are currently available on the Internet, despite of the fact that people prefer them to RA.

To circumvent the shortcomings of current IIMT, our goal was to design an IIMT-prototype which would closely fit the individual's decision process because we argue that this is the determining factor for user satisfaction and his/her intention to use a system. By breaking down decision strategies in the basic steps which need to be supported, we were able to define which IIMT were necessary to support all different kinds of strategies.

Next, we tried to find the best design for these IIMT. To this end, we retrieved several design criteria from research on IS and decision-making behavior: adaptivity, consistency, control, flexibility, low effort, and transparency. In an iterative process, we designed and evaluated our IIMT-prototype INTACMATO in two usability studies across these criteria. However, the "adaptivity" criteria was ignored since it would have added another complexity layer to the prototype which we like to leave to future work. Although the IIMT can also be used in the screening phase, in all usability studies, we focused only on decision support for product-comparison matrix.

Besides the two qualitative usability studies during the design of INTACMATO, we evaluated the complete INTACMATO from a theoretical and an empirical perspective. In Chap. 7, we developed an extended effort-accuracy framework, where we specified the decision maker's effort for each decision strategy with and without support of INTACMATO. This theoretical analysis revealed that the prototype is able to reduce effort for various kinds of decision-making behavior. Finally, we wanted to know how a large group of users would evaluate the prototype. In a quantitative study with 115 students, users were randomly assigned to either our prototype, a prototype with reduced functionality, or a product-comparison matrix without further DSS. The results showed that users perceived increased ease of use, usefulness, enjoyment, confidence and satisfaction, the more IIMT are offered. Furthermore, the evaluation across the different design criteria was again very positive. In the study, we further found that *FILTER* was the predominantly used IIMT, even though respondents only saw six different cell phones in the matrix. The more users became familiar with a particular IIMT, the more willing they were to use other IIMT. In contrast to our expectations, we were not able to influence decision-making behavior by restricting people to only using specific IIMT. Further research is needed to test this idea. We suspect that different ways of determining the applied decision strategies would improve the analysis.

To sum up, in the second part of the thesis, we provided a theory driven design approach for IIMT. With the first and the second part, we have completed the full complementary research cycle of rigor, build and relevance: we designed a new artifact based on current theory and this artifact itself became part of new theory testing in a behavioral experiment and will hopefully stimulate continued research in the future.

9.2 Implications for Web Stores

In this section, we point out the practical relevance of the present work and give advice to the management-oriented audience and webdesigners. Taking our most important results into account, we make four recommendations on how to design a webstore or any other interface for preferential decision problems. First, we have shown the usefulness of IIMT in several empirical studies. Therefore, we advise to offer IIMT in preferential decision problems as decision support. Second, certain IIMT, such as *FILTER*, are useful to quickly eliminate inferior alternatives. This might be useful in particular in the screening phase when large sets of alternatives are offered since the effort of this IIMT does not increase with the number of alternatives. Other IIMT, in contrast, are only appropriate for an in-depth comparison such as evaluating attribute levels with the IIMT *SCORE*. Consequently, we suggest to separate the interface in two screens, the *screening* and the *in-depth* screen. Third, in general settings, where the choice task complexity is unknown, we suggest to offer a variety of IIMT. Our research has shown that because of heterogenous decision-making behavior, offering many instead of only few IIMT leads to higher user satisfaction. Fourth, in choice tasks with certain complexity, users prefer some IIMT and neglect others. Given that we have knowledge on the choice task complexity, we advise to offer the appropriate IIMT from the beginning on, or to allow the user to personally hide or delete certain IIMT in order to individually adapt the interface to the situation. We will allude to these four recommendations in more detail in the following sections.

9.2.1 Usefulness of IIMT

Users evaluate IIMT in general and, specifically, INTACMATO positively across perceived ease of use, perceived usefulness, confidence, shopping enjoyment, and satisfaction (see Sects. 5.2 and Chap. 8). In many studies it has been shown that these variables have a positive influence on the intention to return to a webpage, the actual usage of the webpage and online purchase behavior (Chen et al. 2002; Chuan-Chuan Lin and Hsipeng 2000; Davis 1989; Gefen et al. 2003; Klopping and McKinney 2004; Lee et al. 2001; Mun and Hwand 2003).

Furthermore, in an extended effort-accuracy framework, we demonstrated theoretically that the usage of INTACMATO always yields a positive net saving of effort (see Chap. 7). Hence, IIMT saves user effort independently of the decision strategy they actually use. Although we have not considered the possible accuracy improvement of IIMT in detail, we would like to point out that offering IIMT is supposed to increase accuracy, since users are likely to make errors when applying certain strategies without decision support. Thus, customers should not only feel satisfied with the web interface but also, in the long-run, with the product they have purchased. The increased user-satisfaction on these different levels and a larger propensity to return to the website would also positively impact the sales volume of the merchandiser. Thus, our research suggests that INTACMATO creates a win-win situation for both customers and merchandisers.

9.2.2 Separation into Screening and In-Depth Phase

We have shown empirically that people like to apply several strategies when making a decision. Specifically, they tend to start comparing information attribute-wise at the beginning and switch to an alternative-wise information acquisition afterwards (see Chap. 3). In line with other researchers (Bettman and Park 1980; Gilbride and Allenby 2006; Luce et al. 1997; Payne 1976), we suggest to separate the choice process into a screening and an in-depth comparison phase. This finding has implications for the decision support, because some IIMT are more appropriate for the screening, and others for the in-depth comparison phase. In the screening phase, often a large amount of products is offered. Amazon.com, for instance, shows 2,266 results when searching for camcorders, and 1,004 when searching for adult bikes. Therefore, we advise to offer such IIMT for the screening phase which make the effort of choosing independent of the number of alternatives. In the extended effort-accuracy framework in Chap. 7, we have identified the effort-reduction for each decision strategy when it is supported by IIMT. The analysis reveals that the two IIMT *FILTER* and *SORT* which support the EBA, LEX, and LED strategy are able to reduce the dependency of effort on the number of alternatives tremendously. In a descriptive study on the distribution of the 100 most important shopping websites, we observed that these two IIMT are the ones which are predominantly offered in the screening phase (see Sect. 5.1.2.2). However, while *FILTER* are in a quite advanced and user-friendly status on current websites, *SORT* often lacks certain features, such as sorting for nominal values (e.g., colors) according to a self-defined preference order, sorting not only for price but all product features, and sorting hierarchically according to several criteria. In short, in the screening phase, we suggest to carry on the current approach of webstores and to offer *FILTER* and *SORT* with an extended functionality.

Whenever the consumer has succeeded in reducing the consideration set to a small amount, the remaining products can be compared in a product-comparison matrix. INTACMATO shows how consumers can be supported in this in-depth comparison phase. Consumers usually put more effort into comparison of few, preferred alternatives (Olshavsky 1979; Payne 1976; Payne et al. 1988; Svenson 1979). Hence, we advise that decision strategies of high accuracy should be supported in this phase. Following the normative model, decision strategies with high accuracy are those that select alternatives with high utility. According to the effort-accuracy models, WADD, EQW, MAJ, and FRQ are examples of such strategies which either maximize utility (WADD) or at least consider all information and somehow approximate a utility-maximizing model by summing up positive and negative attribute levels. All these strategies can be supported by IIMT which allow the user to evaluate attributes and attribute levels. We denoted such IIMT with *SCORE* and *CALCULATE* and made several suggestions in Chap. 6. We advise to lay more emphasize on offering such IIMT in the screening phase. Furthermore, *FILTER* was widely used in our study and should therefore be offered in both phases.

9.2.3 Offering a Variety of IIMT in the In-Depth Comparison Phase

In three empirical studies (see Chaps. 3, 4, and 8), we showed that people apply a variety of decision strategies in the in-depth comparison phase and that they switch from attribute-wise to alternative-wise information acquisition. Thus, a variety of IIMT which support all different kinds of decision-making behavior should be offered in the in-depth comparison phase. In addition to that, we observed that when people first encounter INTACMATO, they predominantly use *FILTER* and $SCORE_{attributeLevel}$ but with increasing familiarity with INTACMATO respondents become more diverse and each IIMT is used at least once by over 5% of respondents. Thus, all IIMT seem to be of relevance.

Since our results also showed that people experienced the variety of offered IIMT to be less effortful and found it more satisfying and enjoyed shopping more in case many IIMT were offered, we advise webdesigners to offer several IIMT in the in-depth comparison phase.

Figure 9.1 shows the number of decision strategies which are supported by each IIMT. *CALCULATE*, for instance, is needed by eight different strategies, followed by *MARK*, which appears in seven strategies. Furthermore, Fig. 9.2 displays how many different decision strategies could be supported if a web store were to offer a combination of IIMT. The IIMT are ordered decreasingly according to the number of strategies which they support. Although *CALCULATE* can be used in eight different strategies, this IIMT alone supports no strategy. In combination with *MARK*, however, three strategies can be supported (DOM, FRQ, MAJ). Offering the three IIMT *CALCULATE*, *MARK*, and *REMOVE* would increase the number of supported strategies already to eight (adding COM, CONJ, SAT+, DIS, and SAT).

9.2.4 Adapting the Set of IIMT to Complexity

In our study in Chap. 3, we learned that people increase depth and breadth of search when products are very similar to each other and when there are a lot of trade-offs. We further found that they spend the additional effort predominantly in the first

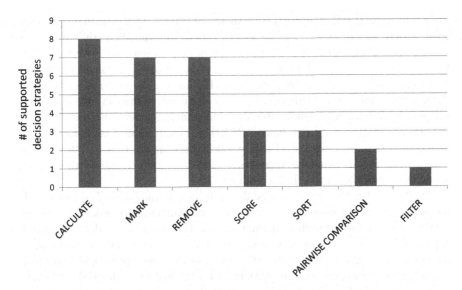

Fig. 9.1 Number of decision strategies which are supported by each decision aid

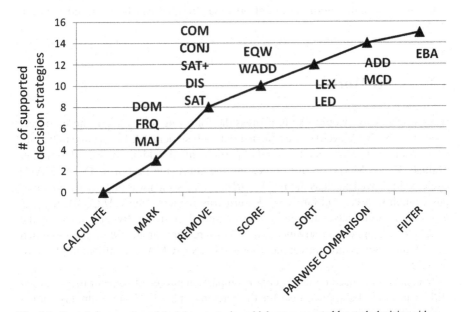

Fig. 9.2 Cumulative number of decision strategies which are supported by each decision aid

stage of the decision process when they eliminate inferior alternatives. This result was supported by our study presented in Chap. 4, where we found an increased usage of EBA that compares attribute-wise and eliminates alternatives in case of similar products with a lot of trade-offs. Thus, in case of high similarity and many trade-offs, a *FILTER* that supports EBA should be offered. However, there are other attribute-wise strategies such as LEX and LED that eliminate alternatives for which we need the IIMT *SORT*. Yet, LEX was rarely used in our study. We think that the other two strategies that are attribute-wise and eliminate alternatives (ADD and MCD, see Table A.1) are less likely to be used because they cost too much effort (see Table 7.3) and are thus not suitable to quickly eliminate alternatives. More research needs to be done, to test which other decision strategies apart from the four ones tested in our study (EBA, LEX, WADD, MAJ) are exactly applied in choice tasks of high complexity. With that knowledge, webdesigners can use Figs. 9.1, 9.2 and the pseudo-code notations (see the Appendix A and Sect. 7.2) to determine which IIMT are needed to support the particular strategies.

Finally, another conclusion can be drawn from our study described in Chap. 4, where we argued that people try to follow a more compensatory process in case of high complexity but fail in their attempt and finally make a choice that can be best explained by a non-compensatory strategy. Hence, depending on the webdesigner's intention, one might think of supporting users in their attempt to apply effortful, compensatory strategies such as WADD and MAJ and offer the IIMT *SCORE*, *MARK* and *CALCULATE* needed to support these strategies. By computing the net saving of effort with the indicated costs of EIP and ECP (see all pseudo-code notations), one can determine the effort-reduction that can be achieved for each strategy.

9.3 Future Work

In future work, we would like to address the following topics. First, our empirical evaluation of INTACMATO was carried out with students. A follow up study with a larger and more representative pool of participants should be conducted to further evaluate INTACMATO. Before repeating the study, the design of INTACMATO could be improved, such as the IIMT $SORT_{drag\&drop}$ which was apparently not obvious enough to users and rarely used. Furthermore, activating $CALCULATE_{weighted}$ by default might have influenced the empirical study. Activating none of the *CALCULATE*-options in advance might be more appropriate. Other aspects, such as customer ratings, are not yet incorporated in INTACMATO at all but might be of interest.

Second, we focused on the in-depth comparison phase but some of the proposed IIMT can easily be applied also for the screening phase. We have already started with including some IIMT in a prototypical screening phase-interface in one of our other works in order to test which IIMT are appropriate and whether we should improve and adapt certain IIMT for the screening phase. For example, we are currently developing an extension of *SORT* which allows to specify a preference order for nominal attributes, for instance color.

Third, we argued that, generally, offering a variety of IIMT is a better approach than offering only certain IIMT because people might feel restricted. Nevertheless, we showed that when we have knowledge of problem characteristics such as complexity, some decision strategies are applied more often than other. In this case, some IIMT appear more relevant than others. In addition to the problem characteristics considered here, decision-making behavior is influenced by social context and personal characteristics. The ideal future system should be able to adapt automatically to problem characteristics, personal characteristics and the social context by, for instance, showing the appropriate IIMT. Moreover, we could learn from the user's behavior in the screening phase and incorporate that knowledge directly when showing the product-comparison matrix: certain product information could be highlighted, other left out; certain IIMT might be offered and other IIMT might be left out. Learning about decision-making behavior in the first phase in order to immediately personalize and customize the interface leads us to our next topic.

As a fourth topic we would like to improve learning decision-making behavior from data. Particularly in Internet applications, it is easy to gather all kinds of process data via clickstream analysis and user profiles, to mention only a few. Currently, we are developing an automated way of assigning decision strategies to clickstream data based on the idea of state machines where each activated state machine represents a potentially applied decision strategy. Since several state machines can be activated during the decision process, this modeling approach also allows for learning mixed decision strategies. A next step will be to incorporate all kinds of data in the algorithm, such as mouse movements, eye-tracking data, etc.

Last but not least, our ideas and our prototype are easily extendable to all other kinds of preferential decision problems. It will be interesting for instance, to test INTACMATO on managerial decisions.

Appendix A
Details on Decision Strategies

Table A.1 Decision strategies and alternative name conventions

Abbr.	Strategy name	Source
1. ADD	Additive difference strategy (for 2 alternatives)	Tversky 1969
	Additive difference model (extended)	Payne 1976
	Addition of utility differences rule	Montgomery and Svenson 1976
2. COM	Compatibility test	Beach 1990
	(Image theory)	Beach and Mitchell 1987
3. CONJ	Conjunctive strategy	Coombs and Kao 1955
4. DIS	Disjunctive strategy	Coombs and Kao 1955
5. DOM	Dominance strategy	Lee 1971
6. EBA	Elimination by aspect strategy	Tversky 1972
	Deterministic version of elimination by aspect strategy	Payne et al. 1988
7. EQW	Equal weight heuristic	Einhorn and Hogharth 1975
	Dawes rule	Dawes and Corrigan 1974
	Equal weight linear model	Dawes 1979
	Equal weighting rule	Thorngate 1980
8. FRQ	Frequency of good and/or bad features heuristic	Alba and Marmorstein 1987
	Maximizing number of attributes with a great attractiveness	Montgomery and Svenson 1976
9. LED	Minimum difference lexicographic strategy	Montgomery and Svenson 1976
	Lexicographic semiorder strategy	Luce 1956
10. LEX	Lexicographic heuristic	Tversky 1969
11. MAJ	Simple majority decision rule	Arrow 1951
12. MCD	Majority of confirming dimensions heuristic	Wright and Barbour 1977
13. SAT	Satisficing heuristic	Simon 1955
14. SAT+	Satisficing-plus heuristic	Park 1978
15. WADD	Weighted additive rule	Tversky 1969
	Additive model	Fishburn 1970
	Multiattribute utility model	Montgomery and Svenson 1976
	Addition of utilities rule	Todd and Benbasat 1991

J. Pfeiffer, *Interactive Decision Aids in E-Commerce*, Contributions to Management Science, DOI 10.1007/978-3-7908-2769-9, © Springer-Verlag Berlin Heidelberg 2012

		compensatory vs. non-compensatory	attribute weights (ratio or ordinal scale)	attribute-wise vs. alternative-wise	pairwise comparison	aspiration levels used	consistency across attributes/alternatives	complete vs. selective	elimination of alternatives	quantitative vs. qualitative evaluation	screening vs. choice
1	ADD	comp	ratio	attr	yes	-	yes	comp	elim	quant	choice
2	COM	n.-comp	-	alt	-	yes	-	sel	elim	qual	screen
3	CONJ	n.-comp	-	alt	-	yes	-	sel	elim	qual	screen
4	DIS	n.-comp	-	alt	-	yes	-	sel	elim	qual	screen
5	DOM	n.-comp	-	attr	-	-	yes	comp	-	qual	choice
6	EBA	n.-comp	ordinal	attr	-	yes	-	sel	elim	qual	screen
7	EQW	comp	-	alt	-	-	yes	comp	-	quant	choice
8	FRQ	comp	-	alt	-	yes	yes	comp	-	quant	choice
9	MAJ	comp	-	attr	yes	-	yes	comp	-	quant	choice
10	MCD	comp	-	attr	-	-	yes	comp	elim	quant	choice
11	LED	n.-comp	ordinal	attr	-	-	-	sel	elim	quant	choice
12	LEX	n.-comp	ordinal	attr	-	-	-	sel	elim	qual	choice
13	SAT	n.-comp	-	alt	-	yes	-	sel	elim	qual	screen
14	SAT+	n.-comp	-	alt	-	yes	-	sel	elim	qual	screen
15	WADD	comp	ratio	alt	-	-	yes	comp	-	quant	choice

Fig. A.1 Characteristics of decision strategies

Table A.2 Summary of studies on choice task complexity

Study	Subjects and task	Design	Method	Independent variables	Dependent variables	Results
Ford et al. (1989)	Meta-study on studies with 9–120 subjects, diverse types of tasks	Within-subjects, between-subjects	Information display board, verbal protocol	Task-based complexity: (1) number of alternatives (2 up to 15), (2) number of attributes (2 up to 15)	(a) depth of search (b) search index (c) time spent on each alternative and each attribute	(1,2:a) depth of search decreases with increasing amount of information; (1,2:b,c) increasing amount of information leads to an attribute-wise search and varying time spent on each alternative and each attribute
Bettman et al. (1993)	34 students, gambles	Within-subjects, (4 alt., 4 att.), 8 choices	Mouselab	Context-based complexity (attribute range and trade-offs): (1) correlation of attribute-vectors, (2) variance of pay-offs	(a) depth of search (b) time (c) variance of time spent on each alternative (d) variance of time spent on each attribute (e) search index (f) relative accuracy (g) utility maximizing choice	(1,2:a,b) decision time and depth of search increases with strongly decreasing (1) and low (2) ; (1,2:c,d,e) increasing negative correlation and low variance of pay-offs leads to decreases of (c) and alternative-wise search, (1,2: f,g) accuracy decreases with increasing (1) and decreasing (2), (1 + 2) strong negative correlation in interaction with low variance increases decision time and the amount of information acquired

(continued)

Table A.2 (continued)

Study	Subjects and task	Design	Method	Independent variables	Dependent variables	Results
Biggs et al. (1985)	11 lending officers, choice between credit users	Within-subjects, 4 choices per subject with varying task-based complexity, 2 choices with varying context-based complexity, no dominant alternatives	Information display board, verbal protocol	Task-based complexity: (1) number of alternatives (3; 10) (2) number of attributes (3;7); context-based complexity (attribute range): (3) variances of attribute levels on a 11-point scale (low variance if less than 3 levels difference per attribute)	(a) depth of search (b) standard deviation of information acquired per alternative	(1,2:a) depth of search decreases with increasing (1), (2); (3:a) depth of search increases with low variance; (1,2,3:b) (b) increases with increasing amount of information, particularly for increasing (2); (b) decreases with higher similarity (decreasing (3)), however in general the effects of task-based complexity are stronger than those of context-based complexity
Böckenholt et al. (1991, study 1)	16 students, choice between summer vacation locations	Within-subjects, (2 alt., 10 att.), 84 choices, prescribed attribute values	Mouselab	Context-based complexity (attribute ranges, overall attractiveness, dominance structure): (1) variances of attribute levels on a 13-point scale (low variance if less than 4 levels different for at least 80% of attributes) (2) overall attractiveness (3) one dominant vs. no dominant alternative	(a) breadth of search	(1,2:a) breadth of search increases with decreasing (1) and (2) (main effect), interaction effect as breadth of search increases more strongly in case of low (2), (3:a) breadth of search increases when there is no dominant alternative

Study	Sample	Design	Method	Complexity	Dependent variable	Results
Böckenholt et al. (1991, study 2)	18 students, choice between restaurants	Within-subjects, (2 alt., 10 att.), 30 choices per subject, self-reported ranking of attribute levels and attribute weights	Mouselab	Context-based complexity (attribute ranges, overall attractiveness, dominance): (1) attractiveness difference (difference of the sum of attribute level ranks on two attributes) (2) overall attractiveness	(a) breadth of search	(1,2:a): breadth of search increases with decreasing (1) and (2) (main effect), no interaction
Fasolo et al. (2003)	123 students, choice between digital cameras	Within-subjects, (5 alt., 8 att.), 4 choices per subject	Mouselab	Context-based complexity (trade-offs): (1) correlations of attribute-vectors	(a) search index (b) self-reported complexity	(1:a): more alternative-wise search with decreasing (1), (1:b) self-reported complexity increases with decreasing (1)
Fasolo et al. (2009)	120 students, choice between cell phones	Between-subjects, (6;24 alt., 5 att.), 1 choice	Questionnaire	Task-based complexity: (1) number of alternatives (6;24), context-based complexity (trade-offs): (2) correlations of attribute-vectors	(a) time (effort) (b) self-reported effort	(1:a) (a) increases with increasing (1), (2:a) (a) increases with decreasing (2), (2:b) (b) decreases with increasing (2)
Garbarino and Edell (1997)	45 students and faculty, choice between abstract, numeric alternatives	Within-subjects, 7 choices	Mouselab	Task-based complexity: (1) number of alternatives (2;3;4), context-based complexity (dominance structure): (2) complexity of displayed fractions (3) dominance of more complex alternative	(a) time spent on each alternative, (b) accuracy as absolute number of correct answers	(1,2:a) (a) increases with increasing (2), this effect is the stronger the higher (1), (1:b) (b) decreases with increasing (1), (1,2;3:b) dominance is recognized in 94% of cases

(continued)

Table A.2 (continued)

Study	Subjects and task	Design	Method	Independent variables	Dependent variables	Results
Iglesias-Parro et al. (2002, study 1)	98 students, choices between job candidates	Between-subjects, (2 alt., 5 att.), 7 choices, prescribed utility function	Mouselab	Context-based complexity (attribute range): (1) variance of attribute values, (2) mean of attribute values	(a) time (effort) (b) self-reported effort (c) search index	(a,b) both correlate strongly positive, (1:a) time increases with decreasing (1), (2:a) (a) increases with (2) approaching 0 (1,2:c) no significant result; in total attribute-wise search
Iglesias-Parro et al. (2002, study 2)	84 students, choices between job candidates	Between-subjects, (2 alt., 5 att.), 1 choice, prescribed utility function	Mouselab	Context-based complexity (attribute range and trade-offs): (1) mean of difference of attribute values (2) correlation of attribute vectors	(a) time (effort) (b) self-reported effort (c) search index	(a,b) both correlate strongly positive, (1:a,b) effort increases with mean approaching 0 (2:a,b) effort increases with negative (2), (1,2:c) no significant influence, in total attribute-wise search
Iglesias-Parro et al. (2002, study 3)	84 students, choices between job candidates	Within-subjects (2 alt., 5 att.), 6 choices, prescribed utility function	Mouselab	Context-based complexity (attribute range and trade-offs): (1) variance of attribute values (2) correlation of attribute vectors	(a) time (effort) (b) self-reported effort (c) search index	(a,b) both correlate strongly positive, (1:a,b) effort increases with increasing (1), (2:a,b) effort increases with negative (2), (1,2:c) no significant influence, in total attribute-wise search

Study	Sample	Design	Tool	Complexity	Dependent variables	Results
Klein and Yadav (1989)	74 students, choice of an MBA program	Within-subjects (18 alt., 5 att.), 3 choices, utility function is determined with conjoint analysis	improved version of Mouselab	Context-based complexity (dominance structure): (1) number of dominated alternatives	(a) self-reported accuracy and effort (b) time (effort) (c) relative accuracy (d) number of elimination steps and the number of eliminated alternatives (sequence of search)	(1:a,b) correlates positive with (b), particular with high (1:b,c) faster and more accurate decisions with increasing (1:d) (d) decreases with increasing (1)
Luce et al. (1997)	41 students, choice between job offers	Between-subjects for (1) and within-subjects for (2), utility function is determined a priori	Mouselab	Context-based complexity (trade-offs): (1) correlations of attribute-vectors (2) trade-offs on important vs. non-important attributes according to individual preferences	(a) self-reported experience of amount of trade-offs (b) time (effort) (c) depth of search (d) search index	(1,2:a) (1) and (2) correlated significantly, particular for important attributes (2), (1:b,c)(b) and (c) increase with decreasing (1), (1,2:c) only the interaction of both (1) and (2) lead to more depth of search, (1,2:d) no significant result
Timmermans (1993)	48 students, choice between personnel	Between-subjects, 1 choice, no dominant alternative	Verbal protocol	Task-based complexity: (1) number of alternatives (2) number of attributes	(a) number of considered attributes (b) depth of search (c) number of mentioned alternatives (d) number of absolute and comparative statements on attributes and alternatives	(1,2:a) (a) increases with increasing (1) and (2) but for (2) only until a threshold is reached, (1,2:b) depth of search decreases with increasing (1) and (2), (1,2:c,d) (c) decreases with increasing (2); more attribute-wise search when (1) and (2) increase; at the end of decision process in total more alternative-wise search

Algorithm	ADD without support of IIMT

// Assign attribute weights.
for $i = 1$ to m **do**
  READ $attr_i$
  EVALUATE $attr_i$ with weight w_i $\Big\}\, 3m$
  STORE w_i
end for
// Compare so far best alternative with next one.
for $j = 2$ to n **do**
  // If j==2, then j=1 is the currently best alternative.
  if $j \neq 2$ **then**
    RETRIEVE currently best alternative $\Big\}\, n\text{-}1$
  end if
  for $i = 1$ to m **do**
    if $j == 2$ **then**
      READ a_{i1}
      EVALUATE a_{i1} with $v_i(a_{i1})$ $\Big\}\, 3m$
      STORE $v_i(a_{ibest}) = v_i(a_{i1})$
    end if
    RETRIEVE $v_i(a_{ibest})$
    READ a_{ij}
    EVALUATE a_{ij} with $v_i(a_{ij})$
    RETRIEVE w_i $\Big\}\, 7m$
    DIFFERENCE $dummy = v_i(a_{ibest}) - v_i(a_{ij})$
    PRODUCT $dummy = w_i * dummy$
    ADD $diff+ = dummy$
    if $i \neq 1$ **then**
      RETRIEVE $diff_{stored}$
      ADD $diff_{stored}+ = diff$ $\Big\}\, 3(m\text{-}1)$
      STORE $diff_{stored}$
    else
      STORE $diff_{stored} = diff$ $\Big\}\, 1$
    end if
  end for
  // Eliminate alternative with lower utility.
  if $diff_{stored} > 0$ **then**
    ELIMINATE alt_j
    STORE new status of alt_j $\Big\}\, 2{*}0$ (worst-case scenario)
  else
    ELIMINATE alt_{best}
    STORE new status of alt_j
    STORE new status of alt_{best} $\Big\}\, 3(n\text{-}1)$ (worst-case scenario)
  end if
end for
CHOOSE remaining alt $\Big\}\, 1$

Overall bracket spanning the inner loop block: $\Big\}\, n\text{-}1$

Fig. A.2 Effort for ADD without support of IIMT

Algorithm   ADD with support of IIMT

CLICK $CALCULATE_{weighted}$ $\left.\right\}$1
// Assign attribute weights.
for $i = 1$ to m **do**
   READ $attr_i$
   EVALUATE $attr_i$ with weight w_i $\left.\right\}$ 3m
   CLICK assign w_i with $SCORE_{attribute}$
end for
// Assign utility values for the first alternative.
for $i = 1$ to m **do**
   READ a_{i1}
   EVALUATE a_{i1} with $v_i(a_{i1})$ $\left.\right\}$ 3m
   CLICK assign $v_i(a_{i1})$ with $SCORE_{attributeLevel}$
end for
CLICK $PAIRWISE\ COMPARISON\ alt_1$ $\left.\right\}$1
// Compare so far best alternative with next one.
for $j = 2$ to n **do**
   // Assign utility values for the next alternative.
   CLICK $PAIRWISE\ COMPARISON\ alt_j$ $\left.\right\}$n-1
   for $i = 1$ to m **do**
      READ a_{ij}
      EVALUATE a_{ij} with $v_i(a_{ij})$ $\left.\right\}$3m(n-1)
      CLICK assign $v_i(a_{ij})$ with $SCORE_{attributeLevel}$ (worst-case
   end for   scenario)
   // Eliminate alternative with lower utility.
   if utility of alt_{best} > utility of alt_j **then**
      CLICK $REMOVE_{alt_j}$ $\left.\right\}$1
   else
      CLICK $REMOVE_{alt_{best}}$ $\left.\right\}$1*0
   end if
end for
CHOOSE remaining alt $\left.\right\}$1

Fig. A.3 Effort for ADD with support of IIMT

Algorithm   COM without support of IIMT

// Assign aspiration levels
for $i = 1$ to m do
  READ $attr_i$
  EVALUATE $attr_i$ with aspiration levels $\Big\}\ 3m$
  STORE updated asp
end for
// Eliminate the alternative if $\sum_{i=1}^{m} asp(a_{ij}) > k$.
for $j = 1$ to n do
  for $i = 1$ to m do
    RETRIEVE asp
    if COMPARE $asp(a_{ij}) == 1$ then $\Big\}2mn$
      if $i \neq 1$ then
        RETRIEVE $aspirationLevelsViolated$ $\Big\}n(m\text{-}1)$
      end if   (worst-case
      ADD $aspirationLevelsViolated+ = asp(a_{ij})$ scenario)
      STORE $aspirationLevelsViolated$ $\Big\}3mn$
      if COMPARE $aspirationLevelsViolated > k$ then (worst-case
        ELIMINATE alt_j scenario)
        STORE new status of alt_j $\Big\}2(n\text{-}1)$
        BREAKLOOP
      end if   (worst-case
    end if   scenario)
  end for
end for
CHOOSE remaining alt $\Big\}1$

Fig. A.4 Effort for COM without support of IIMT

Algorithm   COM with support of IIMT

```
// Assign aspiration levels
for i = 1 to m do
    READ attr_i
    EVALUATE attr_i with aspiration levels          } 3m
    STORE updated asp
end for
// Activate the possibility to highlight attribute levels.
CLICK CALCULATE_markings                            } 1
// Eliminate the alternative if ∑_{i=1}^{m} asp(a_ij) > k.
for j = 1 to n do
    for i = 1 to m do
        RETRIEVE asp
        if COMPARE asp(a_ij) == 1 then
            CLICK MARK_manually a_ij                 } 4mn
            if COMPARE CALCULATE_markings > k then        (worst-case
                CLICK REMOVE_alt_j                            scenario)
                BREAKLOOP                            } n-1
            end if                                        (worst-case
        end if                                            scenario)
    end for
end for
CHOOSE remaining alt                                } 1
```

Fig. A.5 Effort for COM with support of IIMT

Algorithm   CONJ without support of IIMT

```
// Assign aspiration levels
for i = 1 to m do
    READ attr_i
    EVALUATE attr_i with aspiration levels          } 3m
    STORE updated asp
end for
// Eliminate the alternative if ∑_{i=1}^{m} asp(a_ij) >= 1.
for j = 1 to n do
    for i = 1 to m do
        RETRIEVE asp
        if COMPARE asp(a_ij) == 1 then              } 2mn
            ELIMINATE alt_j
            STORE new status of alt_j               } 2(n-1)
            BREAKLOOP                                     (worst-case
        end if                                            scenario)
    end for
end for
CHOOSE remaining alt                                } 1
```

Fig. A.6 Effort for CONJ without support of IIMT

Algorithm   CONJ with support of IIMT

// Assign aspiration levels
for $i = 1$ to m do
  READ $attr_i$
  EVALUATE $attr_i$ with aspiration levels $\Big\}$ $3m$
  STORE updated asp
end for
// Eliminate the alternative if $\sum_{i=1}^{m} asp(a_{ij}) >= 1$.
for $j = 1$ to n do
  for $i = 1$ to m do
    RETRIEVE asp
    if COMPARE $asp(a_{ij}) == 1$ then $\Big\}2mn$
      CLICK $MARK_{manually}$ a_{ij} $\Big\}$n-1 (worst-case
      BREAKLOOP   scenario)
    end if
  end for
end for
$REMOVE_{markings}$
CHOOSE remaining alt $\Big\}2$

Fig. A.7 Effort for CONJ with support of IIMT

Algorithm   DIS without support of IIMT

// Assign aspiration levels
for $i = 1$ to m do
  READ $attr_i$
  EVALUATE $attr_i$ with aspiration levels $\Big\}$ $3m$
  STORE updated asp
end for
// Eliminate the alternative if $\sum_{i=1}^{m} asp(a_{ij}) == m$.
for $j = 1$ to n do
  for $i = 1$ to m do
    RETRIEVE asp $\Big\}2mn$ (worst-case
    if COMPARE $asp(a_{ij}) == 1$ then   scenario)
      if $i \neq 1$ then $\Big\}n(m-1)$
        RETRIEVE $aspirationLevelsViolated$ (worst-case
      end if   scenario)
      ADD $aspirationLevelsViolated+ = asp(a_{ij})$
      STORE $aspirationLevelsViolated$ $\Big\}3mn$
      if COMPARE $aspirationLevelsViolated == k$ then (worst-case
        ELIMINATE alt_j scenario)
        STORE new status of alt_j $\Big\}2(n-1)$
        BREAKLOOP   (worst-case
      end if   scenario)
    end if
  end for
end for
CHOOSE remaining alt $\Big\}1$

Fig. A.8 Effort for DIS without support of IIMT

Algorithm DIS with support of IIMT	
// Assign aspiration levels	
for $i = 1$ to m **do**	
READ $attr_i$	
EVALUATE $attr_i$ with aspiration levels	$\}\,3m$
STORE updated asp	
end for	
// Activate the possibility to highlight attribute levels.	
CLICK $CALCULATE_{markings}$	$\}1$
// Eliminate the alternative if $\sum_{i=1}^{m} asp(a_{ij}) >== m$.	
for $j = 1$ to n **do**	
for $i = 1$ to m **do**	
RETRIEVE asp	
if COMPARE $asp(a_{ij}) == 1$ **then**	
CLICK $MARK_{manually}$ a_{ij}	$\}\,4mn$ (worst-case
if COMPARE $CALCULATE_{markings} == m$ **then**	scenario)
CLICK $REMOVE_{alt_j}$	
BREAKLOOP	$\}\,n{-}1$
end if	(worst-case
end if	scenario)
end for	
end for	
CHOOSE remaining alt	$\}1$

Fig. A.9 Effort for DIS with support of IIMT

Algorithm   DOM without support of IIMT

```
// Determine highest attribute value per attribute.
for i = 1 to m do
    for j = 1 to n do
        READ a_ij
        EVALUATE a_ij with v_i(a_ij)              } 2nm (worst-case scenario)
        if j == 1 then
            STORE v_i(a_ij) as v_i(a_ibest)        } m (worst-case scenario)
        else
            RETRIEVE v_i(a_ibest)
            COMPARE v_i(a_ij) and v_i(a_ibest)     } 2(n-1)m (worst-case scenario)
            if v_i(a_ij) > v_i(a_ibest) then
                // There is no dominant alt if the current dominant alt is dominated
                // This can be checked by comparing the indices of alternatives.
                RETRIEVE alt_dominant
                if (i ≥ 2) && (dominant < best) then   } (n-1)m (worst-case scenario)
                    return
                end if
                STORE v_i(a_ij) as v_i(a_ibest)         } (n-1)m (worst-case scenario)
            end if
        end if
    end for
    if i == 1 then
        STORE alt_best as alt_dominant                  } 1
    end if
end for
RETRIEVE alt_dominant
CHOOSE alt_dominant                                     } 2 (worst-case scenario)
```

$$\} 2nm \text{ (worst-case scenario)}$$

$$\} m \text{ (worst-case scenario)}$$

$$\} 2(n-1)m \text{ (worst-case scenario)}$$

$$\} (n-1)m \text{ (worst-case scenario)}$$

$$\} (n-1)m \text{ (worst-case scenario)}$$

$$\} 1$$

$$\} 2 \text{ (worst-case scenario)}$$

Fig. A.10 Effort for DOM without support of IIMT

Algorithm   DOM with support of IIMT

// Determine highest attribute value per attribute.
CLICK $MARK_{diff/comm}$ $\}1$
// Activate the possibility to highlight attribute levels.
CLICK $CALCULATE_{markings}$ $\}1$
for $i = 1$ to m of only attributes with highlighted differences **do**
  for $j = 1$ to n **do**
    READ a_{ij}
    EVALUATE a_{ij} with $v_i(a_{ij})$ $\}2nm$ (worst-case scenario)
    if $j == 1$ **then**
      STORE $v_i(a_{ij})$ as $v_i(a_{ibest})$ $\}m$ (worst-case scenario)
    else
      RETRIEVE $v_i(a_{ibest})$
      COMPARE $v_i(a_{ij})$ and $v_i(a_{ibest})$ $\}2(n\text{-}1)m$ (worst-case scenario)
      if $v_i(a_{ij}) > v_i(a_{ibest})$ **then**
        // There is no dominant alt if the current dominant alt is dominated
        // This can be checked by comparing the indices of alternatives.
        if $(i \neq$ first attribute with differences$)$ && (index of marked alternative $<$ best) **then**
          return
        end if
        STORE $v_i(a_{ij})$ as $v_i(a_{ibest})$ $\}(n\text{-}1)m$ (worst-case scenario)
      end if
    end if
  end for
  if $i == 1$ **then**
    CLICK $MARK_{manually}$ of $v_i(a_{ibest})$ $\}1$
  end if
end for
CHOOSE marked alternative $\}1$ (worst-case scenario)

Fig. A.11 Effort for DOM with support of IIMT

Algorithm   EQW without support of IIMT

// Compute utility of each alternative.
for $j = 1$ to n do
  for $i = 1$ to m do
    READ a_{ij}
    EVALUATE a_{ij} with $v_i(a_{ij})$ **} 2m**
    if $i \neq 1$ then
      RETRIEVE $utility_j$
      ADD $utility_j + = v_i(a_{ij})$ **} 3(m-1)** **} n**
      STORE $utility_j$
    else
      STORE $utility_j = v_i(a_{ij})$ **} 1**
    end if
  end for
  // Eliminate alternative with lower utility.
  if $j > 1$ then
    RETRIEVE $utility_{j-1}$
    COMPARE $utility_{j-1}$ and $utility_j$ **} 3(n-1)**
    ELIMINATE alt with lower $utility$
  end if
end for
CHOOSE remaining alt **} 1**

Fig. A.12 Effort for EQW without support of IIMT

Algorithm   EQW with support of IIMT

// Compute utility of each alternative.
for $j = 1$ to n do
  for $i = 1$ to m do
    READ a_{ij}
    EVALUATE a_{ij} with $v_i(a_{ij})$
    CLICK assign $v_i(a_{ij})$ with $SCORE_{attributeLevel}$ **} 3nm**
  end for   **(worst-case**
end for   **scenario)**
CLICK $CALCULATE_{simple}$
CHOOSE alt with highest utility   **} 2**

Fig. A.13 Effort for EQW with support of IIMT

Algorithm FRQ without support of IIMT	
// Assign aspiration levels	
for $i = 1$ to m **do**	
READ $attr_i$	
EVALUATE $attr_i$ with aspiration levels	$\}\ 3m$
STORE updated asp	
end for	
// Count number of attribute levels which fulfill aspiration level.	
for $j = 1$ to n **do**	
for $i = 1$ to m **do**	
READ a_{ij}	
RETRIEVE asp	$\}\ 3mn$
if COMPARE $asp(a_{ij}) == 0$ **then**	
if $i \neq 1$ **then**	
RETRIEVE $goodCount_j$	
ADD $goodCount_j + = 1$	$\}\ 3(m-2)n+1$
STORE $goodCount_j$	(worst-case
else	scenario)
STORE $goodCount_j = 1$	$\}n$
end if	
end if	
end for	
// Eliminate alternative with lower sum.	
if $j > 1$ **then**	
RETRIEVE $goodCount_{j-1}$	
COMPARE $goodCount_{j-1}$ and $goodCount_j$	$\}\ 3(n-1)$
ELIMINATE alt with lower $goodCount$	
end if	
end for	
CHOOSE remaining alt	$\}1$

Fig. A.14 Effort for FRQ without support of IIMT

Algorithm   MAJ without support of IIMT

// Determine highest attribute value per attribute.

for $i = 1$ to m **do**

  READ a_{i1}

  EVALUATE a_{i1} with $v_i(a_{i1})$

  STORE $a_{ibest} = v_i(a_{i1})$ $\Big\}$ *3m*

  for $j = 2$ to n **do**

    READ a_{ij}

    EVALUATE a_{ij} with $v_i(a_{ij})$

    RETRIEVE $v_i(a_{ibest})$ $\Big\}$ *4m (n-1)*

    COMPARE $v_i(a_{ij})$ and $v_i(a_{ibest})$

    if $v_i(a_{ij}) > v_i(a_{ibest})$ **then**

      STORE $a_{ibest} = v_i(a_{ij})$ $\Big\}$ *m(n-1)*

    end if   (worst-case

  end for   scenario)

  if $i \neq 1$ **then**

    RETRIEVE $sum_{alt_{best}}$

    ADD $sum_{alt_{best}} + = 1$ $\Big\}$ *3(m-1)*

    STORE $sum_{alt_{best}}$

  else

    STORE $sum_{alt_{best}} = 1$ $\Big\}$ *1*

  end if

end for

// Choose alternative with highest score.

for $j = 1$ to n **do**

  RETRIEVE sum_{alt_j}

  RETRIEVE $sum_{alt_{best}}$

  COMPARE sum_{alt_j} and $sum_{alt_{best}}$ $\Big\}$ *4n*

  ELIMINATE alt with lower sum

end for

CHOOSE remaining alt $\Big\}$ *1*

Fig. A.15 Effort for MAJ without support of IIMT

Algorithm   FRQ with support of IIMT

```
// Assign aspiration levels
for i = 1 to m do
    READ attr_i
    EVALUATE attr_i with aspiration levels          } 3m
    STORE updated asp
end for
// Activate the possibility to highlight attribute levels.
CLICK CALCULATE_markings                            } 1
// Compute utility of each alternative.
for j = 1 to n do
    for i = 1 to m do                               } 3mn (worst-case
        READ a_ij                                           scenario)
        RETRIEVE asp
        if COMPARE asp(a_ij) == 0 then              } (m-1)n+1
            CLICK MARK_manually                            (worst-case
        end if                                             scenario)
    end for
end for
CHOOSE alt with highest utility                     } 1
```

Fig. A.16 Effort for FRQ with support of IIMT

Algorithm   MAJ with support of IIMT

```
CLICK MARK_diff/com                                 } 2
CLICK CALCULATE_markings
// Determine highest attribute value per attribute.
for i = 1 to m do
    READ a_i1
    EVALUATE a_i1 with v_i(a_i1)                     } 3m
    STORE a_ibest = v_i(a_i1)
    for j = 2 to n do
        READ a_ij
        EVALUATE a_ij with v_i(a_ij)                } 4m (n-1)
        RETRIEVE v_i(a_ibest)
        COMPARE v_i(a_ij) and v_i(a_ibest)
        if v_i(a_ij) > v_i(a_ibest) then            } m(n-1)
            STORE a_ibest = v_i(a_ij)                    (worst-case
        end if                                          scenario)
    end for
    CLICK MARK_manually alt_best                     } m
end for
// Choose alternative with highest score.
CHOOSE alt with highest score                        } 1
```

Fig. A.17 Effort for MAJ with support of IIMT

Algorithm   MCD without support of IIMT

// Compare so far best alternative with next one.
for $j = 2$ to n **do**
  // If j==2, then j=1 is the currently best alternative.
  if $j \neq 2$ **then**
    RETRIEVE currently best alternative $\left. \right\} n\text{-}1$
  end if
  for $i = 1$ to m **do**
    if $j == 2$ **then**
      READ a_{i1}
      EVALUATE a_{i1} with $v_i(a_{i1})$ $\left. \right\} 3m$
      STORE $a_{ibest} = v_i(a_{i1})$
    end if
    RETRIEVE $v_i(a_{ibest})$
    READ a_{ij}
    EVALUATE a_{ij} with $v_i(a_{ij})$ $\left. \right\} 4m$
    COMPARE $v_i(a_{ibest})$ with $v_i(a_{ij})$
    if $v_i(a_{ibest}) > v_i(a_{ij})$ **then**
      if $i \neq 1$ **then**
        RETRIEVE $diff_{stored}$
        ADD $diff_{stored}+ = 1$ $\left. \right\} 3(m\text{-}1)$
        STORE $diff_{stored}$
      else
        STORE $diff_{stored} = 1$ $\left. \right\} 1$
      end if
    else
      if $i \neq 1$ **then**
        RETRIEVE $diff_{stored}$
        ADD $diff_{stored}- = 1$ $\left. \right\} 3(m\text{-}1)$
        STORE $diff_{stored}$
      else
        STORE $diff_{stored} = -1$ $\left. \right\} 1$
      end if
    end if
  end for
  // Eliminate alternative with lower utility.
  if $diff_{stored} > 0$ **then**
    ELIMINATE alt_j
    STORE new status of alt_j $\left. \right\} 2*0$ (worst-case scenario)
  else
    ELIMINATE alt_{best}
    STORE new status of alt_j $\left. \right\} 3(n\text{-}1)$ (worst-case scenario)
    STORE new status of alt_{best}
  end if
end for
CHOOSE remaining alt $\left. \right\} 1$

(Brackets on the right: the block from "RETRIEVE $v_i(a_{ibest})$" through the "STORE $diff_{stored} = 1$" grouped as $4m$, $3(m\text{-}1)$ and 1 are braced together as $n\text{-}1$; the else branch $3(m\text{-}1)$ and 1 are braced together as 0.)

Fig. A.18 Effort for MCD without support of IIMT

Algorithm MCD with support of IIMT

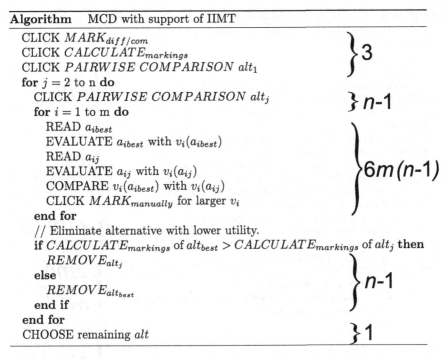

CLICK $MARK_{diff/com}$
CLICK $CALCULATE_{markings}$
CLICK $PAIRWISE\ COMPARISON\ alt_1$ $\Big\}\ 3$
for $j = 2$ to n **do**
  CLICK $PAIRWISE\ COMPARISON\ alt_j$ $\}\ n-1$
  for $i = 1$ to m **do**
    READ a_{ibest}
    EVALUATE a_{ibest} with $v_i(a_{ibest})$
    READ a_{ij}
    EVALUATE a_{ij} with $v_i(a_{ij})$ $\Big\}\ 6m\,(n-1)$
    COMPARE $v_i(a_{ibest})$ with $v_i(a_{ij})$
    CLICK $MARK_{manually}$ for larger v_i
  end for
  // Eliminate alternative with lower utility.
  if $CALCULATE_{markings}$ of $alt_{best} > CALCULATE_{markings}$ of alt_j **then**
    $REMOVE_{alt_j}$
  else $\Big\}\ n-1$
    $REMOVE_{alt_{best}}$
  end if
end for
CHOOSE remaining alt $\}\ 1$

Fig. A.19 Effort for MCD with support of IIMT

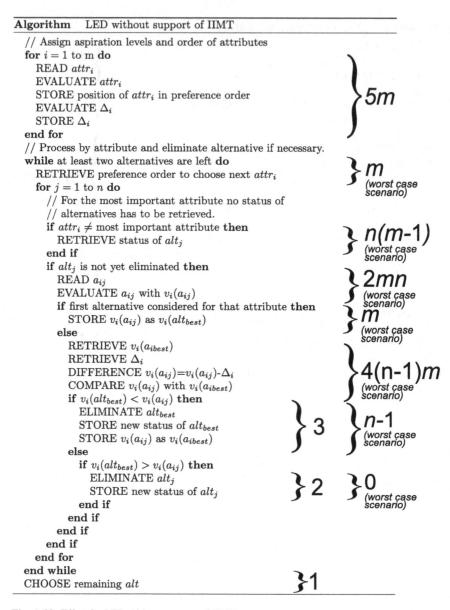

Fig. A.20 Effort for LED without support of IIMT

Algorithm   LED with support of IIMT

// Assign aspiration levels and order of attributes
for $i = 1$ to m do
   READ $attr_i$
   EVALUATE $attr_i$
   STORE position of $attr_i$ in preference order $\left.\rule{0pt}{6em}\right\} 5m$
   EVALUATE Δ_i
   STORE Δ_i
end for
// Process by attribute and eliminate alternative if necessary.
repeat
   RETRIEVE preference order to choose next $attr_i$ $\}\, 1$
   for $j = 1$ to n do
      READ a_{ij}
      EVALUATE $v_i(a_{ij})$ $\}\, 2n$
   end for
   SELECT $SORT_{hierarchically}$ for $attr_i$
   RETRIEVE Δ_i $\}\, 2$
until no alternatives are equivalent on considered attributes
CHOOSE most left alt $\}\, 1$

$\left.\rule{0pt}{6em}\right\} m$ (worst-case scenario)

Fig. A.21 Effort for LED with support of IIMT

Algorithm   SAT without support of IIMT

// Assign aspiration levels
for $i = 1$ to m do
   READ $attr_i$
   EVALUATE $attr_i$ with aspiration levels $\}\, 3m$
   STORE updated asp
end for
// Eliminate the alternative if $\sum_{i=1}^{m} asp(a_{ij}) >= 1$.
for $j = 1$ to n do
   for $i = 1$ to m do
      RETRIEVE asp
      if COMPARE $asp(a_{ij}) == 1$ then $\}\, 2mn$ (worst-case scenario)
         ELIMINATE alt_j
         STORE new status of alt_j
         BREAKLOOP
      end if
   end for
   if alt_j not removed then
      CHOOSE current alt $\}\, 1$
      BREAKLOOP
   end if
end for

$\}\, 2(n-1)$ (worst-case scenario)

Fig. A.22 Effort for SAT without support of IIMT

Algorithm   SAT with support of IIMT

// Assign aspiration levels
for $i = 1$ to m **do**
  READ $attr_i$
  EVALUATE $attr_i$ with aspiration levels $\Big\}$ 3m
  STORE updated asp
end for
// Eliminate the alternative if $\sum_{i=1}^{m} asp(a_{ij}) >= 1$.
for $j = 1$ to n **do**
  for $i = 1$ to m **do**
    RETRIEVE asp
    if COMPARE $asp(a_{ij}) == 1$ **then** $\Big\}$2mn (worst-case
      $REMOVE\ alt_j$ $\Big\}$n-1   scenario)
      BREAKLOOP   (worst-case
    end if   scenario)
  end for
  if alt_j not removed **then**
    CHOOSE current alt $\Big\}$1
    BREAKLOOP
  end if
end for

Fig. A.23 Effort for SAT with support of IIMT

Algorithm   SAT+ without support of IIMT

// Assign aspiration levels
for $i = 1$ to $m^\star$ **do**
  READ $attr_i$
  EVALUATE $attr_i$ with asp_i $\Big\}$ 3m*
  STORE asp
end for
// Eliminate the alternative if $\sum_{i=1}^{m^\star} asp(a_{ij}) >= 1$.
for $j = 1$ to n **do**
  for $i = 1$ to $m^\star$ **do**
    RETRIEVE asp_i
    if COMPARE $asp(a_{ij}) == 1$ **then** $\Big\}$2m*n (worst-case
      ELIMINATE alt_j $\Big\}$2(n-1) scenario)
      STORE new status of alt_j
      BREAKLOOP
    end if
  end for
  if alt_j not removed **then**
    CHOOSE current alt $\Big\}$1
    BREAKLOOP
  end if
end for

Fig. A.24 Effort for SAT+ without support of IIMT

Algorithm   SAT+ with support of IIMT

// Assign aspiration levels
for $i = 1$ to $m^\star$ **do**
   READ $attr_i$
   EVALUATE $attr_i$ with asp_i $\Big\}$ **3m***
   STORE asp
end for
// Eliminate the alternative if $\sum_{i=1}^{m^\star} asp(a_{ij}) >= 1$.
for $j = 1$ to n **do**
   for $i = 1$ to $m^\star$ **do**
      RETRIEVE asp
      if COMPARE $asp(a_{ij}) == 1$ **then** $\Big\}$**2m*n** (worst-case scenario)
         CLICK $REMOVE_{alt_j}$ $\Big\}$**n-1** (worst-case scenario)
         BREAKLOOP
      end if
   end for
   if alt_j not removed **then**
      CHOOSE current alt $\Big\}$**1**
      BREAKLOOP
   end if
end for

Fig. A.25 Effort for SAT+ with support of IIMT

Appendix B
Details on IIMT-Prototype

J. Pfeiffer, *Interactive Decision Aids in E-Commerce*, Contributions to Management
Science, DOI 10.1007/978-3-7908-2769-9, © Springer-Verlag Berlin Heidelberg 2012

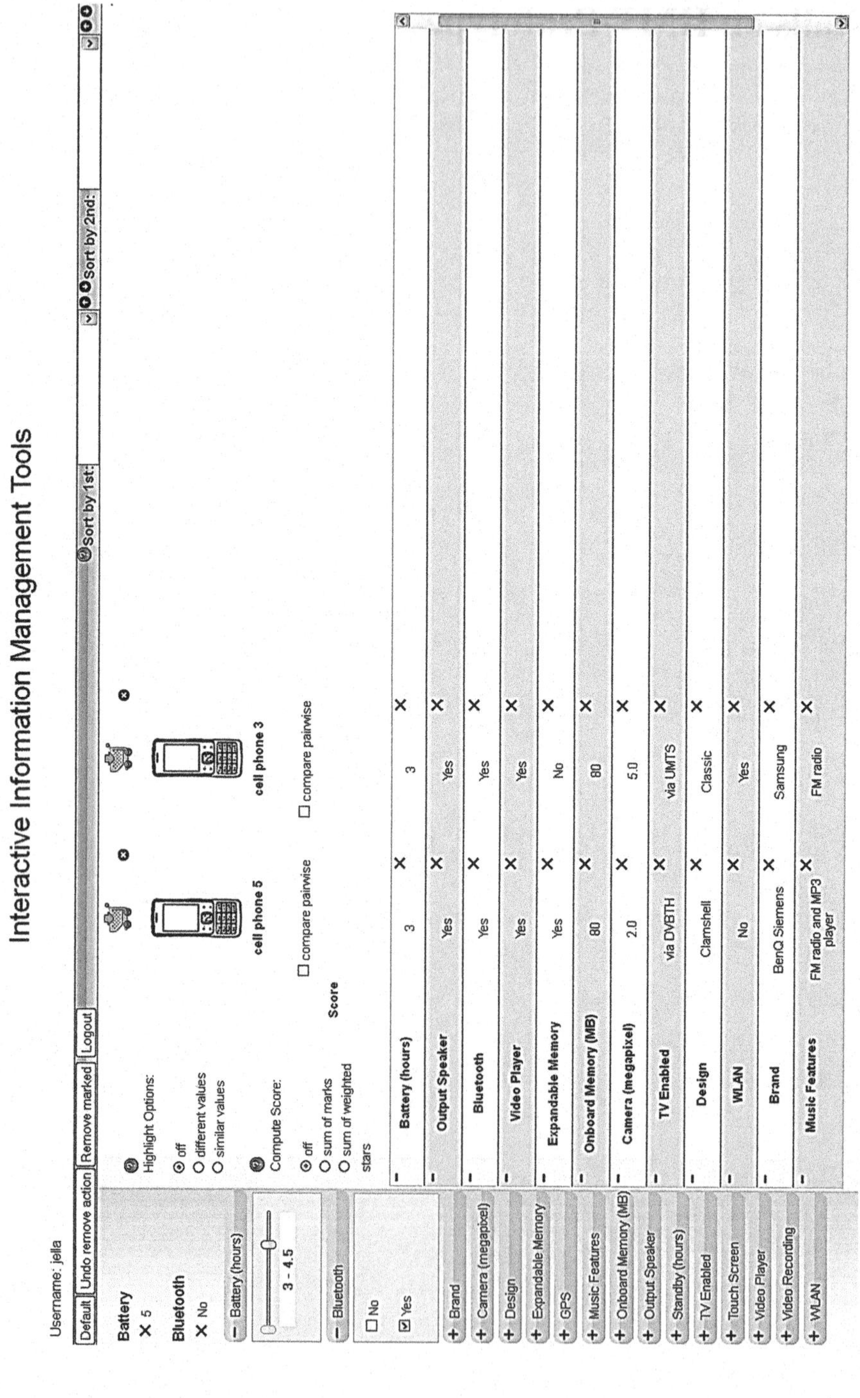

Interactive Information Management Tools

Username: jella

| Default | Undo remove action | Remove marked | Logout |

Battery
X 5

Bluetooth
X No

— Battery (hours)

3 - 4.5

— Bluetooth

☐ No
☑ Yes

Highlight Options:
⊙ off
○ different values
○ similar values

Compute Score:
⊙ off
○ sum of marks
○ sum of weighted stars

☐ compare pairwise   ☐ compare pairwise

Score

○ Sort by 1st: ○ ○ Sort by 2nd:

cell phone 5   cell phone 3

	Battery (hours)	3	X	3	X
	Output Speaker	Yes	X	Yes	X
+ Brand	**Bluetooth**	Yes	X	Yes	X
+ Camera (megapixel)	**Video Player**	Yes	X	Yes	X
+ Design	**Expandable Memory**	Yes	X	No	X
+ Expandable Memory	**Onboard Memory (MB)**	80	X	80	X
+ GPS	**Camera (megapixel)**	2.0	X	5.0	X
+ Music Features	**TV Enabled**	via DVBTH	X	via UMTS	X
+ Onboard Memory (MB)	**Design**	Clamshell	X	Classic	X
+ Output Speaker	**WLAN**	No	X	Yes	X
+ Standby (hours)	**Brand**	BenQ Siemens	X	Samsung	X
+ TV Enabled	**Music Features**	FM radio and MP3 player	X	FM radio	X
+ Touch Screen					
+ Video Player					
+ Video Recording					
+ WLAN					

Fig. B.1 Final design of IIMT: *FILTER*

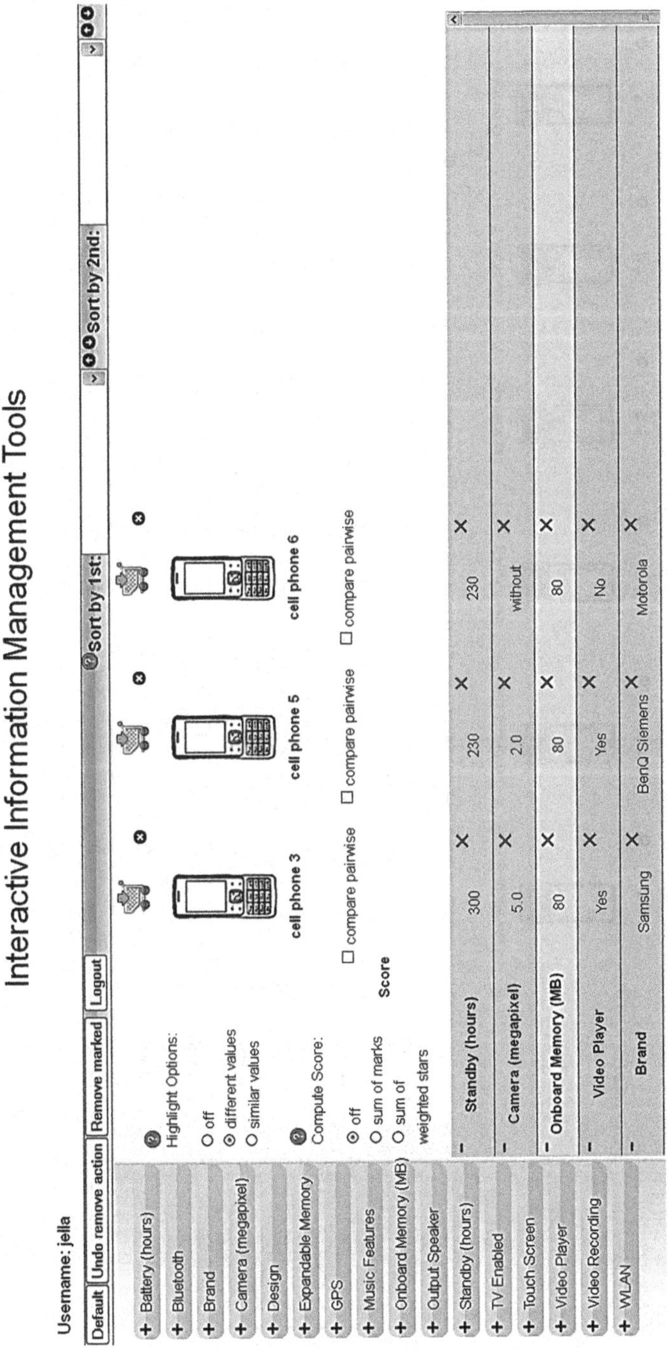

Fig. B.2 Final design of IIMT: $MARK_{diff}$

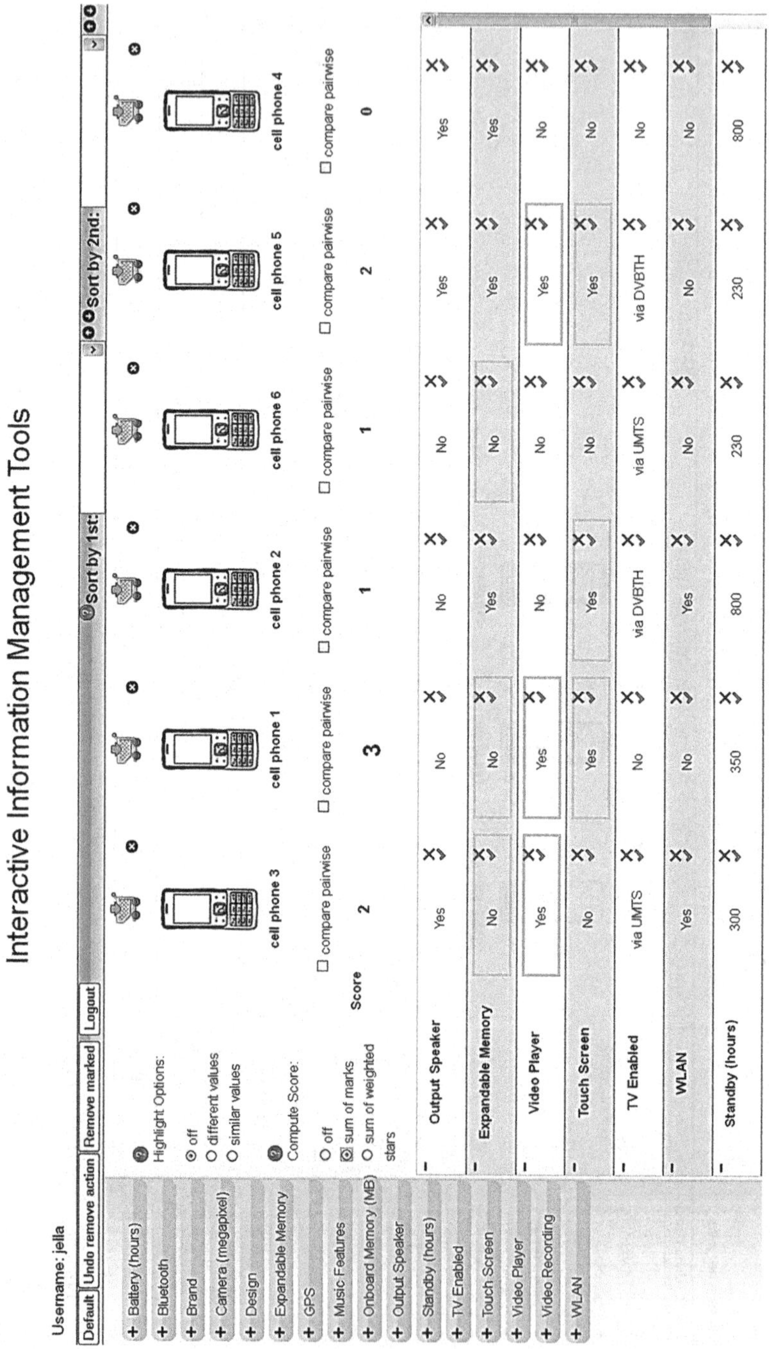

Fig. B.3 Final design of IIMT: $MARK_{manually}$ as a positive attribute level and $CALCULATE_{markings}$

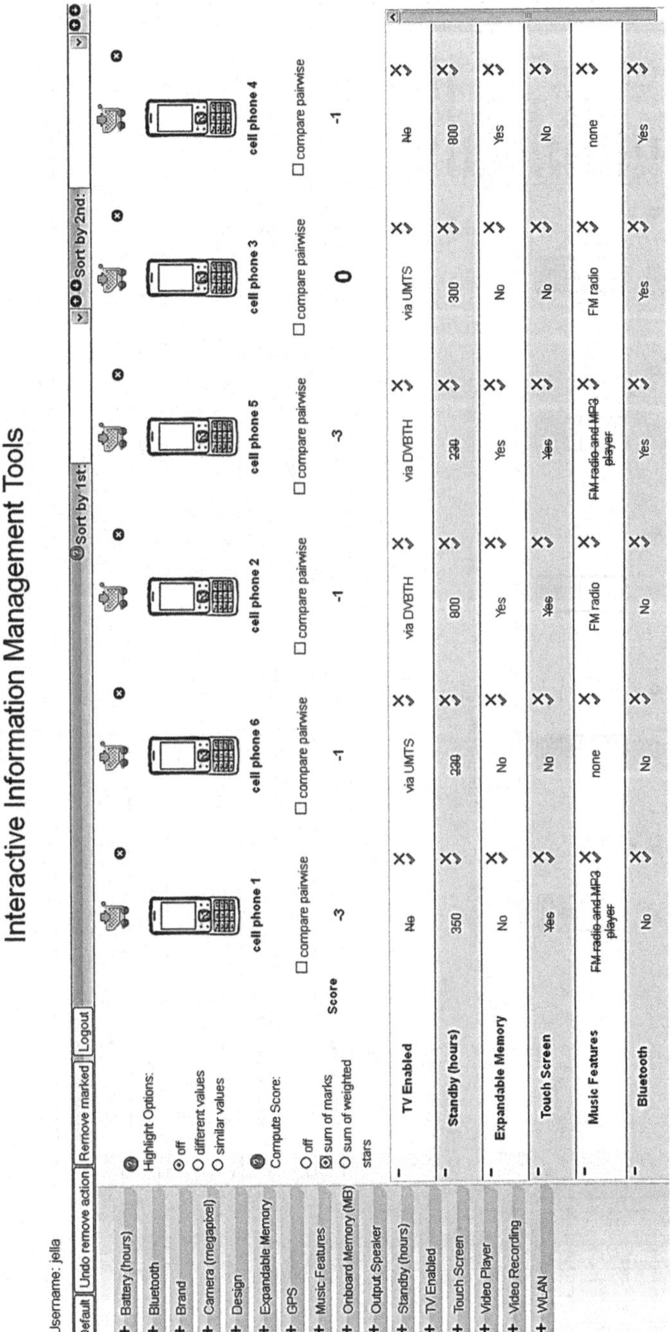

Fig. B.4 Final design of IIMT: *MARK$_{manually}$* as a negative attribute level

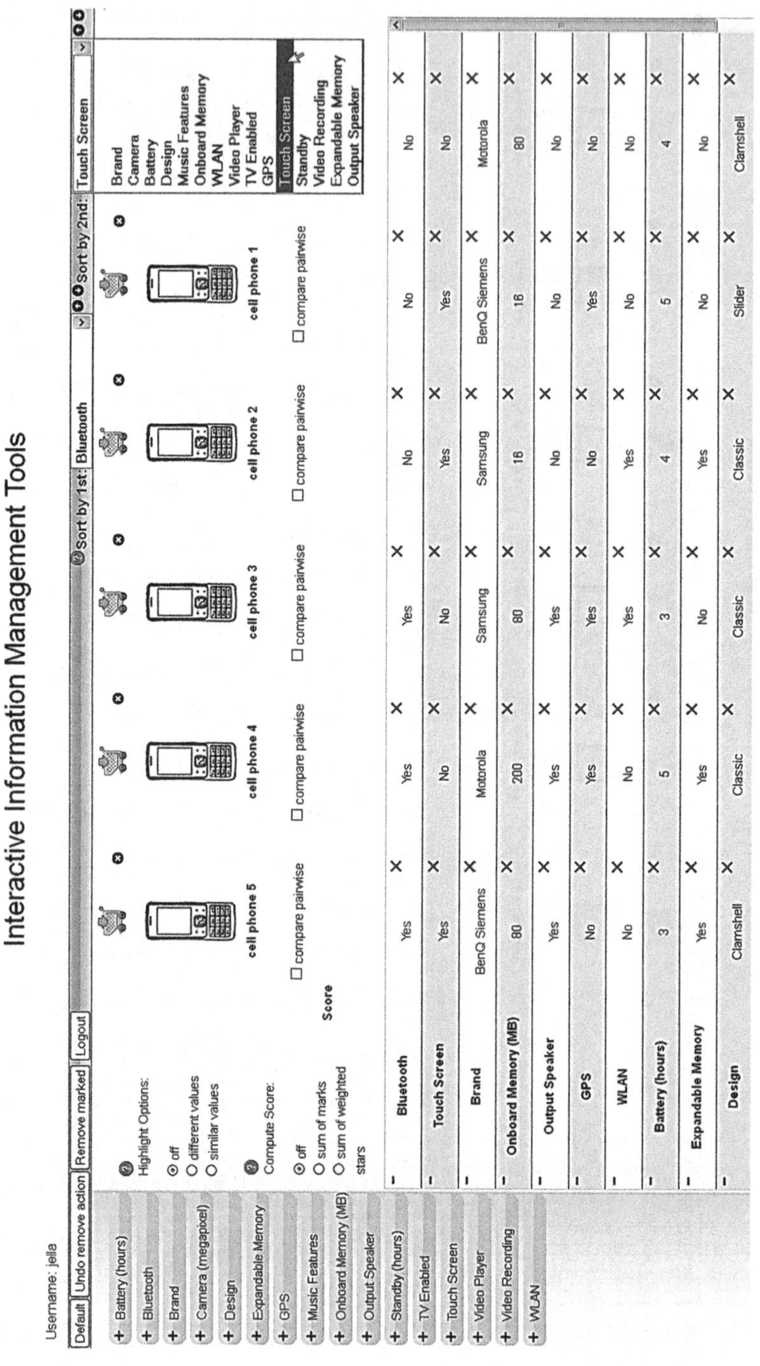

Fig. B.5 Final design of IIMT: *SORT*$_{hierarchically}$

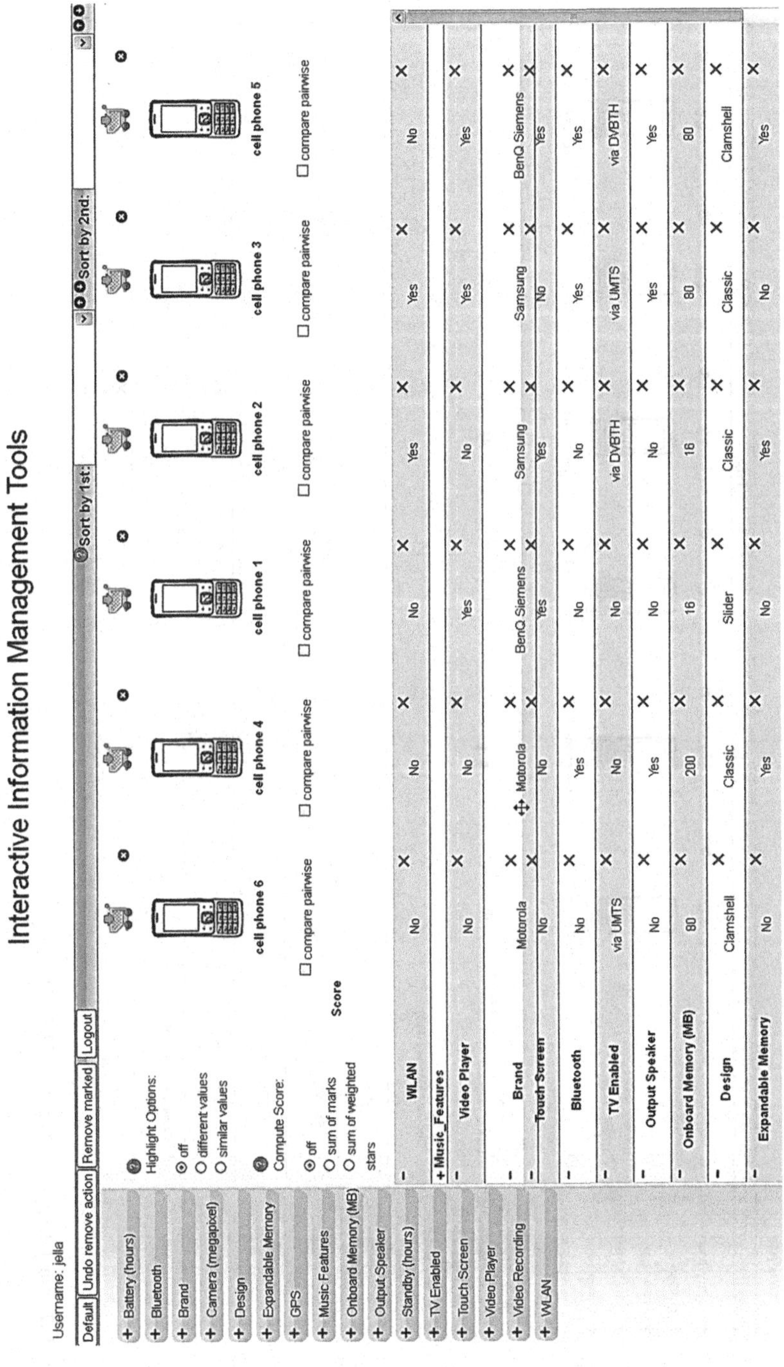

Interactive Information Management Tools

Username: jella

Default | Undo remove action | Remove marked | Logout

Highlight Options:
- ⊙ off
- ○ different values
- ○ similar values

Compute Score:
- ⊙ off
- ○ sum of marks
- ○ sum of weighted stars

Feature list: Battery (hours), Bluetooth, Brand, Camera (megapixel), Design, Expandable Memory, GPS, Music Features, Onboard Memory (MB), Output Speaker, Standby (hours), TV Enabled, Touch Screen, Video Player, Video Recording, WLAN

	cell phone 6	cell phone 4	cell phone 1	cell phone 2	cell phone 3	cell phone 5
	compare pairwise	compare pairwise	compare pairwise	compare pairwise	compare pairwise	compare pairwise
WLAN	No	No	No	Yes	Yes	No
+ Music Features						
Video Player	No	No	Yes	No	Yes	Yes
Brand	Motorola	Motorola	BenQ Siemens	Samsung	Samsung	BenQ Siemens
Touch Screen	No	No	Yes	Yes	No	Yes
Bluetooth	No	Yes	No	No	Yes	Yes
TV Enabled	via UMTS	No	No	via DVBTH	via UMTS	via DVBTH
Output Speaker	No	Yes	No	No	Yes	No
Onboard Memory (MB)	80	200	16	16	80	80
Design	Clamshell	Classic	Slider	Classic	Classic	Clamshell
Expandable Memory	No	Yes	No	Yes	No	Yes

Score

Fig. B.6 Final design of IIMT: *SORT manually*

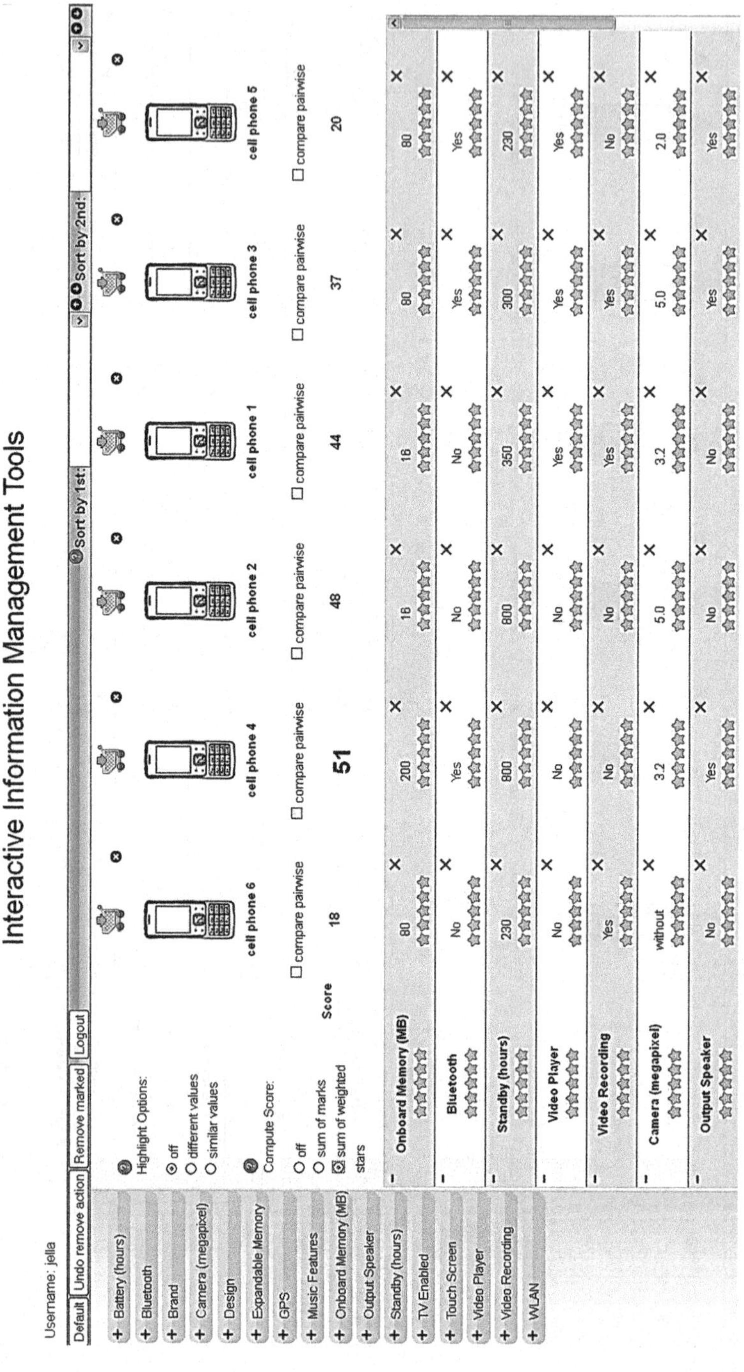

Fig. B.7 Final design of IIMT: $CACLULATE_{weighted}$

Appendix C
Details on Empirical Studies

Table C.1 The list is based on data from Google PageRank, January 2009. Detailed information about the Google PageRank algorithm is available at http://en.wikipedia.org/wiki/Pagerank. The companies with the numbers 18, 48, 70, and 96 did not have an Internet shop in January 2009. Hence, we included the ranks 101 through 104 in our empirical study

Rank	Company	Web site	PageRank
1	Amazon	www.amazon.com	9
2	Dell	www.dell.com	9
3	Apple	www.apple.com	9
4	Barnes And Noble	www.barnesandnoble.com	9
5	Think Geek	www.thinkgeek.com	8
6	Palm	www.palm.com	8
7	PC Mall	www.pcmall.com	8
8	B&H Photo Video	www.bhphotovideo.com	8
9	Cafe Press	www.cafepress.com	8
10	CDW	www.cdw.com	8
11	American Greetings	www.americangreetings.com	7
12	Buy	www.buy.com	7
13	Blockbuster	www.blockbuster.com	7
14	Wal- Mart	www.walmart.com	7
15	Netflix	www.netflix.com	7
16	compUSA	www.compusa.com	7
17	Cabela's	www.cabelas.com	7
18	Audible	www.audible.com	7
19	Ritz Camera	www.ritzcamera.com	7
20	Discovery Store	www.discoeverystore.com	7
21	Bestbuy	www.bestbuy.com	7
22	Powell's Books	www.powells.com	7
23	Panasonic	www.panasonic.com	7
24	Target	www.target.com	7
25	Books-A-Million	www.booksamillion.com	7

(continued)

J. Pfeiffer, *Interactive Decision Aids in E-Commerce*, Contributions to Management Science, DOI 10.1007/978-3-7908-2769-9, © Springer-Verlag Berlin Heidelberg 2012

Table C.1 (continued)

Rank	Company	Web site	PageRank
26	RadioShack	www.radioshack.com	7
27	Ballard Designs	www.ballardDesigns.com	7
28	Gateway	www.gateway.com	7
29	Restoration Hardware	www.restorationhardware.com	7
30	TigerDirect	www.tigerdirect.com	7
31	1-800-Flowers	www.1800flowers.com	7
32	Costco	www.costco.com	7
33	Sony	www.sonystyle.com	7
34	AbeBooks	www.abebooks.com	7
35	CBSSportsStore	www.cbssportsstore.com	7
36	CD Baby	www.cdbaby.com	7
37	Chapters.indigo.ca	www.chapters.indigo.ca	7
38	Zappos	www.zappos.com	7
39	Zazzle	www.zazzle.com	7
40	Napster	www.napster.com	7
41	Shop PBS	www.shoppbs.org	7
42	Alibris	www.alibris.com	7
43	Major League Baseball	www.mlb.com	7
44	HSN	www.hsn.com	7
45	Allposters	www.allposters.com	7
46	DeepDiscount	www.deepdiscount.com	6
47	Drugstore	www.drugstore.com	6
48	Safeway Inc.	www.safeway.com	6
49	Design Within Reach	www.dwr.com	6
50	Saks Fifth Avenue	www.saksfifthavenue.com	6
51	Coldwater Creek	www.coldwatercreek.com	6
52	Sam Ash	www.samash.com	6
53	eBags	www.ebags.com	6
54	eCampus	www.ecampus.com	6
55	Golfballs	www.golfballs.com	6
56	eCOST	www.ecost.com	6
57	Ralph Lauren	www.polo.com	6
58	Christian Book	www.christianbook.com	6
59	Quixtar	www.quixtar.com	6
60	QVC	www.qvc.com	6
61	redEnvelope	www.redenvelope.com	6
62	Dick's Sporting Goods	www.dickssportinggoods.com	6
63	CVS/ Pharmacy	www.cvs.com	6
64	Dillard's	www.dillards.com	6
65	Cooking	www.cooking.com	6
66	Sephora	www.sephora.com	6
67	American Blinds	www.decoratetoday.com	6
68	West Marine	www.westmarine.com	6
69	Replacements, Ltd.	www.replacements.com	6
70	The Sharper Image	www.sharperimage.com	6

(continued)

Table C.1 (continued)

Rank	Company	Web site	PageRank
71	REI	www.rei-outlet.com	6
72	Crateandbarrel	www.createandbarrel.com	6
73	Crutchfield	www.crutchfield.com	6
74	csn Stores	www.csnstores.com	6
75	Sheet Music Plus	www.sheetmusicplus.com	6
76	ShopNBC	www.shopnbc.com	6
77	Pottery Barn	www.potterybarn.com	6
78	kmart	www.kmart.com	6
79	Magellan's	www.magellans.com	6
80	HP	www.HPShopping.com	6
81	Mountain Equipement	www.mec.ca	6
82	The Home Depot	www.homedepot.com	6
83	Modell's	www.modells.com	6
84	HERSHEY's	www.hersheys.com	6
85	Musican's Friend	www.musicansfriend.com	6
86	Kenneth Cole	www.kennethcole.com	6
87	Harry And David	www.harryanddavid.com	6
88	Neiman Marcus	www.neimanmarcus.com	6
89	Newegg	www.newegg.com	6
90	Macy's	www.macys.com	6
91	MacConnection	www.macconnection.com	6
92	Lancome	www.lancome-usa.com	6
93	J&R	www.jr.com	6
94	Lands' End	www.landsend.com	6
95	Leap Frog	www.leapfrog.com	6
96	Jockey	www.jockey.com	6
97	Lego	www.lego.com	6
98	Levenger	www.levenger.com	6
99	Lillian Vernon	www.lillianvernon.com	6
100	JCPenney	www.jcpenney.com	6
101	Linens Things	www.lnt.com	6
102	Lowes	www.lowes.com	6
103	NFL-Shop	www.nflshop.com	6
104	Hallmark	www.hallmark.com	6

Table C.2 Measures (A). RA vs. IIMT. Experimental version (German) and original version (English)

Item #	Item text
Perceived ease of use, $\alpha = 0.891$	
PEU1[Eng]	The task of selecting the product using the recommendation agent was too complex. (Wang and Benbasat 2009)
PEU1[Ger]	Das gewünschte Produkt auszusuchen, empfand ich als zu schwierig.
PEU2[Eng]	Selecting the product using the recommendation agent required too much effort. (Wang and Benbasat 2009)
PEU2[Ger]	Das gewünschte Produkt zu finden empfand ich als zu aufwendig.
PEU3[Eng]	The task of selecting the product using the recommendation agent took to much time. (Wang and Benbasat 2009)
PEU3[Ger]	Das gewünschte Produkt auszuwühlen, dauerte mir zu lange.
PEU4[Eng]	I found it easy to get the recommendation agent to do what I want it to do. (Wang and Benbasat 2009)
PEU4[Ger]	Ich fand es einfach den Product Advisor entsprechend meiner Vorstellungen zu bedienen.
PEU5[Eng]	It would be easy for me to become skillful at using the recommendation agent. (Wang and Benbasat 2009)
PEU5[Ger]	Mit etwas Übung, kann ich mich schnell in die Benutzung des Product Advisors einarbeiten.
PEU6[Eng]	My interaction with the recommendation agent was clear and understandable. (Wang and Benbasat 2009)
PEU6[Ger]	Die Benutzung des Product Advisors war klar und verständlich.
Perceived usefulness, $\alpha = 0.703$	
PU1[Eng]	Using the recommendation agent in this webstore improved my decision making efficiency. (Kamis and Davern 2005)
PU1[Ger]	Durch die Nutzung des Product Advisors konnte ich die Effizienz meines Entscheidungsprozesses steigern.
PU2[Eng]	Using the recommendation agent in this webstore improved my decision making. (Kamis and Davern 2005)
PU2[Ger]	Die Nutzung des Product Advisors verbesserte meine Entscheidungsfindung.

Table C.3 Measures (B). RA vs. IIMT. Experimental version (German) and original version (English). Original versions are in brackets

Item #	Item text
Confidence, $\alpha = 0.721$	
CON1[Eng]	I am convinced that the recommendation agent recommended alternatives which most closely matched my preferences. (Pereira 2000)
CON1[Ger]	Ich bin sicher, dass mir der Product Advisor alle Produkte aufgezeigt hat, die meinen Präferenzen am nächsten kommen.
CON2[Eng]	The recommendation agent can be trusted to recommend alternatives which closely match the preferences I expressed. (Pereira 2000)
CON2[Ger]	Ich kann dem Product Advisor vertrauen, und glaube, dass er genau die Produkte für mich heraussucht, welche mit meinen Präferenzen übereinstimmen.
CON3[Eng]	The recommendation agent can be relied on to use my preference specifications when it recommends alternatives to me. (Pereira 2000)
CON3[Ger]	Der Product Advisor hat alle meine Präferenzangaben berücksichtigt.
CON4[Eng]	I am sure that my input on price limits, weights (most vs. least important, etc.) match my preferences. (NEW)
CON4[Ger]	Ich bin mir sicher, dass meine Angaben von Preisgrenzen, Gewichtungen (unwichtig vs. sehr wichtig) beim Product Advisor meinen wirklichen Präferenzen entsprechen.
Satisfcation, $\alpha = 0.8$	
SAT1[Eng]	The recommendation agent was advantageous when searching for the laptop.(NEW)
SAT1[Ger]	Der Product Advisor war beim Suchen des passenden Laptops von Vorteil.
SAT2[Eng]	If I could do it over again, I'd rather not use this system to select a laptop [car] (reverse). (Wang and Benbasat 2009)
SAT2[Ger]	Dürfte ich den Vorgang wiederholen, würde ich lieber keinen Product Advisor zur Einschränkung meiner Wahl benutzen.
SAT3[Eng]	If my friend was searching for information in order to purchase a laptop [car], and I knew that a system such as this was available, I would be very likely to recommend this system to him. (Wang and Benbasat 2009)
SAT3[Ger]	Wenn ein Freund von mir einen Laptop kaufen wollte und ein Product Advisor wie dieser wäre verfügbar, wäre es sehr wahrscheinlich, dass ich ihm diesen empfehlen würde.
SAT4[Eng]	This system was very useful in helping me to select the best laptop [car model] to suit my requirements.(Wang and Benbasat 2009)
SAT4[Ger]	Der Product Advisor war sehr hilfreich für mich, um einen Laptop zu finden, der meinen Anforderungen entspricht.
FRQ1[Eng]	I have used the recommendation agents for my decision. (NEW)
FRQ1[Ger]	Ich habe den Product Advisor bei meiner Entscheidung verwendet.

Table C.4 Measures (A). Evaluation of INTACMATO. Experimental version (German) and original version (English). The translations for PEU3, PEU4, PU1 had to be adapted quite a bit in order to meet our purpose. Original versions are in brackets

Item #	Item text
Perceived ease of use, $\alpha = 0.812$	
PEU1[Eng]	The task of selecting a car [cell phone] using this system took too much time. (Pereira 2000)
PEU1[Ger]	Ich musste viel Zeit investieren, um die Produktinformationen zu vergleichen, die für meine Entscheidung wichtig waren.
PEU2[Eng]	I had to be very attentive to shop in the webstore. (NEW)
PEU2[Ger]	Für den Einkauf in diesem Webshop musste ich sehr aufmerksam sein.
PEU3[Eng]	I find a computer easy to use (Venkatesh and Davis 1996)
PEU3[Ger]	Das gewünschte Mobiltelefon auszusuchen, empfand ich als zu schwierig.
PEU4[Eng]	Interacting with a computer does not require a lot of my mental effort. (Venkatesh and Davis 1996)
PEU4[Ger]	Den Einkauf in diesem Webshop empfand ich als anstrengend.
PEU5[Eng]	I easily found the information I was looking for (Pereira 2000)
PEU5[Ger]	Informationen, die wichtig waren, um mein Mobiltelefon auszuwählen, waren leicht zu finden.
PEU6[Eng]	Selecting a cell phone [car model] using this system required to much effort. (Pereira 2000)
PEU6[Ger]	Das gewünschte Produkt zu finden, empfand ich als zu aufwendig.
Perceived usefulness, $\alpha = 0.771$	
PU1[Eng]	Using WordPerfect would enhance my effectiveness in my degree program. (Venkatesh and Davis 1996)
PU1[Ger]	Nach der Nutzung des Webshops hatte ich das Gefühl, meine Entscheidung effizient getroffen zu haben.
PU2[Eng]	Using the webstore improved my decision making. (Kamis and Davern 2005)
PU2[Ger]	Die Nutzung des Webshops verbesserte meine Entscheidungsfindung.
PU3[Eng]	The webstore is useful. (Venkatesh and Davis 1996)
PU3[Ger]	Der Webshop ist nützlich.

Table C.5 Measures (B). Evaluation of INTACMATO. Experimental version (German) and original version (English). Original versions are in brackets

Item #	Item text
Confidence, $\alpha = 0.686$	
CON1[Eng]	The webstore realized all my specifications. (NEW)
CON1[Ger]	Der Webstore hat alle meine Eingaben umgesetzt.
CON2[Eng]	I trust the functionality of the website. (NEW)
CON2[Ger]	Ich vertraue den Funktionen der Website.
CON3[Eng]	The system accurately executed my commands. (NEW)
CON3[Ger]	Die Website hat meine Eingaben und Aktionen akkurat umgesetzt.
Satisfcation, $\alpha = 0.853$	
SAT1[Eng]	In total, I am satisfied with the webstore.(NEW)
SAT1[Ger]	Alles in allem bin ich mit dem Webshop zufrieden.
SAT2[Eng]	If I had to select a cell phone [car] in future, and a system such as this was available, I would be very likely to use it. (Pereira 2000)
SAT2[Ger]	Wenn ich nochmal ein Produkt aussuchen müsste, würde ich den Shop wieder verwenden.
SAT3[Eng]	I am satisfied with the possibilities to compare product information in this webstore.(NEW)
SAT3[Ger]	Mit der Möglichkeit, Produktinformationen in diesem Webshop zu vergleichen, bin ich zufrieden.
Shopping Enjoyment, $\alpha = 0.86$	
ENJ1[Eng]	I found my visit interesting. (Koufaris 2002)
ENJ1[Ger]	Der Besuch des Webshops war interessant.
ENJ2[Eng]	I found my visit exciting. (Koufaris 2002)
ENJ2[Ger]	Der Besuch des Webshops war unerhaltsam.
ENJ3[Eng]	I found my visit fun. (Koufaris 2002)
ENJ3[Ger]	Der Besuch des Webshops hat Spaß gemacht.

Table C.6 Measures (C). Evaluation of INTACMATO. Experimental version (German) and original version (English). Original versions are in brackets

Item #	Item text
Adaptivity, $\alpha = 0.678$	
ADA1[Eng]	Such a webstore could be easily adapted to my personal shopping behavior. (NEW)
ADA1[Ger]	Solch eine Webseite könnte leicht an mein persönliches Kaufverhalten angepasst werden.
ADA2[Eng]	It would be easy to adapt the user interaction of such a webstore customer specifically. (NEW)
ADA2[Ger]	Es wäre leicht, die Bedienung einer solchen Webseite käuferspezifisch anzupassen.
Consistency, $\alpha = 0.584$	
COS1[Eng]	The fonts on the webstore are consistent. (NEW)
COS1[Ger]	Die Schrift auf der Webseite ist einheitlich.
COS2[Eng]	Interaction with the webstore is consistent. (NEW)
COS2[Ger]	Die Bedienung der Webseite war konsistent.
Control, $\alpha = 0.692$	
COT1[Eng]	While using the webstore [during my last visit to Booksamillion.com] I felt confused. (recoded) (Koufaris 2002)
COT1[Ger]	Während ich den Webshop verwendet habe, fühlte ich mich verwirrt.
COT2[Eng]	While using the webstore [during my last visit to Booksamillion.com] I felt in control. (Koufaris 2002)
COT2[Ger]	Während ich den Webshop verwendet habe, hatte ich stets das Gefühl die Kontrolle zu haben.
COT3[Eng]	While using the webstore [during my last visit to Booksamillion.com] I felt frustrated. (recoded) (Koufaris 2002)
COT3[Ger]	Während ich den Webshop verwendet habe, fühlte ich mich frustriert.

Table C.7 Measures (D). Evaluation of INTACMATO. Experimental version (German) and original version (English)

Item #	Item text
Flexibility, $\alpha = 0.776$	
FLE1[Eng]	There was only a restricted number of possibilities to compare cell phones with one another. (NEW)
FLE1[Ger]	Ich hatte nur begrenzte Möglichkeiten, die Mobiltelefone miteinander zu vergleichen.
FLE2[Eng]	I find the possibilities to compare products with another limited. (NEW)
FLE2[Ger]	Die Möglichkeiten, um Produkte zu vergleichen, sind mir zu eingeschränkt.
FLE3[Eng]	The webstore enabled me to be flexible in my cell phone choice. (NEW)
FLE3[Ger]	Die Webseite hat es mir ermöglicht, flexibel ein passendes Handy auszusuchen.
Transparency, $\alpha = 0.515$	
TRA1[Eng]	My interaction with the webstore was clear and understandable. (Wang and Benbasat 2009)
TRA1[Ger]	Meine Interaktion mit dem Webshop war klar und verständlich.
TRA2[Eng]	I was aware what would happen whenever I had used an element of the webstore. (NEW)
TRA2[Ger]	Mir war immer klar, was passiert, nachdem ich ein Element des Webshops geklickt hatte.
TRA3[Eng]	My input caused an immediate action by the webstore. (NEW)
TRA3[Ger]	Meine Eingaben erzeugten eine sofortige Reaktion der Webseite.

References

Adamowicz W, Bunch D, Cameron T, Dellaert B, Hanneman M, Keane M, Louviere J, Meyer R, Steenburgh T, Swait J (2008) Behavioral frontiers in choice modeling. Market Lett 19(3):215–228

Adomavicius G, Tuzhilin A (2005) Toward the next generation of recommender systems: A survey of the state-of-the-art and possible extensions. IEEE Trans Knowl Data Eng 17(6):734–749

Agarwal R, Karahanna E (2000) Time flies when you're having fun: Cognitive absorption and beliefs about information technology usage. MIS Quart 24(4):665–694

Alba J, Hutchinson J (1987) Dimensions of consumers expertise. J Consum Res 13:411–454

Alloy LB, Tabachnik N (1984) Assessment of covariation by humans and animals: The joint influence of prior expectations and current situational information. Psychol Rev 91(1):112–149

Applegate LM (1999) Rigor and relevance in IS research - introduction. MIS Quart 23(1):1–2

Ariely D (2000) Controlling the information flow: Effects on consumer's decision making and preferences. J Consum Res 27(2):233–248

Arrow KJ (1951) Social choice and individual values. Wiley, New York

Bäck T, Fogel DB, Michalewicz Z (eds) (1997) Handbook of evolutionary computation. Institute of Physics Publishing, Bristol/Oxford University Press, New York

Ball C (1997) A comparison of single-step and multiple-step transition analyses of multiattribute decision strategies. Organ Behav Hum Decis Process 69(3):195–204

Ball C, Langholtz H, Auble J, Sopchak B (1998) Resource allocation strategies: A verbal protocol analysis. Organ Behav Hum Decis Process 76:70–88

Batley R, Daley A (2006) On the equivalence between elimination-by-aspects and generalised extreme value models of choice behavior. J Math Psychol 50(5):456–467

Beach L (1990) Image theory: Decision making in personal and organizational contexts. Wiley, Chichester

Beach L (1997) The psychology of decision making: People in organizations. Sage, Thousand Oaks

Beach L, Mitchell T (1978) A contingency model for the selection of decision strategies. Acad Manag Rev 3:439–449

Bechwati N, Xia L (2003) Do computers sweat? the impact of perceived effort of online decision aids on consumers' satisfaction with the decision process. J Consum Psychol 13(1&2):139–148

Bettman J, Johnson EJ, Luce MF, Payne JW (1993) Correlation, conflict, and choice. J Exp Psychol Learn Mem Cognit 19:931–951

Bettman J, Johnson EJ, Payne JW (1990) A componential analysis of cognitive effort in choice. Organ Behav Hum Decis Process 45(1):111–139

Bettman J, Johnson EJ, Payne JW (1991) Consumer decision making. In: Robertson T, Kassarjian H, (eds) Handbook of consumer behavior. Prentice-Hall, Englewood Cliffs, pp 50–84

Bettman J, Kakkar P (1977) Effects of information presentation format on consumer information acquisition. Adv Consum Res 3:316–320

Bettman J, Luce MF, Payne JW (1998) Constructive consumer choice processes. J Consum Res Interdisciplinary Quart 25(3):187–217

Bettman J, Park CW (1980) Effects of prior knowledge and experience and phase of the choice process on consumer decision processes: A protocol analysis. J Consum Res 7:234–248

Bettman J, Zins M (1979) Information format and choice task effects in decision making. J Consum Res 6(2):141–153

Bettman JR, John DR, Scott CA (1986) Covariation assessment by consumers. J Consum Res 13(3):316–326

Biggs S, Bedard J, Gaber B, Linsmeier T (1985) The effects of task size and similarity on the decision behavior of bank loan officers. Manag Sci 31:970–987

Billings R, Marcus S (1983) Measures of compensatory and noncompensatory models of decision behavior: Process tracing versus policy capturing. Organ Behav Hum Perform 31:331–352

Böckenholt U, Albert D, Aschenbrenner M, Schmalhofer F (1991) The effects of attractiveness, dominance, and attribute differences on information acquisition in multiattribute binary choice. Organ Behav Hum Decis Process 49(2):258–281

Böckenholt U, Hynan L (1994) Caveats on a process-tracing measure and a remedy. J Behav Decis Making 7(2):103–117

Brehmer B (1994) The psychology of linear judgement models. Acta Psychol, 87:137–154

Bröder A (2000) Assessing the empirical validity of the "take-the-best" heuristic as a model of huam probability inference. J Exp Psychol Learn Mem Cognit 26:1332–1346

Bröder A, Schiffer S (2003a) Bayesian strategy assessment in multi-attribute decision research. J Behav Decis Making 16:193–213

Bröder A, Schiffer S (2003b) Take the best versus simultaneous feature matching: Probabilistic inferences from memory and effects of respresentation format. J Exp Psychol Gen 132(2):277–93

Brunswick E (1955) Representative design and probabilisty theory in a functional psychology. Psychol Rev 62:193–217

Brynjolfsson E, Hu Y, Smith M (2006) From nices to riches: The anatomy of the long tail. Sloan Manag Rev 47(4):67–71

Buber R, Holzmüller H (2007) Qualitative markforschung: Konzepte - Methoden - Analysen. Gabler, Wiesbaden

Caplin A, Dean M (2011) Search, choice, and revealed preference. Theor Econ 6(1):19–48

Chen L, Gillenson M, Sherell D (2002) Enticing online consumers: An extended technology acceptance perpective. Inform Manag 39(8):705–719

Chewning EJ, Harrell A (1990) The effect of information load on decision makers' cue utilization levels and decision quality in a financial distress decision task. Account Org Soc 15(6):527–542

Chu P, Spires EE (2000) The joint effects of effort and quality on decision strategy choice with computerized decision aids. Decis Sci 31(2):259–288

Chu PC, Spires EE (2003) Perceptions of accuracy and effort of decision strategies. Organ Behav Hum Decis Process 91(2):203–214

Chuan-Chuan Lin J, Hsipeng L (2000) Towards an understanding of the behavioural intention to use a web site. Int J Inform Manag 20(3):197–208

Cohen J (1988) Statistical power analysis for the behavioral sciences, vol 2. Academic Press, New York

Cohen J (1992) A power primer. Psychol Bull, 112(1):155–159

Conlon B, Dellaert B, van Soest A (2001) Complexity and accuracy in consumer choice: The double benefits of being the consistently better brand. Technical report, Tilburg University, Center for Economic Research. Discussion Paper

Cook GJ (1993) An empirical investigation of information search strategies with implications for decision support system design. Decis Sci 24(3):683–697

Coombs CH, Kao RC (1955) Nonmetric factor analysis Engineering Research Institute Bulletin No. 38 University of Michigan Press

Cortina J (1993) What is coefficient alpha? an examination of theory and applications. J Appl Psychol 78:98–104

Covey J, Lovie A (1998) Information selection and utilization in hypothesis testing: A comparison of process tracing and structural analysis techniques. Organ Behav Hum Decis Process 75:56–74

Creyer EH, Bettman JR, Payne JW (1990) The impact of accuracy and effort feedback and goals on adaptive decision behavior. J Behav Decis Making 3:1–16

Crow LE, Olshavsky RW, Summers JO (1980) Industrial buyers' choice strategies: A protocol analysis. J Consum Res 17:34–44

Cutting J (2000) Accuracy, scope, and flexibility of models. J Math Psychol 44:3–19

Davis FD (1989) Perceived usefulness, perceived ease of use, and user acceptance of information technology. MIS Quarterly 13(3):319–340

Davis FD, Bagozzi RP, Warshaw PR (1989) User acceptance of computer-technology: A comparison of two theoretical models. Manag Sci 35(8):982–1003

Dawes R, Corrigan B (1974) Linear models in decision making. Psychol Bull 81(2):95–106

Dawes RM (1979) The robust beauty of improper linear models in decision making. Am Psychol 34:571–582

Dellaert BD, Brazell JD, Louviere JJ (1999) The effect of attribute variation on consumer choice consistency. Market Lett 10(2):139–147

DeShazo J, Fermo G (2002) Designing choice sets for stated preference methods: The effect of complexity on choice consistency. J Environ Econ Manag 44:123–143

Dhami M, Ayton P (2001) Bailing and jailing the fast and frugal way. J Behav Decis Making 14:141–168

Dieckmann A, Dippold J, Dietrich H (2009) Compensatory versus noncompensatory models for predicting consumer preferences. Judgment Decis Making 4(3):200–123

Donges J, Mai S, Buttermann A (2001) E-Commerce und wirtschaftspolitik. Lucius & Lucius, Stuttgart

Duchowski AT (2007) Eye tracking methodology: Theory and practice, vol 2. Springer, New York

Edmunds A, Morris A (2000) The problem of information overload in business organisations: A review of the literature. Int J Inform Manag 20(1):17–28

Eighmey J, McCord L (1998) Adding value in the information age: Uses and gratifications of sites on the world wide web. J Bus Res 41(3):187–194

Einhorn H, Hogarth R (1981) Behavioral decision theory: Processes of judgment and choice. Annu Rev Psychol 32:53–88

Eisenfuhr F, Weber M (2002) Rationales entscheiden. Springer, Berlin

Eppler MJ, Mengis J (2004) The concept of information overload: A review of literature from organization science, accounting, marketing, MIS, and related disciplines. Inform Soc 20:325–344

Ericsson K, Simon H (1980) Verbal protocols as data. Psychol Rev 87:215–251

Ericsson K, Simon H (1993) Protocol analysis: Verbal reports as data. The MIT Press, Cambridge

Faltings B, Pu P, Torrens M, Viappiani P (2004) Designing example-critiquing interaction. In: Proceedings of the 9th International Conference on Intelligent User Interfaces. ACM Press, New York, pp 22–29

Fasolo B, Carmeci FA, Misuraca R (2009) The effect of choice complexity on perception of time spent choosing: When choice takes longer but feels shorter. Psychol Market 26(3):213–228

Fasolo B, McClelland G, Lange K (2005) The effect of site design and interattribute correlations on interactive web-based decisions. In: Haugtvedt C, Machleit K, Yalch R (eds) Online consumer psychology: Understanding and influencing behavior in the virtual world. Lawrence Erlbaum Associates, pp 325–342

Fasolo B, Misuaraca R, McClelland G (2003) Individual differences in adaptive choice strategies. Res Econ 57(3):219–233

Fidler E (1983) The reliability and validity of concurrent, restrospective, and interpretative verbal reports: An experimental study. In: Humphreys P, Svenson O, Vári A (eds) Advances in psychology. Analysing and aiding decision processes, vol 14. Elsevier, Amsterdam, pp 429–440

Field A (2009) Discovering statistics using SPSS. Sage Publications, Los angeles, California

Fishburn PC (1970) Utility Theory of Decision Making. Krieger, Huntington

Fitzsimons GJ, Lehmann DR (2004) Reactance to recommendations: When unsolicited advice yields contrary responses. Market Sci 23(1):82–94

Ford JK, Schmitt N, Schechtman SL, Hults BM, Doherty ML (1989) Process tracing methods: contributions, problems, and neglected research questions. Organ Behav Hum Decis Process 43(1):75–117

Garbarino EC, Edell JA (1997) Cognitive effort, affect, and choice. J Consum Res 24(2):147–158

Garcia-Retamero R, Hoffrage D, Dieckmann A (2007) When one cue is not enough: combining fast and frugal heuristics with compound cue processing. Quart J Exp Psychol 60(9):1197–1215

Gefen D, Karahanna E, Straub D (2003) Trust and tam in online shopping: An integrated model. MIS Quarterly 27(1):51–90

Gensch D (1987) A two-stage disaggregate attribute choice model. Market Sci 6:223–231

Gettys C, Pliske R, Manning C, Casey J (1987) An evaluation of human act generation performance. Organ Behav Hum Decis Process 39:23–51

Gigerenzer G, Selten R (2001) Bounded rationality: The adaptive toolbox. MIT Press, Cambridge

Gilbride TJ, Allenby, Greg M (2004) A choice model with conjunctive, disjunctive, and compensatory screening rules. Market Sci 23(3):391–406

Gilbride TJ, Allenby, Greg M (2006) Estimating heteroogeneous eba and economic screening rule choice models. Market Sci 25(5):494–509

Glöckner A (2009) Investigating intuitive and deliberate processes statistically: The multiple-measure maximum likelihood strategy classifcation method. Judgment Decis Making 4(3):186–199

Glöckner A, Betsch T (2008) Multiple-reason decision making based on automatic processing. J Exp Psychol Learn Mem Cognit 34(5):1055–1075

Glover F, Kochenberger GA (eds) (2003) Handbook of metaheuristics. Kluwer, Boston

Goldberg DE (1989) Genetic algorithms in search, optimization and machine learning. Addison–Wesley Longman, Bonn

Goodhue D (1995) Understanding user evaluations of information systems. Manag Sci 41(12):1827–1844

Goodhue D (1998) Development and measurement validity of a task-technology fit instrument for user evaluations of information systems. Decis Sci 29(1):105–138

Goodhue D, Thompson R (1995) Task-technology fit and individual performance. MIS Quarterly 19(2):213–236

Gretzel U, Fesenmaier D (2006) Persuasion in recommender systems. Int J Electron Commerce 11(2):81–100

Gupta P, Yadav MS, Varadarajan R (2009) How task-facilitative interactive tools foster buyers' trust in online retailers: A process view of trust development in the electronic marketplace. J Retailing 85(2):159–176

Haaijer R, Wedel M (2007) Conjoint choice experiments: General characteristics and alternative model specifications. In: Gustafsson A, Herrmann A, Huber F (eds) Conjoint measurement: Methods and applications, vol 4. Springer, Berlin, pp 199–229

Harte JM, Koele P (2001) Modelling and describing human judgement processes: The multiat-tribute evaluation case. Think Reas 7(7):29–49

Hassanein K, Head M (2007) Manipulating perceived social presence through the web interface and its impact on attribute towards online shopping. Int J Hum Comput Stud 65(8):689–708

Häubl G, Murray KB (2003) Preference construction and persistence in digital marketplaces: The role of electronic recommendation agents. J Consu Psychol 13(1&2):75–91

Häubl G, Murray KB (2006) Double agents: Assessing the role of electronic product recommendation systems. MIT Sloan Manag Rev 47(3):8–12

Häubl G, Trifts V (2000) Consumer decision making in online shopping environments: The effects of interactive decision aids. Market Sci 19(1):4–21

Hauser JR, Toubia O, Theodoros E, Silinskiai D, Berfurt R (2010) Disjunctions of conjunctions, cognitive simplicity and consideration sets. J Market Res 47(3):485–496

Hays WL (1973) Statistics for the social sciences. Holt Rinhehart and Winston, New York

Hevner AR, March ST, Park J, Ram S (2004) Design science in information systems research. MIS Quarterly 28:75–105

Hinz O, Eckert J (2010) The impact of search and recommendation systems on sales in electronic commerce. Bus Inform Syst Eng Optim 2(2):67–77

Hoch S, Bradlow E, Wansing B (1999) The variety of an assortment. Market Sci 18(4):527–546

Hoffman DL, Novak TP (1996) Marketing in hypermedia computer-mediated environments: conceptual foundations. J Market 60:50–68

Hoffrage U, Hertwig R, Gigerenzer G (2000) Hindsight bias: A by-product of knowledge updating? J Exp Psychol Learn Mem Cognit 26:566–581

Hogarth R (1987) Judgment and Choice, vol 2. Wiley, Chichester

Holland JH (1975) Adaptation in natural and artificial systems. University of Michigan Press, Ann Arbor

Horrigan J (2008) Online shopping: Internet users like the convenience but worry about the security of their financial information. Technical report, Pew Internet & American Life Project

Hostler RE, Yoon VY, Guimaraes T (2005) Assessing the impact of internet agent on end users' performance. Decis Support Syst 41(1):313–323

Huang Z, Chen H, Guo F, Xu JJ, Wu S, Chen, W.-H. (2006) Expertise visualization: an implementation and study based on cognitive fit theory. Decis Support Syst 42(3):1539–1557

Huber O (1980) The influence of some task variables on cognitive operations in an information-processing decision model. Acta Psychol 45:187–196

Iglesias-Parro S, De la Fuente EI, Ortega A (2002) The effect of context variables on cognitive effort in multiattribute binary choice. Theor Decis 52(2):101–125

Iglesias-Parro S, Ortega AR, De la Fuente EI, Martín I (2001) Context variables as cognitive effort modulators in decision making using an alternative-based processing strategy. Qual Quantity 35(3):311–323

Jacoby J, Speller D, Berning C (1974) Brand choice behavior as a function of information load: Replication and extension. J Consum Res 1(1):22–42

Jarvenpaa SL, Todd PA (1997) consumer reactions to electronic shopping on the world wide web. Int J Eletron Commerce 1(2):59–88

Jasper J, Shapiro J (2002) Mousetrace: A better mousetrap for catching decision processes. Behav Res Meth Instrum Comput 34:364–374

Johnson EJ (1979) Deciding how to decide: The effort of making a decision. Working paper, University of Chicago

Johnson EJ, Meyer RJ (1984) Compensatory choice models of noncompensatory processes: The effect of varying context. J Consum Res 11(3):528–541

Johnson EJ, Payne JW (1985) Effort and accuracy in choice. Manag Sci 31(4):395–414

Jorgensen AH (1990) Thinking-aloud in user interface design: A method promoting cognitive ergonomics. Ergonomics 33(4):501–507

Joseph A, Lynch J, Weitz B, Janiszewski C, Lutz R, Sawyer A, Wood S (1997) Interactive home shopping: Consumer, retailer, and manufacturer incentives to participate in electronic marketplaces. J Market 61:38–53

Kamis AA, Davern MJ (2005) An exploratory model of decision quality and its antecedents for category novices using multiple-stage shopping engines. e Serv J 4(1):3–27

Kasper GM (1996) A theory of decision support system design for user calibration. Inform Syst Res 7(2):215–232

Keeney R, Raiffa H (1993) Decisions with multiple objectives: Preferences and value tradeoffs, vol 14. Wiley, New York

Keller L, Ho J (1988) Decision problem structuring: Generating options. IEEE Trans Syst Man Cybern 18:715–728

Kelly GA (1955) The Psychology of personal constructs. Norton, New York

Klayman J (1985) Children's decision strategies and their adaptation to task characteristics. Organ Behav Hum Decis Process 35(2):179–201

Klein NM, Yadav MS (1989) Context effects on effort and accuracy in choice: An enquiry into adaptive decision making. J Consum Res 15(4):411–421

Kline P (2000) The handbook of psychological testing, vol 2. Routledge, Londen

Klopping IM, McKinney E (2004) Extending the technology acceptance model and the task-technology fit model to consumer e-commerce. Inform Tech Learn Perform J 22:35–47

Kohli R, Devaraj S, Mahmood MA (2004) Understanding determinants of online consumer satisfaction: A decision process perspective. J Manag Inform Syst 21(1):115–136 (1277688)

Kohli R, Jedidi K (2007) Representation and inference of loexicographic preference models and their variants. Market Sci 26(3):380–399

Koufaris M (2002) Applying the technology acceptance model and flow theory to online consumer behavior. Inform Syst Res 13(2):205–223

Kwak M (2001) Web sites learn to make smarter suggestions. MIT Sloan Manag Rev 42(4):17

Lee BK, Lee WN (2004) The effect of information overload on consumer choice quality in an on-line environment. Psychol Market 21(3):159–183

Lee D, Park J, Ahn J (2001) On the explanation of factors affecting e-commerce adoption. In: Proceedings of the Twenty-Second International Conference in Information Systems, pp 109–120

Lee M, Cheung C, Chen Z (2005) Acceptance of internet-based learning medium: the role of extrinsic and intrinsic motivation. Inform Manag 42(8):1095–1104

Lee M, Cummins T (2004) Evidence accumulation in decision making: Unifying the "take the best" and the "rational" models. Psychonomic Bull Rev 11:343–352

Lee WL (1971) Decision theory and human behavior. Wiley, New York

Lenk P, DeSarbo W, Green P, Young M (1996) Hierarchical bayes conjoint analysis: Recovery of partworth heterogeneity from reduced experimental designs. Market Sci 15(2):173–191

Lim KH, Benbasat I (2000) The effect of multimedia on perceived equivocality and perceived usefulness of information systems. MIS Quarterly 24(3):449–471

Lohse G, Johnson E (1996) A comparison of two process tracing methods on choice tasks. Organ Behav Hum Decis Process 68(1):28–43

Louviere J, Meyer R (2007) Formal choice models and informal choices: What choice modeling research can (and can't) learn from behavioral theory. Rev Market Res 4:3–32

Luce D (1956) Semiorders and a theory of utility discrimination. Econometrica 24(2):178–191

Luce MF, Bettman JR, Payne JW (1997) Choice processing in emotional difficult decisions. J Exp Psychol Learn Mem Cognit 23(2):384–405

Maes P, Guttman RH, Moukas AG (1999) Agents that buy and sell. Comm ACM 42(3):81–91

Malhorta N (1982) Information load and consumer decision making. J Consum Res 8(4):419–430

Maule A, Svenson O (1993) Theoretical and empirical approaches to behavioral decision making and their relation to time constraint. In: Svenson O, Maule A (eds) Time pressure and stress in human judgment and decision making. Plenum Press, New York

Meißner M, Decker R, Pfeiffer J (2010) Ein empirischer vergleich der prozessasufzeichnungsmeth-oden mouselab und eyetracking bei präferenzmessungen mittels choice-based conjoint analyse. Market Z Forsch Prax 3(3):133–143

Monsuwé, T., Dellaert B, Ruyter K (2004) What drives consumers to shop online? A literature review. Int J Serv Ind Manag 15(1):102–121

Montaner M, Lopez B, de la Rosa JL (2003) A taxonomy of recommender agents on the internet. Artif Intell Rev 19(4):285–330

Montgomery A, Hosanager K, Krishnan R, Clay K (2004) Designing a better shopbot. Manag Sci 50(2):189–206

Montgomery H, Svenson O (1976) On decision rules and information processing strategies for choices among multiattribute alternatives. Scand J Psychol 17:283–291

Moon J-W, Kim Y-G (2001) Extending the tam for a world-wide-web context. Inform Manag 38:217–230

Mun YY, Hwand Y (2003) Predicting the use of web-based information systems: Self-efficacy, enjoyment, learning goal orientation, and the technology acceptance model. Int J Hum Comput Stud 59(4):431–449

Murray KB, Häubl G (2008) Interactive consumer decision aids. In: Wierenga B (ed) Handbook of marketing decision models. Springer Science + Business Media, New York, pp 55–77

Myers J, Alpert M (1968) Determinant buying attitudes: Meaning and measurement. J Market 32(4):13–20

Myung JI, Pitt MA (2009) Optimal experimental design for model discrimination. Psychol Rev 116(3):499–518

Netzer O, Toubia O, Bradlow E, Dahan E, Evgeniou T, Feinberg F, Feit E, Hui S, Johnson J, Liechty J, Orlin J, Rao V (2008) Beyond conjoint analysis: Advances in preference measurement. Market Lett 19(3):337–354

Newell A, Simon H (1972) Human problem solving. Prentice Hall, Englewood Cliffs

Nielsen J (1993) Noncommand user interfaces. Comm ACM 36(4):83–99

Nielsen J (1994) Usability engineering. Morgan Kaufmann, San Francisco

Nisbett R, Wilson T (1977) Telling more than we can know: Verbal resports on mental processes. Psychol Rev Market Res 84(3):231–259

Nitzsch R, Weber M (1993) The effect of attribute ranges on weights in multiattribute utility measurements. Manag Sci 39(8):937–943

Norman E, Schulte-Mecklenbeck M (2010) Take a quick click at that! mouselab and eye-tracking as tools to measure intuition. In: Glöckner A, Wittemann C (eds) Tracing intuition: Recent methods in measuring intuitive and deliberate processes in decision making. Psychology Press/Routledge, London, pp 24–44

Nunamaker JF, Chen M (1991) Systems development in information systems research. In: Proceedings of the 23rd International Conference on System Science, pp 631–640

Nunnally J (1967) Psychometric theory. McGraw-Hill, New York

Olshavsky R (1979) Task complexity and contingent processing in decision making: A replication and extension. Organ Behav Hum Perform 24:300–316

Onken J, Hastie R, Revelle W (1985) Individual differences in the use of simplification strategies in a complex decision-making task. J Exp Psychol Hum Percept Perform 11(1):14–27

Osborn A (1963) Applied imagination: Principles and procedures of creative problem-solving. Scribner'S, New York

Park CW (1978) A seven-point scale and a decision maker's simplifying choice strategy: An operationalized satisficing-plus model. Organ Behav Hum Perform 21:252–271

Payne JW (1976) Task complexity and contingent processing in decision making: An information search and protocol analysis. Organ Behav Hum Perform 16(2):366–387

Payne JW, Bettman JR (1994) The costs and benefits of alternative measures of search behavior: Comments on böckenholt and hynan. J Behav Decis Making 7(2):119–122. 10.1002/bdm.3960070204

Payne JW, Bettman JR, Coupey E, Johnson EJ (1992) A constructive process view of decision making: Multiple strategies in judgment and choice. Acta Psychol 80(1–3):107–141

Payne JW, Bettman JR, Johnson EJ (1988) Adaptive strategy selection in decision making. J Exp Psychol Learn Mem Cognit 14(3):534–552

Payne JW, Bettman JR, Johnson EJ (1993) The adaptive decision maker. Cambridge University Press, Cambridge

Payne JW, Bettman JR, Schkade DA (1999) Measuring constructed preferences: Towards a building code. J Risk Uncertainty 19(1–3):243–270

Payne JW, Branunstein ML, Carroll JS (1978) Exporing predecisional behaior: An alternative approach to decision research. Organ Behav Hum Perform 22:17–44

Payne JW, Braunstein ML (1978) Risky choice: An examination of information acquisition behavior. Mem Cognit 6(5):554–561

Pedersen P (2000) Behavioral effects of using software agents for product and merchant brokering: An experimental study of consumer decision making. Int J Electron Commerce 5:125–141

Pereira RE (2000) Optimizing human-computer interaction for the electronic commerce environment. J Electron Commerce Res 1(1):23–44

Pfeiffer J, Duzevik D, Rothlauf F, Yamamoto K (2009a) A genetic algorithm for analyzing choice behavior with mixed decision strategies. In: Raidl G (ed) Proceedings of the genetic and evolutionary computation conference. ACM Press, Montreal

Pfeiffer J, Riedl R, Rothlauf F (2009b) On the relationship between interactive decision aids and decision strategies: A theoretical analysis. In: Hansen HR, Karagiannis D, Fill H-G (eds) Proceedings of the 9th international Tagung Wirtschaftsinformatik

Pfeiffer T (2010) Understanding Multimodel Deixis with Gaze and Gesture in Conversational Interfaces. PhD thesis, University of Bielefeld

Pu P, Chen L (2008) User-involved preference elicitation for product search and recommender systems. AI Mag 29(4):93–102

Qiu L, Benbasat I (2009) Evaluating anthropomorphic product recommendation agents: A social and relational perspective to designing information systems. J Manag Inform Syst 25(4):145–182

Raidl GR, Julstrom BA (2000) A weighted coding in a genetic algorithm for the degree-constrained. In: Carroll J, Damiani E, Haddad H, Oppenheim D (eds) Proceedings of the 2000 ACM symposium on applied computing. ACM Press, New York, pp 440–445

Reeves C, Rowe J (2003) Genetic algorithms: Principles and perspectives. Kluwer, Boston

Reisen N, Hoffrage U, Mast FW (2008) Identifying decision strategies in a consumer choice situation. Judgment Decis Making 3(8):641–658

Reynolds TJ, Gutman J (1988) Laddering theory, method, analysis and interpretation. J Advert Res 28(1):11–31

Riedl R, Brandstätter E, Roithmayr F (2008) Identifying decision strategies: A process and outcome-based classification method. Behav Res Meth 20(3):795–807

Rieskamp J, Hoffrage U (1999) When do people use simple heuristics, and how can we tell? In: Gigerenzer G, Todd P, and the ABC Research Group (eds) Simple heuristics that make us smart. Oxford University Press, Oxford

Rieskamp J, Hoffrage U (2008) Inferences under time pressure: How opportunity costs affect strategy selection. Acta Psychol 127:258–276

Rosenthal R (1991) Meta-analytic procedures for social research, vol 2. Sage, Newbury Park

Rosnow R, Rosenthal R (2005) Beginning behavioral research: A conceptual primer, vol 5. Pearson/Prentice Hall, Englewood Cliffs

Rothlauf F (2009) An encoding in metaheuristics for the minimum communication spanning tree problem. INFORMS J Comput 21(4):575–584

Russo JE (1978) Eye fixations can save the world: A critical evaluation and a comparison between eye fixations and other information processing methodologies. In: Hunt HK (ed) Advances in consumer research, vol 21. Association for Consumer Research, Ann Arbor, pp 561–570

Russo JE, Dosher B (1983) Strategies for multiattribute binary choice. J Exp Psychol Learn Mem Cognit 9(4):676–696

Russo JE, Johnson EJ, Stephens D (1989) The valdity of verbal protocols. Mem Cognit 17:759–769

Russo JE, Leclerc F (1994) An eye-fixation analysis of choice processes for consumer nondurables. J Consum Res 21(2):274–290

Sawtooth (2008) CBC v6.0. Technical Paper

Scammon D (1977) Information load and consumers. J Consum Res 4(3):148–155

Schmalhofer F, Albert D, Aschenbrenner KM, Gertzen H (1986) Process trace of binary choices: Evidence for selective and adaptive decision heuristics. Quart J Exp Psychol 38(A):59–76

Scholz SW, MeiSSner M, Decker R (2010) Measuring consumer preferences for complex products. J Market Res 47(4):685–698

Selart M, Gärling T, Montgomery H (1998) Compatibility and the use of information processing strategies. J Behav Decis Making 11(1):59–72

Seth A, Dienes K, Cleeremans Z, Overgaard A, Pessoa L (2008) Measuring consciousness: Relating behavioural and neurophysiological approaches. Trends Cognit Sci 12(8):314–321

Shapiro M (1994) Think-alound and though-list procedures in investigating mental processes. In: Lang A (ed) Measuring psychological responses to media. Hillsdale, New York, pp 1–15

Shephard R (1964) On subjectively optimum selection among multiattribute alternatives. In: Human judgments and optimality. Wiley, New York, pp 257–281

Shields MD (1980) Some effects of information load on search patterns used to analyze performance reports. Account Org Soc 5(4):429–442

Shneiderman B (1983) Direct manipulation: A steo beyond programming languages. IEEE Comput 16(8):57–69

Shneiderman B, Plaisant C (2009) Designing the user interface: Strategies for effectivehuman-computer interaction, 5th edn. Pearson/Addison-Wesley, Boston

Shugan SM (1980) The cost of thinking. J Consum Res 7:99–111

Silver M (1988) User perceptions of decision support systems restrictiveness. J Manag Inform Syst 5(1):51–65

Silverman BG, Bachann M, Al-Akharas K (2001) Implications of buyer decision theory for design of e-commerce websites. Int J Hum Comput Stud 55(5):815–844 (511885)

Simon H (1955) A behavioral model of rational choice. Quart J Econ 69(1):99–118

Simon HA (1996) The sciences of the artificial, vol 3. MIT Press, Cambridge

Simonson I (2005) Determinant of customers' responses to customized offers: Conceptual framework and research propositions. J Market 69(1):32–45

Sinha R, Swearingen K (2002) The role of transparency in recommender systems. In: Terveen L (ed) Proceedings of the ACM CHI 2002 Conference on Human Factors in Computing Systems. ACM Press, New York, pp 830–831

Sismeiro C, Bucklin R (2004) Modeling purchase behavior at an e-commerce web site: A task-completion approach. J Market Res 41(3):306–323

Smith SL, Mosier JN (1986) Guidelines for designing user interface software. The Mitre Corporation, Bedford

Someren MV, Barnard Y, Sandberg J (1994) The think aloud method. Academic Press, London

Song J, Jones D, Gudigantala N (2007) The effects of incorporating compensatory choice strategies in web-based consumer decision support systems. Decis Support Syst 43(2):359–374

Spiekermann S, Paraschiv C (2002) Motivating human-agent interaction: Transferring insights from behavioral marketing to interface design. Electron Commerce Res 2(3):255–285

Staelin R, Payne JW (1976) Studies of the information-seeking behavior of consumers. Lawrence Erlbaum, Hillsdale, pp 185–202

Sternberg S (1966) High-speed scanning in human memory. Science 153:652–654

Stone DN, Schkade DA (1994) Effects of attribute scales on process and performance in multiattribute choice. Organ Behav Hum Decis Process 59(2):261–287

Storer RH, Wu SD, Vaccari R (1992) New search spaces for sequencing problems with application to job shop scheduling. Manag Sci 38(10):1495–1509

Svenson O (1979) Process descriptions of decision making. Organ Behav Hum Perform 23:86–112

Svenson O (1989) Eliciting and analysing verbal protocols in process studies of judgment and decision making. In: Montgomery H, Svenson O (eds) Process and structure in human decision making. Wiley, Chichester, pp 65–81

Swait J, Adamowicz W (2001) The influence of task complexity on consumer choice: A latent class model of decision strategy switching. J Consum Res 28(1):135–148

Swearingen K, Sinha R (2002) Interaction design for recommender systems. In: Proceedings of the conference on designing interactive systems, ACM Press, Londen

Timmermans D (1993) The impact of task complexity on information user in multi-attribute decision making. J Behav Decis Making 6(2):95–111

Todd P, Benbasat I (1991) An experimental investigation of the impact of computer based decision aids on decision making strategies. Inform Syst Res 2:87–115

Todd P, Benbasat I (1992) An experimental investigation of the impact of computer based decision aids on processing effort. MIS Quarterly 16(3):373–393

Todd P, Benbasat I (1993) Decision makers, decision aids and decision making effort: An experimental investigation. Inform Syst Oper Res 31:80–100

Todd P, Benbasat I (1994a) The influence of decision aids in choice strategies: An experimental analysis of the role of cognitive effort. Organ Behav Hum Decis Process 60(1):36–74

Todd P, Benbasat I (1994b) The influence of decision aids on choice strategies und conditions of high cognitive load. IEEE Trans Syst Man Cybern 24(4):537–547

Todd P, Benbasat I (2000) Inducing compensatory information processing through decision aids that facilitate effort reduction: An experimental assessment. J Behav Decis Making 13(1):91–106

Tuckey JW (1995) Exploratory data analysis, vol 19. Addison-Wesley, Reading

Tversky A (1969) Intransitivity of preferences. Psychol Rev 76:31–48

Tversky A (1972) Elimination by aspects: A theory of choice. Psychol Rev 79:281–299

Tversky A, Kahneman D (1981) The framing of decisions and the psychology of choice. Science 211:453–458

Urban GL, Hauser JR (2003) "listening in" to find unmet customer needs and solutions. J Market 68:72–87

Van den Poel D, Leunis J (1999) Consumer acceptance of the internet as a channel of disitribution. J Bus Res 45(3):249–256

Van der Heijden H, Verhagen T, Creemers M (2003) Understandung online purchase intentions: contributions from technolgy and trust perspectives. Eur J Inform Sys 12:41–48

Venkatesh V (1999) Creation of favorable user perceptions: Exploring the role of intrinsic motivation. MIS Quarterly 23(2):239–260

Venkatesh V (2000) Determinants of perceived ease of use: Integrating control, intrinsic motivation, and emotion into the technology acceptance model. Inform Syst Res 11(4):342–365

Venkatesh V, Davis FD (1996) A model of the antecedents of perceived ease of use: Development and test. Decis Sci 27(3):451–481

Verlegh P, Schifferstein H, Wittink D (2002) Range and number-of-levels effects in derived and stated measures of attribute importance. Market Lett 13(1):41–52

Vessey I (1991) Cognitive fit: A theory-based analysis of the graphs versus tables literature. Decis Sci 22:219–240

Vessey I, Galletta D (1991) Cognitive fit: An empirical study of information acquisition. Inform Syst Res 2:63–84

Wang W, Benbasat I (2005) Trust in and adoption of online recommendation agents. J Assoc Inform Syst 6(3):72–101

Wang W, Benbasat I (2008) Analysis of trust formation in online recommendation agents. J Manag Inform Syst 24(4):249–273

Wang W, Benbasat I (2009) Interactive decision aids for consumer decision making in e-commerce: The influence of perceived strategy restrictiveness. Manag Inform Syst Quart 33(2):293–320

West PM, Ariely D, Bellman S, Bradlow E, Huber J, Johnson E, Kahn B, Little J, Schkade D (1999) Agents to the resscue. Market Lett 10(3):285–300

White C, Hoffrage U (2009) Testing the tyranny of too much choice against the allure of more choice. Psychol Market 26(3):280–298

Wilkie W (1975) New perspectives for consumer information processing research. Comm Res 2(3):216–231

Wixom BH, Todd P (2005) A theoretical integration of user satisfaction and technology acceptance. Inform Syst Res 16(1):85–102

Woods D (1993) Process-tracing methods for the study of cognition outside of the experimental psychology laboratory. In: Klein GA, Orasanu J, Calderwood R (eds) Decision making in action: models and methods. Ablex, Norwood, pp 228–251

Wright P, Barbour F (1977) Phased decision strategies: Sequels to an initial screening. In: Starr MK, Zeleny M (eds) Multiple criteria decision making. TIMS studies in the management sciences, vol 6. Elsevier Science Pub, Amsterdam, pp 99–109

Xiao B, Benbasat I (2007) E-commerce product recommendation agents: Use, characteristics, and impact. Mis Quart 31(1):137–209

Yee M, Dahan E, Hauser JR, Orlin J (2007) Greedoid-based noncompensatory inference. Market Sci 26(4):532–549

Yuan S-T (2003) A personalized and integrative comparison-shopping engine and its applications. Decis Support Syst 34(2):139–156

Zack MH (1993) Interactivity and communication mode choice in ongoing management groups. Inform Syst Res 4(3):207–239

Zhang J, Pu P (2006) Performance evaluation of consumer decision support systems. Int J E-Bus Res 2(3):28–45

Index